THE
POWER
OF
RESILIENCE

◆ ◆ ◆ ◆ ◆ ◆ ◆ ◆

THE
POWER
OF
RESILIENCE

Achieving Balance, Confidence, and Personal Strength in Your Life

◆ ◆ ◆ ◆ ◆ ◆ ◆ ◆

Robert Brooks, Ph.D., and
Sam Goldstein, Ph.D.

New York Chicago San Francisco Lisbon London Madrid Mexico City
Milan New Delhi San Juan Seoul Singapore Sydney Toronto

Library of Congress Cataloging-in-Publication Data

Brooks, Robert B.
    The power of resilience : achieving balance, confidence, and personal strength in your life /
Robert Brooks, Sam Goldstein.
        p.   cm.
    Includes bibliographical references and index.
    ISBN 0-07-139104-5 (hardcover) — ISBN 0-07-143198-5 (paperback)
    1. Resilience (Personality trait).   2. Resilience (Personality trait)—Problems, exercises,
etc.   I. Goldstein, Sam, 1952–   II. Title.

    BF698.35.R47.B76   2003
    155.2'4—dc21   2003051561

16 17 18 19 20 21 22 23 24 25 26   QFR/QFR   1 5 4 3

ISBN 978-0-07-143198-9
MHID   0-07-143198-5

McGraw-Hill books are available at special quantity discounts to use as premiums and sales
promotions or for use in corporate training programs. To contact a representative, please visit the
Contact Us pages at www.mhprofessional.com.

This book is printed on acid-free paper.

In loving appreciation of my parents, Nathan and Sarah, and of the life they worked so hard to create for me. And, as always, to my family, Janet, Allyson, and Ryan.

S.G.

Resilience springs forth from our connections with others. I am grateful to my parents, Eva and David, for having served as models of unconditional love; to my wife, Marilyn, for her unwavering support and love; to my sons, Rich and Doug, for continually enriching my life; to their wonderful wives, Cybèle and Suzanne, for enhancing this enrichment; and to my first grandchild, Maya Kaitlyn, for whom I wish a life's journey filled with love, joy, and hope.

R.B.

Thanks to Kathleen Gardner for unfailing support and editorial assistance; to our agent, James Levine; and our editor, Matthew Carnicelli.

R.B.
S.G.

Contents

Preface ix

1 Resilient Mindsets, Negative Scripts, and
Personal Control 1

2 Changing the Words of Life: Rewriting Your
Negative Scripts 23

3 Choosing the Path to Become Stress Hardy
Rather than Stressed Out 49

4 Viewing Life Through the Eyes of Others 73

5 Communicating Effectively 99

6 Accepting Oneself and Others 125

7 Making Connections and
Displaying Compassion 151

8 Dealing Effectively with Mistakes 183

9 Dealing Well with Success in Building
Islands of Competence 209

10 Developing Self-Discipline and Self-Control 237

11 The Lessons of Resilience: Maintaining a
Resilient Lifestyle 261

Appendix A: Worksheets for Resilient Living 269

Appendix B: A Guide to Resilient Living 297

Endnotes 303

Recommended Reading 307

Index 309

Preface

A five-year-old child watched helplessly as his younger brother drowned. In the same year, glaucoma began to darken his world, and his family was too poor to afford the medical help that might have saved his sight. Both of his parents died during his teens. Eventually he was sent to a state institution for the blind. Because he was an African-American he was not permitted access to many activities, including music. Given the obstacles he faced, one could not have predicted that he would someday become a world-renowned musician. His name is Ray Charles.

In an interview he poignantly observed, "My mom, to me, was the most fantastic woman in the world. As I think of her today, she didn't have a lot of what people say you're supposed to have. I mean, she didn't have a college education. She only went to fifth grade. We were in a very small town and very poor, and there were no such things as psychologists to teach her how to raise a kid who was an oddity in that town. I was the only blind kid in this little town, so that made me odd to all the other kids. But my mom, she somehow knew that there's nothing wrong with my brain. I just couldn't see."[1]

The words of Ray Charles reflect the power of parents to nurture a resilient mindset in their children. In our books *Raising Resilient Children: Fostering Strength, Hope, and Optimism in Your Child* and *Nurturing Resilience in Our Children: Answers to the Most Important Parenting Questions*, we emphasized that for children to develop resilience required what the late psychologist Dr. Julius Segal called a *charismatic adult*, an adult from whom they "gathered strength."

Though our two books focused on what adults could do to nurture hope and resilience in children, many adults have asked us how to develop and maintain a resilient mindset and lifestyle of their own—not just as parents, but in all aspects of their lives.

Interest in applying the concept of a resilient mindset to adults was not unexpected. We have responded to these questions for years. However, the theme of resilience has found a more prominent place in our landscape since the terrorist attacks of September 11, 2001, which provoked anger, sadness, and anxiety in Americans. The word *resilient* has increasingly appeared in the media and in numerous speeches by government leaders, often to describe the people of New York and the United States.

In research literature, resilience has been conceived of as a buffering process, one that may not eliminate risks or adverse conditions but does help individuals deal with them effectively. However, as author and researcher Dr. Emmy Werner has suggested, resilience may also reflect the concept of "reserve capacity." That is, a resilient mindset helps us prepare for future adversity and enables the potential for change and continued personal growth throughout our lives.

Dr. Werner's perspective encourages us to adopt a more comprehensive view of resilience. Although the term *resilience* has typically been reserved for people who have overcome great adversity, such as Ray Charles, it is a concept that should apply to every person. We can never predict with certainty who will face great pressure and hardship. While we know that particular factors in childhood contribute to stress and vulnerability, such as poverty or domestic violence, we also know that some children and adults, leading seemingly calm lives filled with love, may suddenly face unexpected situations that tax their mental and physical health. As a vivid illustration, think of the many children, husbands, wives, and parents who lost loved ones on the morning of September 11, 2001. They have to deal not only with the painful loss of a cherished relative but with all of the uncertainties associated with not having a spouse, child, or parent in their lives.

We should not focus on and nurture resilience primarily as a safeguard against the possibility of confronting unfathomable tragedy and crisis. Rather, we believe that developing a resilient mindset will serve us well in every aspect of ordinary living—in all the roles we play and in all our interactions with others. Even for those fortunate enough to grow up in loving homes with many advantages, a resilient mindset provides a basic foundation and reservoir of emotional strength that can be called on to manage daily challenges.

The need to appreciate the importance of resilience as a central force in all of our lives is supported by the large number of individuals who report encountering daily stress. In a Gallup poll undertaken in December 2001, 42 percent of the adults surveyed said they "frequently" experienced stress and 38 percent said they "sometimes" experienced stress. A report issued by the National Institute of Mental Health in 2002 noted that an estimated 22 percent of Americans aged eighteen and older suffer from a diagnosable mental disorder in a given year. At any given time, almost nineteen million American adults aged eighteen and older suffer from a depressive disorder; a similar number have an anxiety disorder, and some adults have both.

Our experiences as psychologists and parents have taught us that certain guideposts can help people nurture a resilient mindset. This mindset contains assumptions about ourselves that influence our behavior, successes, failures, and relationships with others. The more aware we are of the features of this mindset, the more skillfully we can strive to strengthen and reinforce this style.

We have written this book in a format similar to that used in our previous works, presenting a framework of resilience and illustrating its concepts with many examples. We describe the main features of a resilient mindset and offer specific ideas and strategies to develop this mindset. We also examine obstacles to achieving this mindset. Understanding these obstacles helps us initiate steps to remove them and to discover more productive paths. In addition, we pose questions and exercises for you to consider as you assess your mindset and lifestyle. Given your specific interests and situation, you may want to invest time and energy in one guidepost or strategy more than others. You may also wish to skip ahead to a particular chapter or review a certain chapter many times.

We have included two appendixes at the end of the book. Appendix A contains a set of worksheets for the exercises described throughout the book. As you read, we urge you to complete these exercises, writing your answers on the pages provided and using additional paper if necessary. This will personalize your volume and, more important, allow you to track and access your answers to each of these exercises as you read further. Appendix B contains a chapter-by-chapter listing of the obstacles, guideposts, and strategies involved in reinforcing a resilient mindset and lifestyle.

The many individuals you will read about in this book represent people we have worked with in our clinical practice as well as those who have shared their stories with us in our workshops or through correspondence. Some stories are composites of our experiences, but all of the examples represent the real-life situations of individuals and their families.

It is our hope that the guideposts and examples we provide will encourage you to reflect on your relationships, expectations, goals, and dreams, and that this process will lead you to a more satisfying, resilient life. Remember, this process is dynamic and ongoing. It is not accomplished in a day or a week or a year. Rather, it is a process that enriches us throughout our entire lives.

When asked what helped them succeed against the odds, resilient children, youth, and adults overwhelmingly and exclusively gave the credit to members of their extended family, to neighbors and teachers, to mentors and voluntary associations and church groups.

—EMMY WERNER

The development of resilience may parallel the process of healthy human development, a dynamic process in which personality and environmental influences interact in a reciprocal, transactional relationship.

—BONNIE BENARD

A hundred times every day I remind myself that my inner and outer life depends on the labors of other men, living and dead, and that I must exert myself in order to give in the measure as I have received and I am still receiving.

—ALBERT EINSTEIN

1

Resilient Mindsets, Negative Scripts, and Personal Control

As a young boy, Alex Proctor thought he was "retarded." He grew up during a time when we knew little about learning disabilities. He experienced great difficulty in school, especially learning to read. In the fifth grade, his reading level was equivalent to that of a second grader. He would study a list of words in the evening, only to forget their correct spelling the next day. He was held back in the fifth grade, an intervention that proved ineffective. Not only did his reading difficulties continue, but he also experienced the ongoing humiliation of being called "dumb" and "stupid" by several of his classmates. His teachers, failing to understand the nature of his problems, exhorted him to "study harder," implying he was not giving 100 percent and could succeed if only he possessed the will to do so. The death of his father when Mr. Proctor was in seventh grade added to a stressful home situation.

Mr. Proctor dropped out of high school and went to work as a custodian. He married at the age of twenty-one, and two years later he and his wife had their first child, a son. Two years after the birth of their child, with the support of his wife he began a window cleaning business, offering services for both offices and homes. He sought the advice of a childhood friend in the advertising field for strategies to market his services. Much to Mr. Proctor's surprise, his business began to take off and he soon hired two assistants. A second son was born, the business expanded, and Mr. Proctor and his wife bought a home.

When Mr. Proctor was thirty-two, his younger son, who was struggling in school just as he had, was diagnosed with a learning disability. When the clinician explained the reasons for the diagnosis, Mr. Proctor blurted out,

"That's me! My son has the same problems I have. I finally know I'm not stupid." At the recommendation of this clinician Mr. Proctor was tested and diagnosed with a learning disability. Now possessing an understanding of his learning problems, he fulfilled a long-sought but unfulfilled dream of obtaining his GED. With the encouragement of his wife and the addition of several more employees at his business, he made time to take a class at a local community college in which he earned an A. He continued to take courses and moved on to a four-year college. At the age of forty-two, Mr. Proctor received his bachelor's degree with honors. He observed, "I didn't need the degree for my work. I needed it for myself."

Mr. Proctor has a younger brother, Tim, who also struggled in school. As a teenager Tim followed in his brother's footsteps by dropping out of school. However, rather than finding steady employment, he became addicted to drugs. To support his addiction, he resorted to armed robbery. He was caught and sent to prison. Upon Tim's release, Alex offered him a job in his company. Tim accepted but quickly resumed his drug use and criminal actions. He was apprehended and sentenced to prison again. Alex wondered why he went in one direction and Tim in another.

Resilient Mindsets

What permitted Alex to succeed in life while his brother continued down a path of self-destruction? What are the factors that help some adults to bounce back while others languish in feelings of helplessness and hopelessness? Why do some individuals attain success that could never have been predicted from their life circumstances? What is the inner strength that propels some people to overcome mighty obstacles in their path?

Roslyn Smith, a thirty-six-year-old woman, grew up in poverty. She lived in an area where muggings, homicides, and drug deals were common. One of her brothers was killed in a gang fight, and one of her sisters overdosed on heroin. She was the first member of her family to attend college. She commuted to college while living in an apartment above a bar. She also worked many hours a week to support herself, a younger sibling, and her ailing mother. She spent as much time as possible studying at the college library because the noise level at home was unbearable. After obtaining her college degree she worked for a social welfare agency and went to school in the evening to earn a master's degree in social work.

Successful adults such as Alex Proctor and Roslyn Smith may be viewed as *resilient*. The word *success* should not be confused or equated with one's income. As we will discuss more fully in this book, success in life encompasses such features as positive relationships with others, contentment at work and in our other roles (for example, as a mother, father, or coworker), and a feeling of optimism. Although in some scientific circles the word *resilient* has been applied only to individuals who have overcome stress and hardship, it is a concept that should be expanded to become a primary focus of each person's life, whether or not that person has experienced great adversity. All of us encounter some degree of stress and challenge in everyday life. No one can predict which of us will at some point face unimagined adversity.

Resilient individuals are those who have a set of assumptions or attitudes about themselves that influence their behaviors and the skills they develop. In turn, these behaviors and skills influence this set of assumptions so that a dynamic process is constantly operating. We call this set of assumptions a mindset. A resilient *mindset* is composed of several main features:

- Feeling in control of one's life
- Knowing how to fortify one's "stress hardiness"
- Being empathic
- Displaying effective communication and other interpersonal capabilities
- Possessing solid problem-solving and decision-making skills
- Establishing realistic goals and expectations
- Learning from both success and failure
- Being a compassionate and contributing member of society
- Living a responsible life based on a set of thoughtful values
- Feeling special (not self-centered) while helping others to feel the same

Possessing a resilient mindset does not imply that one is free from stress, pressure, and conflict, but rather that one can successfully cope with problems as they arise.

We also use the word *mindset* to capture an important premise of this book: *mindsets can be changed*. The development of mindsets, or assumptions about oneself and others, is a complex process based on the interaction of one's unique temperament with one's life experiences. However, mindsets are not cast in stone. The more we understand the beliefs that guide our behaviors, the more successfully we can engage in the process of replacing counterproductive, self-defeating assumptions with those that will lead to a more resilient, fulfilling life. There are guideposts we can follow and activities we can engage in that will facilitate the process of strengthening a resilient mindset. Unfortunately, there are also roadblocks to developing a resilient mindset, roadblocks that may be viewed as *negative scripts*.

Negative Scripts: Obstacles to a Resilient Mindset

Have you ever found yourself engaging in the same behaviors repeatedly with negative results? If you answered "yes," you are not alone. In our clinical practice and workshops we have heard countless examples of individuals following the same script day after day with predictable negative results. It is as if they are actors who have rehearsed their lines and cannot deviate from the script. The script can dictate a man ending a relationship when he is asked to make a commitment, a woman being fearful of showing anger even when justified, parents telling their children for ten years to clean their rooms with little success, a father asking his son immediately when coming home from work each evening, "Did you do your homework?" or a couple insisting their marriage would be better if only the other person would change.

When we repeat behaviors that lead to positive outcomes, such as a man telling his wife and children each day that he loves them, a woman conveying appreciation to her staff, or a project leader delegating responsibilities to those in his group in order to reinforce their sense of ownership, we are justified in calling these behaviors *positive scripts*. However, when our predictable behaviors are counterproductive or self-defeating but we continue to engage in them, a negative script is operating. These negative scripts, which can influence all aspects of our personal and professional lives, are obstacles to developing a resilient mindset.

Some individuals are not aware that they are trapped in a negative script, even if it is obvious to their friends and relatives. Some individuals blame their behavior on others, shouting the refrain, "If only my kids [or wife, or coworker, and so on] would change, then I would be more relaxed." Often the first drafts of negative scripts are written in childhood and acted throughout our adult lives. Until you can recognize these scripts and take responsibility for your actions, they will continue unabated. Unfortunately, the longer they exist, the more entrenched they are likely to become, precluding opportunities for improvisation and spontaneity.

"They Just Don't Get It!"

Jeremy Butler was an innovative, brilliant engineer. He left college at the end of his junior year to concentrate all of his time and energy to develop his own company. His work engulfed him. After several frustrating years, a product he designed was successful. By the time he was thirty-five years old, his company was worth millions. He had many employees, but happiness eluded him. At the age of thirty he had married, but the marriage ended within two years. Mr. Butler and his wife did not have any children. After the divorce, he had no other serious relationships.

Mr. Butler came to see us when he was thirty-seven at the recommendation of his physician because of anxiety, depression, and insomnia. In the course of our evaluation Mr. Butler focused his remarks on his work. He described all of his efforts to build up his company even when some people doubted him. As he spoke of his accomplishments there was little evidence of any joy or satisfaction. Instead, a sense of sadness pervaded the conversation.

He explained, "My father was the kind of person who thought he knew what was best for me and everyone. He was always telling me what to do, even when I was a kid. When I quit college, he went wild and told me what a big mistake it was, that it was too risky. I told him if the business didn't work out I could always go back to school, but he couldn't understand. I also had a professor for a couple of courses who really reminded me of my father. He always came across in class as having the right answer. Although he said he welcomed views different from his own, when they were offered he had numerous ways of putting them down. When I told him I was leaving college, he said I didn't have the skills to start my own business, that I wasn't disciplined enough. I showed them."

We asked about the business today. He responded, "It's doing OK, but I wish I had a better group of managers. They just don't get it! I've tried to delegate responsibility, but they just don't seem to have the creativity to come up with new ideas. Several of my managers have left. When I ask why, they say I don't really listen to them, that I'm too critical. But when I try to give them responsibility, when I encourage them to come up with ideas, they fail miserably—so what can I do? It's little wonder that I'm feeling down and anxious. I'm surrounded by people who are incompetent and may cause my business to suffer. I've got to learn to hire better people. I wouldn't be sitting here today feeling anxious if I knew that I had managers I could count on. And to think that they blame me for not listening to them! How can I listen if they don't respond to what I ask them to do?"

Mr. Butler continued to attribute his problems to his managers. Because this was his focus we asked him to describe some of the interactions he had with them. He said, "I can tell you something that happened a few weeks ago that is a perfect example of what I'm talking about. We are developing a new product. I sat down with the four managers involved in the project. I outlined the goals of the project and then asked each of them to come back to me the following week with their plans to meet these goals. I really wanted them to take some initiative. When we met the following week I shouldn't have been surprised. I heard ideas that were not very sophisticated or creative. This has happened so often."

We asked how he reacted.

"I was frustrated, as I often am, and I said, 'Is that the best you can do? I expect more. We'll never be successful if you keep coming up with these kinds of ideas!' "

"How did the managers respond?"

Mr. Butler said, "They sat there. I could tell they were annoyed, but someone has to light a fire under them." He then paused and said, "One handed in his resignation letter the next day. He just couldn't take the pressure. I hope I can find someone who can."

In reading Mr. Butler's exchange with his managers, you might wonder why such an intelligent man would say things that obviously create friction with his staff. You don't need an advanced degree in psychology to predict that his behavior would contribute to an unhappy, unproductive group of managers. Yet it was as if he were wearing blinders, unable to see what was so obvious to others. He continued to act out his negative script and was upset when his employees did not improve.

In our work with Mr. Butler, which we will describe in greater detail later in this book, we focused not only on helping him to become more aware of how his behavior influenced others but also on discovering the roots of his negative script.

Spontaneity and venturing beyond prescribed scripts can serve as a source of joy, adventure, and personal discovery. However, if we didn't follow any scripts, then each relationship and experience would be unpredictable and chaotic. Tradition and security often prove to be the foundation for providing us the insight and courage to move beyond current scripts and write new ones. Unfortunately, there are times when particular counterproductive scripts become increasingly entrenched and do not easily invite change. If anything, we are not even aware of the presence of these scripts, expecting others to modify their behaviors without reflecting on our contribution to the situation.

Whose Life Is It Anyway? The Significance of Personal Control

Taking ownership of our behavior and becoming more resilient requires us to recognize that we are the authors of our lives. We must not seek our happiness by asking someone else to change, but instead should always ask, *What is it that I can do differently to change the situation?* Assuming personal control and responsibility is a fundamental underpinning of a resilient mindset, one that affects all other features of this mindset and serves as a catalyst to change negative scripts. For greater clarity and emphasis we will highlight the concept of personal control in a later chapter, but you will discover that the notion of personal control permeates our thoughts throughout this book.

Stephen Covey, author of *The Seven Habits of Highly Effective People*, has eloquently written that effective people focus on what they can control, spending little, if any, time and energy on matters that are beyond their sphere of influence. We are reminded of the words of the Serenity Prayer used by Alcoholics Anonymous:

> *Grant me the serenity to accept the things I cannot change,*
> *the courage to change the things I can,*
> *and the wisdom to know the difference.*

You Should Change First

In our clinical practices and workshops we have heard numerous examples of well-intentioned individuals who continue to experience a high level of stress and unhappiness because they wait for someone else to change or they focus on an event or situation they cannot control.

Alan and Barbara Manter came to us for marital counseling. They had been married for two years, although they had lived together for a year before marrying. Their marital struggles had many features, and one of the strongest was that each expected the other to change first. Both viewed their happiness as dependent on the actions their spouse should take.

During our first meeting we asked what they thought would help their marriage. Mr. Manter immediately jumped in and said, "Before we were married, Barbara seemed more affectionate and loving. I think our marriage would be better if she could be that way again."

Mrs. Manter responded immediately, "Well, if I seem less affectionate, maybe it's because you're less considerate. You neglect to call when you're going to be home late for dinner. Just last night that happened, and when I asked you why you couldn't call, all you could say is that you couldn't find the time."

Mr. and Mrs. Manter continued this line of discussion for a few more minutes, suggesting how the other might change to improve the marriage. We explained, "You've been able to tell each other how to change. Before our next session it might be helpful to think about what *you* might do differently to help with your marital problems." We wanted them to begin to reflect on their contribution to what was transpiring in their relationship and to focus on what each could control.

At the beginning of the next session, Mr. Manter offered that he thought a great deal about what he might do differently. "Barbara is right. I can be more considerate and call if I am going to be late for dinner." *What a quick, positive response to therapy*, we thought. However, this thought was immediately erased when Mr. Manter added what we frequently refer to as the *but statement*: "But it would make it easier for me to be considerate if Barbara would show more affection and caring."

Not surprisingly, Mrs. Manter responded with obvious anger, "Maybe I could be more affectionate if I felt you were more caring and considerate!"

Their mindsets had quickly resorted to "If only the other one would change first" or "I would be happy if the other one would change." Though we understand this kind of thinking and recognize that it commonly occurs in relationships, it works against becoming resilient because it places the responsibility for change on someone else. We are not suggesting that other people shouldn't change, but rather that we must first look within ourselves and ask what we can do differently to improve a situation.

Are we casting blame? By advocating that people examine the ways they can change, are we implying that they are the cause of the problem? Not at all. We are not encouraging self-blame games in which people set themselves up as martyrs. We prefer to replace self-blame with responsibility. If there is a situation that you do not like, you must assume responsibility to change the situation, regardless of its roots. This stance is not one of blame, but rather one that empowers.

Having control over one's life appears to be a basic drive for all human beings. Research exists to support the importance of personal control as a major force in emotional and physical well-being. As reported in the British journal *Lancet*, research conducted by Michael Marmot of University College in London found that clerks and secretaries were more likely to die of heart attacks than senior executives were. Even taking into consideration such variables as smoking and poor nutrition, the researchers found that the "lower the job category and the less the control," the more likely people were to suffer from heart disease.[1]

Marmot's group noted, "Greater attention to the design of work environments may be one important way to reduce inequalities in health." Others concurred, noting that it was probably easier to provide people more control at work than to change their social status. Leonard Syme and Jennifer Balfour, commenting on the Marmot study, contended, "Although it may be difficult to intervene on social class inequalities in health, there are more opportunities to intervene on control. It may also be possible to change environmental forces in the workplace or the community so that more flexibility and control is available."[2]

Similar findings were reported by Laura Kubzansky, a researcher at the Harvard School of Public Health. Kubzansky, taking into account such risk factors for heart disease as smoking, high cholesterol, blood pressure, drinking, and family history, found that men in their sixties were less likely to develop coronary heart disease if they possessed an optimistic outlook on life. She noted, "This shows again there's a link between how people look at the world and what happens to them physically. This also shows that optimism can be protective."[3] A major component of optimism was reported to be the belief that the future will be more pleasant because, to a great extent, we can control important events in our lives.

These two studies and others highlight that a sense of personal control plays a major role in emotional and physical well-being and in dealing effectively with stress and pressure. This feeling of control is a major feature of a resilient mindset.

The Power of Resilience

In this book we will describe the components of a resilient mindset as well as strategies for developing these components. We will also highlight obstacles to strengthening these components. Awareness of the features that nurture resilience and of the roadblocks to achieving a more satisfying, fulfilling life will equip you to achieve a resilient mindset and stress hardiness. The ten keys for resilient living are as follows:

1. Changing the words of life: rewriting your negative scripts
2. Choosing the path to become stress hardy rather than stressed out
3. Viewing life through the eyes of others
4. Communicating effectively
5. Accepting oneself and others
6. Making connections and displaying compassion
7. Dealing effectively with mistakes
8. Dealing well with success in building islands of competence
9. Developing self-discipline and self-control
10. The lessons of resilience: maintaining a resilient lifestyle

Let's briefly examine each of these keys to developing a resilient mindset. We will elaborate on each in subsequent chapters.

1. Changing the Words of Life: Rewriting Your Negative Scripts

As we noted, well-meaning, intelligent people often resort to repeating self-defeating behaviors in their personal and professional lives. In many ways Mr. Butler was trapped, blindly following a prescribed script that did not allow for change or creativity. We have worked with many individuals who adhere to a self-defeating script year after year. Some are aware that they are engaging in counterproductive behaviors but feel helpless to change. Others deflect responsibility from themselves, placing blame on those they interact with, as was so vividly illustrated by Mr. Butler's reaction to his managers.

We have often been asked, "Are people stuck with negative scripts for their entire lives? Can people change?" We recall a woman who appeared to be in her mid-sixties who attended one of our workshops called "Fostering Family Closeness and Respect." At the end of the workshop, when we discussed the theme of negative scripts, she asked, "Is it ever too late? Can people change their ways of behaving at any age?"

We responded that we know of people who were able to alter long-entrenched scripts. She smiled and said, "I knew my husband should have been here tonight!" While she smiled, it was also obvious that aspects of her relationship with her husband required modification.

We begin with the assumption that people can move from less satisfying, less productive scripts to ways of thinking, feeling, and behaving that foster a resilient mindset. We believe that following a sequence of steps can help one accomplish this transformation. While these steps provide direction for change, change may take time, depending on how long and how frequently the script has been used, awareness of the script, openness to change, and how effectively the person can deal with the obstacles that typically emerge when attempting to modify lifelong patterns.

The main steps in the sequence are as follows:

1. Identify negative scripts in oneself and take responsibility for change (don't look for others to change first).
2. Define short- and long-term goals related to the issue at hand.
3. Consider possible new scripts or plans of action that are in accord with your goals.
4. Select from these new scripts the one that you believe has the greatest chance for success, and list criteria for assessing the success of the new script.
5. Anticipate the potential obstacles to success and how these obstacles might be managed.
6. Perform the new script you have selected and assess its effectiveness.
7. Change goals or scripts or approach if the selected course of action proves unsuccessful.

As we noted earlier, the mindset and accompanying steps to change negative scripts may seem very apparent to an outsider. However, as anyone who has attempted to change his or her behavior has learned, some things are not as apparent as they seem and not as easy to change as we might wish. Blind spots and obstacles litter the road to success.

2. Choosing the Path to Become Stress Hardy Rather than Stressed Out

Not surprisingly, a basic characteristic of resilient people is their capacity to manage stress and pressure. We have often been asked what factors contribute to some people living a more stressful existence than others. Certainly, inborn temperament plays a role, as do one's life experiences. Research on temperament reveals that some people are predisposed from birth to feeling stress more intensely than others; however, temperament is not the sole variable in determining stress. Temperament is influenced by the many life situations one encounters, including interactions with others.

Does the mindset of people who are less stressed differ from that of those who are more stressed? The obvious answer is yes—but in what ways do they differ? In Chapter 3 we will articulate these differences; for now, think about what these differences entail.

3. Viewing Life Through the Eyes of Others

Resilient individuals have satisfying relationships in their lives. A cornerstone of such relationships is the capacity to be empathic and to walk in the shoes of others, metaphorically speaking. Dr. Daniel Goleman described empathy as an important feature of emotional intelligence and cited studies to advocate that empathy can be learned.

In our workshops and clinical practice we emphasize that empathic people not only ask, *In anything I say or do, what do I hope to accomplish?* but, just as important, *Am I saying or doing things in a way that others will be most willing to listen and respond to me?* and, *Am I treating others in the same way that I would like to be treated?* Empathy does not imply that you agree with another person, but simply that you appreciate and validate that person's point of view.

While most people consider themselves to be empathic, we have found that it is easier to be empathic toward those people whose ideas agree with ours and who are cooperative and helpful. It is much more difficult to be empathic when we are upset, angry, annoyed, or disappointed with others.

Mr. Butler's behavior represented a failure of empathy. His stated goal was to motivate his managers to develop new ideas. However, as we shall see, because of excess baggage from his past he had not asked, *Am I treating my managers as I would like to be treated?* If he had asked himself that question, he might not have continued to say to them, "Is that the best you can do? I expect more. We'll never be successful if you keep coming up with these kinds of ideas!" It was only after he learned to assume an empathic stance that he could successfully reach his managers.

4. Communicating Effectively

The ability to communicate effectively is an integral component of resilience and is linked closely to empathy. Effective communication includes both an appreciation of how our verbal and nonverbal messages are perceived and a capacity for *active listening.* When we listen actively we attempt to understand and validate what other people are communicating. Validation does not suggest agreement, but rather understanding without belittling. As we noted earlier, Mr. Butler's negative response to his managers reflected a failure in effective communication.

Many people believe they communicate effectively. However, when others do not respond in ways they would like, they tend to blame them. In our clinical practices we have often heard such comments as, "My husband [wife, children, colleagues, students] never listens to me" or "They just don't understand me" or "They just tune me out when I try to tell them something." When others appear not to listen to our messages, we must ask, "How might I change the way I have been saying things so that others may be more receptive to what I have to say?"

Carl and Andrea Pace consulted us about marital issues. They had been married for three years. When we asked about their marriage, Mr. Pace immediately answered, "We are growing apart. I don't know what's the matter with Andrea. Nothing seems to please her. There's really little joy in our house."

Mrs. Pace responded, "Carl is right. There is little joy. I guess I'm to blame. To be honest, I've been feeling pretty depressed for the past year."

Mr. Pace responded, "But Andrea, there's no reason for you to be depressed. We have a nice home and good jobs, and we go on great vacations. You're just letting yourself get depressed."

Mrs. Pace put her head down and began to cry. Mr. Pace looked at us and said, "This is what I'm talking about. All I have to say is one thing and she begins to cry. She's crying over nothing. I don't know what I can do to help."

Mrs. Pace continued to cry. After a couple of minutes she looked at us with a forlorn expression and said with both sadness and anger, "Why can't he realize that I feel terrible about being depressed, but I *am* depressed, even with a nice home, a good job, and great vacations?"

This one vignette poignantly captures a failure to validate another person's feelings, leading a husband and wife to grow farther apart and lessening their resilience. Consider what might have happened if instead of saying, "There's no reason for you to be depressed," Mr. Pace had responded to his wife's distress by assuring her, "I know that you're feeling depressed. I don't understand all of the reasons, but I'm glad we're getting help." Not only would he be validating what his wife said, but by using the word *we* he would introduce the notion that they are unified in helping her with her sadness.

Communication is an essential part of our lives. It is a window to our inner world and a conduit for our relationships with others. The more effectively we learn to convey our feelings, thoughts, and beliefs verbally and nonverbally, the more successful and resilient we will be. In order to achieve this success we will examine the roadblocks that interfere with successful communication and the steps we must take to overcome these obstacles.

5. Accepting Oneself and Others

If we are to nurture a resilient mindset, we must learn to accept ourselves. Acceptance implies possessing realistic expectations and goals, recognizing our strengths as well as our vulnerabilities, and leading an authentic, balanced life in which our behaviors are in accord with our values and goals.

When people are not authentic, when their actions do not reflect their values, they are likely to experience increased stress and pressure. Many, caught up in the day-to-day hassles of everyday life, are not even aware of discrepancies among their goals, values, and behavior. Yet these discrepancies serve as major obstacles to feeling a sense of integrity and leading a fulfilling life.

We frequently ask people to make a list of five things that are very important to them and to consider why these things are important. It is not unusual that health and relationships find a prominent place on this list. We next request that they review each item on the list and reflect on how much time and energy they expend to achieve what they have listed. Many people are surprised to observe the discrepancy between the list they have created and their behavior.

Ross Sargent, an executive at a financial consulting firm, represents a vivid illustration of this point. He came to see us because of increased anxiety, a loss of sexual interest, and a "constant feeling of tiredness." Eventually our individual work with Mr. Sargent included marital therapy, but we will describe our first few sessions with him in terms of his struggles to adhere to an authentic life. When we asked him to make a list of what is important to him, he wrote, "My role as a husband, my role as a father to my three children, my health, my church, and success at work."

In a pattern we have observed all too often, although he listed "success at work" in fifth place his work consumed almost all of his time and attention. There were many days when he left before his three young children were awake and did not come home until they were asleep. Time spent with his wife and children was limited. He explained that when he came home from work, he was frequently so exhausted that all he wanted to do "was eat a quick meal and go to bed." He no longer exercised, he ate poorly, and he had gained twenty-five pounds in the previous eighteen months. When we spoke to him about his church activities, he said that he found a certain comfort while in church but this positive feeling was isolated from the rest of his life.

He observed sadly, "If you looked at my life it would be obvious that most of it is spent at work, yet I feel little satisfaction at work, even when things go well."

In our fast-paced world, many people fall into the same trap as Mr. Sargent—namely, behaving in ways that do not reflect their priorities or placing too much emphasis on one priority (such as work) at the expense of other priorities. A life that is not balanced or authentic is one ripe for discontent, shallow relationships, and stress, all characteristics that are not in accord with a resilient mindset.

As we learn to accept ourselves, as we gain a clear picture of our strengths and vulnerabilities, and as we articulate our values, we will be in a position to remove those factors that serve as obstacles to realizing a more satisfying, honest, rich life.

6. Making Connections and Displaying Compassion

Much has been written in the past decade of the importance of feeling connected to others as a source of emotional well-being and resilience. Our friend and colleague Dr. Ned Hallowell has described the power of connections and what he terms "human moments" as a reservoir of strength.[4]

We must remember that even as adults we require charismatic adults in our lives. Regardless of our sense of security or confidence, the importance of having people from whom we gather strength on an ongoing basis can never be underestimated. Spouses, siblings, parents, or friends may all play that role.

In our clinical practice and workshops we typically ask, "What two or three people serve as charismatic adults in your life?" We then ask, "Think of a couple of examples of what these people have said or done that prompted you to list them as charismatic adults."

Reflect on how you would answer the questions we just posed. It is interesting to learn the various reasons people offer for what qualifies someone as their charismatic adult. A reason that consistently emerges is a feeling of unconditional love and acceptance on the other person's part.

We also ask, "What people would say that you are the charismatic adult in their lives, and why do you think they would say this?" This is an important question because many articles have been written describing the emergence of a "helper's high," an exhilarating feeling rooted in both physical and emotional changes after showing compassion or helping others. When people display compassion, not only do they enhance their resilience by connecting with others, but they also nurture the belief that they make a positive difference in their world.

It is intriguing to observe the struggle that many individuals experience in answering who would list them as their charismatic adult. Once again, reflect on your answer. A husband might name his wife, a wife her husband, or parents their children. However, what is often triggered is uncertainty. For instance, one man said, "I was going to quickly say that my wife and two kids would say I am a charismatic adult to them, but I wonder if they would."

We asked, "Why do you have doubts?"

He responded, "I know that I can be loving, but I can also be critical when my family doesn't do what I think they should do. I have yelled at my kids about forgetting a homework assignment or forgetting to put the dishes in the dishwasher. I have complained to my wife about little incidents. My wife once told me that my love has a lot of strings attached to it, that it is not unconditional. I read once that one negative comment can easily erase ten or more positive comments. Also, I know it's not just a question of saying 'I love you,' but of showing it. However, I still have difficulty hugging my kids or expressing my love."

This man's struggle is not unique. The importance of strengthening our connections cannot be understated. Connections to other people and to values and causes provide the nutriments for a resilient life.

7. Dealing Effectively with Mistakes

The ways in which we understand and respond to mistakes and failure are an integral part of a resilient mindset. Resilient individuals tend to view mistakes as experiences for learning and growth. This does not mean they are overjoyed when they make mistakes, but rather that they are not easily discouraged, instead looking for opportunities that might be a by-product of setbacks. In contrast, people lacking resilience often perceive mistakes as evidence that they are failures. They tend to attribute mistakes to conditions that cannot be easily corrected, such as lacking intelligence. Given this pessimistic outlook, they are prone to rely on self-defeating coping behaviors, such as making excuses ("I did not have the right tools"), quitting ("No one could do that—I'm not going to continue"), avoiding ("Why would anyone want to try that?"), denying ("This is stupid and has no relevance in my life"), or blaming others ("I would do fine if only I had a better boss").

Mr. Butler managed his feelings of insecurity by saying, "I'm surrounded by people who are incompetent and may cause my business to suffer." In part, he relied on this rationalization to protect his vulnerable self-esteem and sense of failure. In essence, he was saying, "Mistakes that occur in my company are not my fault but rather the fault of my incompetent staff." While this outlook may afford temporary relief, it serves as a major obstacle to leading a resilient life. It robs one of the opportunity to develop a sense of personal control and impedes asking, *What is it that I can do to learn from mistakes and setbacks?*

In this scenario, a vicious cycle is set in place. If you believe that you cannot learn from mistakes, you will flee from challenges to avoid further humiliation and increasingly resort to counterproductive coping behaviors. The more you run from mistakes, the less likely you are to experience success, and the greater the probability you will continue down a path marked by insecurity, anger, and sadness.

We have worked with many individuals who "wake up" in their forties or fifties and realize that they have spent most of their lives running from the fear of failure rather than leaving their comfort zones and taking appropriate risks. They begin to realize how fearful they have been and sadly look back at lost opportunities, haunted by the question *What if?*—that is, *What if I had not been so afraid of making mistakes, but instead confronted challenges in my life?*

Are there steps you can take to change the way you view mistakes? Our answer is an unqualified "yes." The first step is to examine your beliefs about mistakes and how these beliefs shape your behavior. To assist with this examination, in Chapter 8 we will describe the components of a negative mindset that influence the way we think about mistakes. Once we understand these components we can begin to slowly change our view and adopt the notion that most mistakes afford an opportunity for growth and learning.

8. Dealing Well with Success in Building Islands of Competence

While the manner in which we understand and respond to setbacks is an integral part of a resilient mindset, so too is the way we react to successes in our lives. Jill Alexander and Marian Baker each completed a project for their respective companies. Both were congratulated for what they had accomplished. When Ms. Alexander received positive feedback, she thought, "I really worked hard on this project. I really put in a lot of energy. I feel very good. I think I'm ready for a more challenging project." Ms. Alexander believed that she was a major contributor to her success, and because of this she could experience a sense of pride and accomplishment. She could describe her *islands of competence*, or areas of strength, and became increasingly aware of how to reinforce these islands while engaged in future projects.

In contrast, Ms. Baker's response to success was devoid of the satisfaction that Ms. Alexander experienced. As people congratulated her, she thought, "I was lucky on this project. I'm surprised it worked. I bet all of my faults will be exposed sooner or later." Success did not bring happiness. A feeling of ownership for success was absent. If anything, success magnified Ms. Baker's feelings of inadequacy, and she was convinced that before long all of her "faults would be exposed for everyone to see." Such an attitude compromises a feeling of accomplishment and lessens the possibility of future success.

Just as we can alter a negative mindset with regard to mistakes, we can take steps to develop a more empowering, positive mindset with regard to our achievements. We will outline these steps in Chapter 9 and describe our interventions with Ms. Baker and others.

9. Developing Self-Discipline and Self-Control

Self-discipline and self-control play a significant role in all of our daily activities. When we think before we act, when we consider the feelings of others (when we are empathic), when we reflect on possible solutions to a problem, when we behave in a rational and thoughtful way, when we engage in developing a business plan, when we keep from screaming at someone who has done something to make us angry, we are displaying self-discipline and self-control. It is little wonder that Daniel Goleman also highlighted self-discipline as a major component of emotional intelligence.

How many of us like to work for someone who is unpredictable and inconsistent, who changes expectations from one moment to the next? How many of us enjoy living with someone who is impulsive and arbitrary and has a bad temper? We want to emphasize that impulsiveness and arbitrariness should not be confused with flexibility and spontaneity. Flexibility implies thoughtfulness together with openness, characteristics that are absent in individuals with limited self-discipline. Spontaneity, when used to foster resilience, is associated with changing scripts, engaging in activities that are fun, and adding a little humor to life.

At our workshops for parents, questions about discipline frequently dominate the discussion. We often advise parents that in addition to ensuring a safe and secure home environment, the other main function of discipline is to promote self-discipline and self-control. Self-discipline goes hand in hand with a sense of personal control, which, as we have described, is an integral feature of resilience.

It is not always easy to exercise self-discipline. We know many well-intentioned adults who act impulsively or lose their temper. Some, after reflecting on their behavior, offer a rationalization such as, "It wasn't really me." If our impulsive actions occur rarely, then one might attribute it to a temporary lapse of judgment. However, if we find we are frequently asserting that "it wasn't really me" or if we are often apologizing for our behavior, it suggests that we are experiencing difficulty with self-control. Fortunately there are steps, which we will describe later in this book, that we can take to assume greater control and develop more realistic expectations for ourselves and others.

10. The Lessons of Resilience: Maintaining a Resilient Lifestyle

If we abandon well-established diets and exercise programs, our health will suffer. As we are all aware, such programs must become a way of life lest we lapse into habits that compromise our health. The same principle is true when we consider the maintenance of a resilient lifestyle. Once we have developed the features associated with a resilient mindset and lifestyle, we cannot sit back and assume that our mindset and behaviors will go into automatic pilot. Expected and unexpected challenges emerge that will test our ability to be resilient.

The more we understand the characteristics of resilient individuals, the more we can engage in daily and long-term "exercises" to maintain and even strengthen a resilient mindset. Just as we enlist the aid of financial planners or develop a financial plan of our own, so too must we have a "resilience plan" to ensure as much as possible that our future will be filled with satisfaction and accomplishment.

A Resilient Mindset and Lifestyle: Obstacles and Achievements

Some may assume that with the proper guideposts, the road toward nurturing a resilient mindset and lifestyle will be straightforward and direct. As we shall explore, even with clearly defined guideposts this road often contains obstacles and detours that interfere with reaching our destination. However, the more knowledgeable we are about the components of a resilient mindset and the roadblocks to attaining it, the better equipped and confident we will be to discover those paths that will lead to a productive, fulfilling life and to experience the power of resilience.

2

Changing the Words of Life

Rewriting Your Negative Scripts

We are the authors of our lives. Our words and behaviors, echoed again and again in similar situations, in similar ways, with predictable outcomes, become the scripts of living. Many patterns of thinking, feeling, and behaving find their roots in childhood. If these patterns result in satisfaction, if they reinforce healthy interpersonal relationships, and if they permit flexibility and change, they represent the building blocks of positive scripts and should be repeated.

In contrast, when our words and actions, although repeated for weeks, months, and in some instances years, are self-defeating, ineffective, or counterproductive, it is wise to modify or abandon them. Yet frequently we continue to follow these scripts, sometimes more forcefully than before. In fact, our current adherence to a negative script appears to best predict returning to it in the future.

We all want to believe that we are flexible, thoughtful, and receptive to new ideas and approaches, but often we fail to model these behaviors, falling prey to the seductive trap of negative scripts. To be resilient is to recognize that if you are dissatisfied with certain aspects of your life, or if you find yourself continually engaging in thoughts or behaviors that lead to frustration, anger, and unhappiness, then it is your responsibility to take the initiative to rewrite the negative scripts that maintain these problems. You must never neglect or ignore the pursuit of your dreams and aspirations, even if this requires having the strength to break away from existing scripts that keep you confined to the seeming safety of your comfort zone.

Certainly there are benefits to perseverance. But why is it that we experience so much difficulty recognizing, acknowledging, and changing our course of action? As we have witnessed countless times in our clinical practice, it is difficult to change counterproductive and self-defeating patterns of thinking, feeling, and behaving. These patterns become increasingly entrenched and predictable. When people become enslaved by these unbending patterns they are unable to assume authorship of their lives or nurture a sense of personal control. Sometimes we are not even aware of the negative scripts we follow because they have become such a "natural part" of our existence. At other times we may recognize these scripts but feel powerless to change them. Instead, as we observed with Mr. Butler and with Mr. and Mrs. Manter, we expect others to change.

Negative scripts serve as powerful obstacles to a resilient lifestyle. They tend to increase conflicts with others. This chapter will help you identify and understand the "incorrect" thoughts, ideas, and attributions that frequently lead to the use of such scripts. We also offer a set of essential steps to help you change your words and write positive scripts. The powerful adversity created by negative scripts is readily apparent when we examine the lives of Marcia Stevens and Paul Castor.

A Brother, a Son

Marcia Stevens, a forty-year-old mother, grew up in what she described as "an emotionally abusive home." She has a forty-three-year-old brother, Al, who "escaped the abuse." She explained, "He could do no wrong and I could do no right. If he stayed out past his curfew my parents would tell him to check his watch next time. If I came in even a minute after my curfew I was grounded the next week. Forgetting a homework assignment led to a lecture about irresponsibility. If he forgot an assignment my parents were there to help him make it up. My parents were more likely to attend his sporting activities than mine. I don't know if it was a boy-girl difference, but I felt like a second-class citizen in my own home. It did quite a number on my self-esteem. I felt so unsure of myself, especially because I rarely heard a positive comment from my parents. I told myself that when I became a mother I would never do something like that to my own kids."

Mrs. Stevens married and had a daughter, Sophie, and three years later a son, Jimmy. She worked as the office manager in a medical practice. She called us at the recommendation of Jimmy's counselor at school. Jimmy was a ten-year-old fifth grader. The counselor was concerned because Jimmy did not complete schoolwork and would often say it was "boring" or would joke around, earning him the title of "class clown." An evaluation by the school psychologist did not reveal any learning disabilities but indicated that behind the clowning was an insecure boy who felt very uncertain about succeeding and worried about failing.

Our meetings with Mrs. Stevens and her husband, Stan, were very revealing. It was obvious that Mrs. Stevens enjoyed the company of her daughter but not her son. When she spoke about Sophie her face lit up with delight. In contrast, when she talked about Jimmy she described him as irresponsible. He always had to be reminded to do things. She commented, "He would rather clown around than do what he was supposed to do."

Mr. Stevens glanced at his wife and said, "I don't want to sound critical because I know Marcia is a loving person, but I have often said to her that I feel she is too negative with Jimmy. It seems he can never do anything right."

Mrs. Stevens answered, "I know I'm more critical of Jimmy than of Sophie, but that's because Sophie is cooperative and meets her responsibilities. What makes me sad is that I promised myself I would not yell at my kids the way my parents yelled at me, but Jimmy gets me so angry that I'm constantly yelling at him. I don't know why he won't change. I know if he did, I would stop yelling and being so critical."

We empathized with Mrs. Stevens's frustration. She was able to acknowledge that her interactions with Jimmy were exasperating and her strategies ineffective. However, rather than consider what actions she might take to improve this situation, she continued to insist that Jimmy had to learn to be more responsible and less angry. We shared her goals for Jimmy to be more responsible, but noted in an empathic way that her interventions were not leading to the desired results.

In an attempt to gain a better understanding of the seeming inflexibility and anger of Mrs. Stevens's script, we asked, "Who does Jimmy remind you of?"

Mr. Stevens responded immediately, "It's really interesting you should ask that. Marcia and I have often discussed how Jimmy not only looks like Marcia's brother, Al, but acts like him also."

We asked Mr. and Mrs. Stevens to describe Mrs. Stevens's brother. Mrs. Stevens used some of the same words to describe Al as she had Jimmy— "irresponsible," "immature," and "uncooperative."

We wondered whether they thought comparing Al and Jimmy influenced the ways in which they responded to Jimmy. Interestingly, Mrs. Stevens said, "I never really thought about that." Though hearing this answer might raise questions about her truthfulness, we have discovered that all of us have particular blind spots that prevent observing what appear to be obvious connections.

Once Mrs. Stevens could make this connection, we asked her how these similarities might influence her view of Jimmy and the ways in which she responded to him. During the next couple of weeks she did a great deal of thinking about her perceptions of Al and Jimmy and demonstrated the courage to examine long-held beliefs.

She said, "Al is an immature, irresponsible adult. If my parents had not made excuses for him, maybe he would be more responsible today. He has been married three times and has had countless jobs. He always blames others for his difficulties. I wanted to make certain that Jimmy didn't turn out the same way. But I've been thinking that what I'm doing is not working and our relationship is getting worse."

With a choked voice and tears in her eyes she added, "I feel very guilty about what I'm going to say. I think so much of my anger toward Jimmy is a lot of pent-up hurt and anger that I have toward my parents and brother."

It was the first time she could appreciate how a script repeatedly recorded in childhood was a major force in directing her feelings and behaviors today. These insights would serve as a catalyst for changes that we will discuss in greater detail later in this book.

"If Only I Could Find a Woman Who Was Loving!"

Paul Castor, a thirty-year-old building contractor, called us after attending one of our workshops about family relationships with his sister and brother-in-law. He said that although he would not normally attend a "psychology lecture," his sister told him that she had heard us before and that he "might find what we had to say interesting."

His sense of humor was apparent during his initial phone call when he said with a laugh, "She enticed me with a nice dinner, but I thought she might have an ulterior motive. She knows I haven't been too happy the last few years. You know how protective older sisters can be."

He then said, "I'm really not certain why I'm calling, but my sister thought it would be a good idea. Can we set up an appointment?"

At our first meeting, Mr. Castor repeated that he was seeing us because his sister thought it was a good idea. As a way of beginning to reinforce a sense of ownership, we asked what he thought.

- Couldn't he see how the same ineffective script was operating with all three women?

An observer might even offer such diagnostic labels as *control freak* or *rigid*. Or an armchair psychologist might provide an interpretation, contending that unconsciously Mr. Castor masked his own problems with commitment by projecting them onto the women in his life.

Rather than addressing the issue of psychological labels and interpretations, we want to focus our remarks on the concept of negative scripts. Mr. Castor actually recognized that he was following a prescribed script, but quickly interpreted this as a sign of consistency rather than an erroneous belief. "I know what I want, and if a woman can't go along, then she isn't the right woman for me." The obvious problem was that this perception kept him from examining his role in these failed relationships. He continued to repeat the same unsatisfying, unsuccessful script, always waiting for the other person to change and comply with his requests. It was not surprising that he often felt unhappy and unfulfilled.

So Why Don't People Change?

Negative scripts are often obvious to others but not to the person living the script. Remarks such as "Don't you see what you keep doing?" or "Aren't you ever going to learn?" or "Why do you keep doing the same thing over and over again?" or "Try using your brain" are triggered when we observe others repeating the same questionable behaviors day in and day out.

However, awareness that we are engaging in ineffective or self-defeating behaviors doesn't appear sufficient to guarantee change. We have often been asked questions such as the following:

- Why do I keep doing the same thing over and over again even when it doesn't work?
- Why do people stick with a negative script?
- What makes it so hard to change?
- You say that people are the authors of their own lives; so why don't many people follow that philosophy?

There are many roadblocks to changing counterproductive behaviors. Awareness of these roadblocks equips us to begin the process of leading a

"I'm not sure. I'm not sure I have a problem, but my sister thinks tha I've been feeling down the past few years."

We asked, "Have you?"

He said, "I guess I have, to some extent. It seems that I can't find a woman I really care about." He then offered an interesting comment: "If only I could find a woman who was loving!"

During the next few sessions we engaged Mr. Castor in a discussion about his relationships with women, what he expected in these relationships, and what exactly he meant by "a woman who was loving." Mr. Castor had been in three relationships over the past five years, all of which had lasted approximately six months. As he described these relationships, a similar pattern emerged. All appeared to go smoothly the first two or three months, but once the relationship reached a certain level of commitment, tension arose. The tension centered on increasing demands made by Mr. Castor.

Mr. Castor said, "People talk about men having trouble with commitments. I could write a book about how women really have that problem. I think if a couple make a commitment to each other, there are certain expectations that go with it."

"Like what?" we asked.

"Like expecting your girlfriend to spend time with you and not as much time with her friends, or expecting her to listen to your suggestions about the clothes she should wear to make her look pretty. I don't think that's too much to ask. I think that's what commitment is all about."

The scenario Mr. Castor described bordered on controlling behavior. Interestingly, each of the three women with whom he had been involved basically told him he was "suffocating" or "controlling," that they did not want to "request his permission" about what to wear or whether they could go out with friends. He immediately interpreted these comments as an expression of a lack of compassion and love, prompting him to establish an ultimatum with each girlfriend: either she acquiesce to his requests or he would leave the relationship. Not one of the three women complied. Mr. Castor was quick to blame the problem on the "women I seem to attract."

As we have noted in other examples, an objective observer might ask a number of questions, including:

- Couldn't Mr. Castor appreciate how his demands and expectations were contributing to the breakup of the relationships?
- Shouldn't he reflect on whether his demands were realistic?

more resilient life. To gain an understanding of the power of these road-blocks, do the following exercise.

On page 269 in Appendix A, list three things in your life that you would like to change. Next to each item, indicate whether you believe that someone else has to change before your change can take place. Also, consider what steps you have taken in the past to make these changes. If these attempts were unsuccessful, what was your next response? Why do you think they were unsuccessful? Next, list three modifications you have made to a script that have proven successful and why you think they were effective.

This task is not an academic exercise but rather a vehicle for encouraging you to reflect on the scripts that guide your life as well as your sense of personal control. Consider your answers to the questions posed in this exercise as you read about the following obstacles to change.

Obstacle One: A Lack of Awareness of the Role Negative Scripts Play in Your Life

Many people, including Mrs. Stevens, Mr. Castor, and Mr. Butler, are unaware that they are following a negative script. Feelings, thoughts, and behaviors may become so routine that we do not realize we are actually adhering to a prescribed script. Mr. Butler appeared to wear blinders as he interacted with his managers, seemingly oblivious to the ways his behavior affected their performance. By constantly blaming them, he short-circuited an opportunity to reflect on his feelings (other than to display annoyance and anger), consider what triggered these feelings, and evaluate how he coped in response to his emotions. Thus, he was unable to develop the insight to change his behavior, instead assuming that others should change first.

The importance of being aware of one's feelings and behavior was evident in a crucial therapy session during which we asked Mr. Butler what words his managers and other employees would use to describe him. He hesitated before answering, "They would probably say that I am opinionated and never listen to their input, that I'm too critical."

Mr. Butler then slipped into his pattern of blaming others. "But if I come across as critical it's because they don't perform effectively. What am I to do, just accept mediocre work? If I did, my company would fail."

We responded that we would not want his company to fail, then posed the following question: "As you look at the relationships you have had, what person might you describe with the same words that you think your staff would use to describe you: opinionated, not considering their input, and being too critical?"

Mr. Butler reflected for a moment and answered, "I never really thought about that. Those would be the words I would use to describe my father. Wow, that wasn't easy to say. I don't like how critical my father has always been, and I hate to think people might see me in the same way. I must say such a comparison hurts."

It was at that moment that Mr. Butler became aware of how he had adopted his father's script. As apparent as it might have been to others, it was not to Mr. Butler. For years he echoed the words and actions of his father in his relationships. Although he did not like his father's critical, judgmental script toward him, he failed to recognize that he was perceived in the same fashion by others. The script he learned from his father served as a major obstacle to success and contentment in his personal and professional life and weakened the development of a resilient mindset. It was only when Mr. Butler began to understand the scripts that guided his life that he could stop blaming others and take ownership for making changes.

As obvious as it may sound, we must first become aware of the scripts that serve as major forces in our lives before we can begin to change those scripts that are counterproductive.

Obstacle Two: Insisting That Others Must Change First

In Chapter 1 we emphasized the role that personal control plays in a resilient mindset. Resilient people not only are aware of their feelings and the ways in which they cope with these feelings, they also take personal responsibility for change. Yet many individuals desperately search for their happiness by expecting others to change first. We witnessed this in our work with Mr. and Mrs. Mantor, who both asserted that the door to a happier marriage could be opened if the other spouse took the initial steps to improve.

When we asked you to list three things you would like to see change in your life and to consider whether these changes were dependent on someone else changing first, how did you answer? Did any of the desired changes you recorded require that someone else take the first step? Such was the case with Mr. and Mrs. Savin. They came in to see us because of problems they were experiencing with their son, Wade. They contended that their lives would be happier if only Wade, a sophomore in high school, would listen to them.

When we asked for a specific example, Mr. Savin said, "Much of our stress comes from Wade's failing to complete homework and his earning Cs when he's capable of Bs and As. He also neglects to do his household chores. We keep telling him that he has to be more responsible and that his poor performance in school is going to catch up with him when he applies to colleges, but it seems to do no good."

We could certainly empathize with Mr. Savin and agreed that he and his wife would be less stressed if their son completed homework and achieved higher grades. However, instead of asking, "What might we do differently when approaching Wade so that he might be more receptive to listening to us and more motivated to do his work?" they continued to exhort him to work harder. When he did not, they accused him of being irresponsible. Not surprisingly, the level of tension in the household rose.

We asked the Savins what they could do differently. Mr. Savin immediately responded, "We've tried everything. It's Wade's responsibility to change. We keep taking away more and more privileges. Eventually, he should get the point. The only other thing we could do is to back off and let him fail, but then the fallout will land on us as well."

Mr. Savin then offered a very revealing comment: "Besides, if we back off and let him do what he wants, he will believe that he has won and take advantage of us. We think there are too many kids who rule the roost these days because their parents are afraid to set limits."

Obviously, Mr. Savin and his wife had attempted many different strategies. At this point, Mr. Savin felt that if he were to back off and change his script of badgering and punishing Wade, the situation would worsen. However, taking away privileges was not working. Many people believe that if they make changes in their script, it suggests that they are weak or that they are giving in to others. Such an attitude serves as a barrier, keeping people from considering new, more creative approaches.

We asked the Savins, "If we interviewed Wade and asked him about his seeming lack of responsibility and how you respond to him, what might he say?"

They answered that they had not really thought about Wade's perception of his behavior or theirs.

Mrs. Savin said, "I guess he would say we're always on his back, that we expect perfection, that all we care about are his grades and not about him."

Mr. Savin said, "He might say that, but he would be wrong. We're just thinking about his future."

We acknowledged how much they cared about Wade but wondered what, if anything, they could do differently because their present approach was ineffective and causing them increased stress.

Once again Mr. Savin said, "Why should we be the ones to do something different? It's his problem. I don't want him to feel he can get away with being irresponsible."

We responded that we also wanted their son to be more responsible but noted, "It may be his problem, but it has become your problem as well. Attempting a new approach does not mean giving in as long as the goal is to help Wade be more responsible without having to continually nag him."

Reframing the issue in terms of finding a more effective strategy for encouraging Wade to become more responsible was immediately helpful to the Savins. Once they abandoned the view that changes on their part were equivalent to "giving in," they were able to explore novel scripts they might adopt. We will describe their new scripts later in this chapter.

Obstacle Three: Being Overwhelmed by the Stress of Everyday Life

Several years ago at the conclusion of one of our all-day workshops, a participant observed, "I love your ideas but I'm too stressed out to try them." While there may have been some humor in her statement, it was also evident that she did not feel she had the energy to author a new script. We have all faced this dilemma, knowing that what we are doing is not working but feeling too physically and emotionally depleted to engage in a different approach.

This state of affairs serves as one of the major obstacles to nurturing a resilient mindset. It is true that writing and experimenting with a new script takes time and energy. While some may question whether the effort is worth it, reflect on the cost of continuing to follow the current, ineffective script week after week, month after month, or even year after year. As most would attest, adhering to a counterproductive script proves more emotionally depleting and stressful than writing and performing a new script.

One of the misconceptions that reinforces the assumption that performing new scripts is emotionally and physically depleting is the mistaken belief that for an intervention to be successful, the script has to be dramatically rewritten. Although it has typically taken years for our scripts to be written, many people want to change the entire script overnight, almost a certain prescription for burnout. While some scripts may require a shorter period of time to change, most demand a longer time filled with a series of small steps.

Unfortunately, as some people consider the new script they would like to adopt, they skip ahead to the final goal, failing to identify the smaller or short-term goals that must be reached along the way. Attempting to make drastic changes all at once is one of the major forces that triggers exhaustion and frustration.

"I Think the Cure Is Worse than the Disease" Larry Whitaker was overweight and had high blood pressure and high cholesterol. His physician warned him that unless he began an exercise and diet program, he was placing himself at risk for a stroke or heart attack. He knew he had to make changes in his lifestyle but had been unsuccessful in the past, prompting even greater distress.

In our consultation with Mr. Whitaker, he poignantly said, "I think the cure is worse than the disease. I actually feel worse when I try to change because I always seem to have difficulty following through, and then I feel like a real failure." He may not have realized how perceptive he was when he added, "Sometimes I feel like I am tackling Mt. Everest without the best training or equipment. I'm doomed to failure after I climb just a few steps."

We asked Mr. Whitaker to describe his previous attempts to alter his lifestyle. It became apparent immediately that these attempts were characterized by a desperate quality that resulted in unrealistic goals and expectations. If there were specific words to his script they would have read, "Major change must take place quickly or I will think they are not effective." When his expectations were not realized he became increasingly discouraged, leading him to abandon his goals rather than change them.

Mr. Whitaker's problems were complicated by his belief that he should be able to correct things on his own without the input or support of professionals. It was as if he were setting out on a canoe trip alone for a destination hundreds of miles away without consulting those more knowledgeable about paddling, even though he was unfamiliar with the technique of paddling and did not know when or where to take rests. Rather than seek the advice of others when attempting these trips, he adhered to the same script of doing things on his own. He explained that he was an "individualist," which is fine, but even individualists need the support of others at times.

The fact that he came to see us on the recommendation of his physician attested to his level of unhappiness and stress and to his deteriorating health. He told us in the first session that he felt "very discouraged and sad." It was only at the urging of his physician that he called us. He said, "I don't think I have the energy to try anything new."

In our sessions, we examined Mr. Whitaker's style of setting unrealistic expectations and goals that were doomed to fail. We observed that this style prompted him to feel even more stressed and tired and less likely to find the strength to pursue alternative strategies. We helped him create a reasonable exercise and diet program with clearly specified and achievable short-term goals along the way. A seemingly simple plan of beginning with a mile rather than five-mile walk and adding a half-mile every couple of weeks led to success. We also suggested that Mr. Whitaker meet a nutritionist, a recommendation that he had received but not pursued in the past. A sensible, realistic diet was established, much different from some of the starvation diets Mr. Whitaker had previously tried, diets that led to dramatic weight loss followed by dramatic weight gain.

The strategies we implemented with Mr. Whitaker were not complicated. Without wishing to minimize their effectiveness, they might even fall under the category of common sense. Yet we have discovered that even commonsense approaches may be neglected when struggling to modify a well-established script.

Obstacle Four: Giving Up

Closely related to this last point but deserving separate attention is the influence of mistakes and failure in directing our lives, a theme we will discuss in greater detail in Chapter 8. Suffice it to say that the journey of rehearsing new scripts does not always result in success. Even with careful planning, new scripts may prove ineffective. When this occurs, some people are prone to give up and view their efforts as a failure rather than considering what they might learn from the situation.

One of the hallmarks of a resilient mindset is the ability to view mistakes or failures as experiences from which to learn rather than to feel defeated. Once we begin to perceive unsuccessful plans as an indictment of our abilities, as a testimony to our failure as humans, we are likely to escape from the task of changing our scripts. People escape in different ways. For example, some blame themselves or others, while some minimize the importance of what they were attempting to accomplish. Whatever ways they cope, the end result is the same: relinquishing a goal or a dream. Feelings of low self-esteem and frustration quickly replace any temporary relief experienced by fleeing from an unsuccessful attempt to change a negative script.

We observed this pattern in our work with Mr. Whitaker. Initially, he attempted to minimize his struggles to adhere to an exercise and diet regimen by asserting, "There are a lot of people with high cholesterol and blood pressure who live into their nineties without major health problems." Then, as he became more comfortable with us, his rationale for not pursuing a new script was to cast blame on himself by claiming that he was "too exhausted" or that he "just didn't have the personality to follow through on things."

He added, "Why keep trying something that isn't working?"

If a plan of action has proved ineffective over a lengthy period of time, you should consider whether it is advantageous to continue using it. However, the part of our philosophy that differed from Mr. Whitaker's is what action to take when a strategy or script is failing. If the strategies you are using to achieve an important goal are ineffective, then you must change the strategies rather than retreat from the goal. If you continually retreat from your goals and dreams, the likely outcome is a lowered sense of dignity together with increased despair. This defeatism may eventually assume the form of what psychologist Martin Seligman called *learned helplessness*, or the belief that "whatever I do will not work, so why try?" Once learned helplessness assumes dominance, a feeling of personal control is weakened and a resilient mindset is more difficult to achieve.

When Mr. Whitaker discovered that a person need not terminate a journey if a certain path proved ineffective in reaching a destination, he was better prepared to seek and discover a more productive road to travel.

Become the Author of Your Life

As we have described, there are obstacles to rewriting negative scripts. Some people may become quickly discouraged as they begin the quest to rewrite their counterproductive scripts, especially when some of the obstacles seem overwhelming. However, you must keep in mind a number of important factors when feeling disheartened.

First, even if the task of changing a script is formidable, it is essential to consider the consequences of not making the necessary changes. Very rarely do negative scripts disappear on their own. If anything, the longer they operate, the more entrenched, the more problematic, and the less open to modification they become. You must assess whether the time and effort required to change these scripts outweighs their continued burden on your life.

Second, while the overall challenge of changing established patterns of thinking, feeling, and behaving may seem daunting, the task can be separated into a sequence of smaller, more manageable steps, as Mr. Whitaker discovered. If you focus on these steps, not only will you have a clearer blueprint of what you must do to change, but you will also have many more opportunities to experience success. As each small step is achieved, you are inspired to tackle the demands of the next step. Success breeds success. We should never underestimate the importance of this kind of ongoing positive feedback, which is not as apparent if we have our sights only on a larger, final goal.

Changing negative scripts involves the following steps:

1. Identify negative scripts in your life and assume responsibility to change them.
2. Define short- and long-term goals related to the particular issue at hand.
3. Consider new scripts or plans of action that accord with your goals.
4. Select from these new scripts the one that you believe has the greatest probability for success. This step also requires considering criteria for assessing the success of the new script.
5. Anticipate the possible obstacles that might interfere with reaching your goal and consider how these obstacles might be handled.
6. Put the new script into action and assess its effectiveness.
7. Change your goals, scripts, or approach if they prove unsuccessful.

Let's examine each of these interrelated steps.

Step One: Identify Negative Scripts

As we have witnessed with Mr. Butler, Mr. Castor, and Mrs. Stevens, many of us are unaware of the existence of negative scripts even when these scripts exert a profound influence on our lives. While some easily identify the negative scripts that guide their behavior, others experience more difficulty. Some individuals move through life experiencing unhappiness and dissatisfaction without appreciating or recognizing the role they play in maintaining the status quo. Unfortunately, the very content of some scripts prevents us from questioning the effectiveness of the script. For instance, when a script attributes one's unhappiness to the behavior of others or to conditions that cannot be changed, it is difficult to reflect on new scripts that might improve the situation.

How do you know when a negative script is operating? Some individuals are forced to confront their self-defeating feelings and activities when a crisis emerges from which they can no longer seek refuge behind rationalizations or blaming others. The observations of trusted relatives or friends may provide the impetus to examine one's life. Or longstanding problems, such as those Mr. Butler experienced—anxiety, depression, and insomnia—may propel a person to seek help, a process that eventually forces identification and confrontation of negative behaviors.

The exercise we described earlier in this chapter can facilitate this process of self-discovery; the task of listing three things in your life that you would like to see changed and then openly and honestly considering whether successful change requires someone else to make the initial move encourages us to be more reflective. We have been impressed by the number of people who have told us that compiling the list served as a revelation.

"I Still Think She Can Hurt Me" Melissa Atkins, a woman who attended one of our all-day workshops, called us to schedule a consultation. When she came in, she said with a smile, "I was listening closely to what you had to say, but I must be honest—I was a little distracted after you asked us to think about what we would like to change in our lives and whether it requires someone else to change first."

Given her smile, we felt comfortable asking, "If it's not too personal, what were you thinking?"

Her sense of humor was immediately apparent when she answered, "What's too personal to tell a psychologist? I don't mind telling you what crossed my mind. I'm thirty-eight years old, married with two kids, and all of my life I've been afraid of my mother. As a kid she would scream and yell at me and tell me I was a failure. My father died when I was four years old. I have no siblings. Financially, my mom and I were OK, but she was always so bitter. Maybe my father's death contributed to it. She never remarried. She seemed to take out her hostility on me."

She paused for a moment and then continued, "She would also slap me. To this day I'm still afraid of her, and I still think she can hurt me. Every time I go over to her house, I feel like a little kid again. I want her to tell me she's sorry for what she did and that I'm a good person. So when you asked what we would like to see changed in our lives, what I immediately thought about was that I want my mother to apologize and accept me. Yet even to this day, when my mother gets angry with me I end up apologizing. I guess I still feel I've done something wrong. Then I hope my mother will also say she's sorry for the way she treated me, but she never has."

Mrs. Atkins continued, "Talk about a negative script on my part! I feed right into my mother's behavior because I keep thinking if I act nice, if I do what she wants, if I apologize, then she will act nice to me. It's such an obvious script, but to be honest it's one that I truly wasn't aware of. But then during your workshop I realized that I keep basing my happiness on having my mother change. If it weren't so sad it would almost be comical. I have to face the fact that there's no chance my mother will change unless I confront her with what she has done. But I've been afraid to say anything because I'm still that scared little girl when I'm with her. But then something dawned on me: if I confront her and she still doesn't change, at least I can move on with my life and not base my happiness on my mother's suddenly seeing the light. I know I have to deal with this script. Not only is it a burden on me, but it affects my relationship with my husband and my two daughters. When I become preoccupied with my mother, which is often, I'm less happy and less available to my family. I'm also more irritable. I've apologized to them about my moodiness, but how often can you apologize without taking some action to change the situation?"

Mrs. Atkins's insight was very impressive. While the questions we posed at our workshop may have served as a catalyst for her to seek a clearer understanding of her behavior and her relationship with her mother, we felt that given the immediate impact of these questions, she had already begun to question her script as a daughter before she attended the workshop. This particular exercise can prompt us to think more precisely about ongoing patterns and relationships in our lives. We will return to Mrs. Atkins shortly.

Because the next six steps of the sequence are intertwined, for the purpose of coherence and continuity we will describe each of the steps first without providing examples of specific people. Once we have outlined all six steps, we will illustrate the entire sequence with examples.

Step Two: Define Your Goals

Once you accomplish Step One and accept responsibility for changing your life, it becomes less difficult to define your goals. If you wait for others to change, setting goals is often an exercise in futility and frustration. The more precise you are in defining goals, the better equipped you will be to write new scripts that will help you reach these goals. As you will come to appreciate, this process is facilitated when you divide goals into short-term and long-term categories, with the short-term goals contributing to the realization of the long-term goals.

Step Three: Consider New Scripts

Having fulfilled Steps One and Two, the next step is to consider possible new scripts that will move you toward your goals. We encourage you to brainstorm during this phase. Think of several new scripts without immediately judging or dismissing any. Be careful to avoid creating a new script, only to resort quickly to a negative attitude and say, "I can't do this" or "It will never work." The goals that have been established during Step Two can offer guideposts for authoring new scripts. As part of this process, it is useful to think about the goals you have defined and the ways in which your old scripts have kept you from reaching these goals.

Don't become discouraged if you have difficulty contemplating new scripts. While some people may be able to develop several new scripts, others may struggle to create one. While having at least two new scripts from which to choose helps one to articulate more clearly the different options available, writing even one new script represents an achievement for many individuals who have been trapped for years in negative patterns of behavior. Some people require the input and support of a counselor as they engage in the task of contemplating the words of a new script.

Step Four: Select Your New Script

Obviously, selecting one script from several applies only when you have more than one script from which to choose. When you do, it is important to think about each new script and whether it will help you to fulfill your goals. You must also anticipate how other people might respond to your "new" behavior in each script and how you might react to their response. One can never predict with certainty the response of others, but it is helpful to engage in this exercise so that you think about different strategies to use based on their responses. This exercise will assist you in deciding which script appears to hold the greatest chance for success.

If you can think of only one new script, it is still important to rehearse it mentally and think about the reactions of others. Doing so will not only prepare you for the various possibilities that may arise but may serve as a catalyst for contemplating additional scripts.

As part of the process of selecting a new script, you should also ask, *How will I know if my new script is successful?* The answer to this question requires that you have clearly defined short- and long-term goals and ways to measure the achievement of these goals. We are not advocating that you use the kind of complex, statistically based criteria better suited for a scientific research project, but that you do have some ways to measure the efficacy of the new script in realizing your goals.

Step Five: Anticipate the Possible Obstacles

In Step Four we advocated anticipating the response of others. This anticipation prepares you for possible roadblocks that may emerge as you begin a new journey with a new script. While some may mistakenly interpret this fifth step as reinforcing a self-fulfilling prophecy for failure, anticipating obstacles alerts you to consider effective ways of dealing with these obstacles. If the anticipated obstacles do not arise, you have not lost anything; if they do arise, you have plans in place to deal with them.

The process of considering possible roadblocks may lead you to make changes in your new script prior to using it. You may recognize flaws in the script that you can correct, thereby minimizing future problems.

Step Six: Put the New Script into Action and Assess Its Effectiveness

Once you have selected your new script, you must put it into practice. When and with whom you put it into practice should be guided by your goals. In addition, you must keep in mind your criteria for assessing the effectiveness of the script and make appropriate changes when indicated.

Step Seven: Change What's Unsuccessful

Perseverance is a valuable trait, but if you have attempted a new script for a reasonable period of time without positive results it may be time to abandon the script and attempt a new one. Of course, an important question is how best to define "reasonable." There is no simple answer. A reasonable amount of time for one situation may not be reasonable for another. The reality is that in some situations all the parties involved are afflicted with calcified scripts that require time to be replaced. In others, in which the existing scripts are more permeable, modifications may be expected to take place more rapidly.

The short- and long-term goals you establish, together with your criteria to assess success, can help you decide when it is reasonable to give up one new script and adopt another. It is for this reason that articulating goals is such a crucial part of the process of reinforcing a resilient lifestyle.

The Courage to Change Negative Scripts

The word *courage* captures the honesty, energy, and anxiety involved in the process of acknowledging and changing particular patterns of thinking, feeling, and behaving that have proved counterproductive. Change is often fraught with uncertainty. However, without this honesty and willingness to venture from familiar paths, we may not be able to reach our destination of a more hopeful, optimistic, resilient mindset. It is our desire that as we describe the journey taken by others who have followed the steps we have outlined, you will be better prepared for the journey that awaits you.

"They Finally Get It Because I Finally Got It"

Let's return to our interventions with Mr. Butler. He initially assumed little, if any, responsibility for the difficulty he was having with his managers, quickly labeling them as incompetent and unresponsive. In our work with Mr. Butler we focused not only on helping him become more aware of how his behavior affected others but also on the roots of his negative script. As you may recall, a turning point in therapy occurred when we asked him what words his managers and other employees would use to describe him. Much to his distress, he said that most likely they would describe him in the same negative way that he would describe his father—namely, opinionated and critical.

The first step in changing negative scripts, recognizing and taking ownership of one's own behavior, could be accomplished only when Mr. Butler realized the parallel between his behavior and the behavior of his father. With this insight he could begin to acknowledge how his style contributed to the problems in his business. We then moved to the second step by asking Mr. Butler to consider his goals at work.

Mr. Butler responded, "One of my main goals is for my managers to do what they are supposed to do without my having to remind them and for them to come up with new ideas without my having to prod them. Of course, if they could do that, then my business would be more successful, which is another goal. And I can think of another goal: that I don't have such a high turnover of managers, because it costs a lot to hire and train new people."

He then added, "If these goals were accomplished I think my anxiety, depression, and sleep problems would disappear."

We discussed the goals he had defined and how they might be divided into the categories of short- and long-term goals. Mr. Butler seemed to enjoy this problem-solving approach. He said that his short-term goals were for his managers to respond "creatively" to his requests for solutions to current problems and "not sit there like lumps" when he requested their input.

We asked him to be a little more specific about these goals.

He said, "There are three new products we are working on. Within the next year, I would like to see two of them completed. I guess that's a long-term goal. In the next three months I would like to see the design for these products completed. I would like to see sales of our existing products increase by 5 percent in the next twelve months. And as another goal I would like to see the turnover rate cut to one or two people for the entire year."

We then challenged Mr. Butler by asking, "What is it that you can do differently to have a chance to realize these goals?"

Not surprisingly, Mr. Butler resorted to his old script by saying, "My managers need to become more productive."

We smiled, and before we could say anything, Mr. Butler also smiled and said, "That's my old script, right?"

Given his display of levity, we responded, "You're very perceptive."

Mr. Butler then said, "I think I have to be clearer in my meetings with my managers, especially when I describe my expectations for them and review the projects they are working on. Maybe I have to give them a little more breathing space. I certainly don't want them to see me the way I saw my father."

We reviewed specific comments that Mr. Butler could make so as to change his script and then, in concert with Step Five, we asked, "What might interfere with implementing your new script?" The difficulty in changing longstanding mindsets was readily apparent in Mr. Butler's response.

"Things may not work out if they continue not to get it and if they continue to come up with inadequate ideas."

In an empathic way, we wondered, "If they continue to have difficulty 'getting it' what is it that you can do differently?"

To assist Mr. Butler, we engaged in a rehearsal of the actual words he might use to make his expectations clearer and to be encouraging rather than critical. As one example, we suggested that he find and acknowledge positive features in some of the ideas his managers presented and say to them, "I appreciate the thinking you've done about this project. I think this point [and offer a specific example] would really be helpful in our work. I see a couple of areas that need some more thought, but it seems we're heading in the right direction."

As we reviewed the possible words of a new script, Mr. Butler questioned how sincere he would seem in saying them. We empathized and said that whenever we change a script, our initial attempts at a new script might have an artificial flavor. We noted, however, that the new script typically becomes more genuine the more we use it, especially if it is successful.

We will long remember the day Mr. Butler came in and with obvious enjoyment said, "They finally get it." He paused and added, "They finally get it because I finally got it."

Mr. Butler's company became more profitable, and resignations among his managers dropped significantly. As he had predicted, his anxiety and depression also decreased, but not for the reasons he had originally expected. Initially he had argued that his mental and physical health would improve when his managers improved. While this was partly true, he omitted an important distinction that he recognized later: namely, that their improvement was largely a result of his actions and the more positive climate he created at work. In changing his script, he felt more in control of his life and less dominated by images of his father, a situation that lessened his anxiety, depression, and insomnia.

"I'm Not That Scared Little Girl Anymore"

In our work with Mrs. Atkins, she stressed that her immediate goals centered around her relationship with her mother, which she felt affected all aspects of her life. We were impressed by the level of ownership she displayed in bringing about a change in her script.

With much feeling she asserted, "I want to be less frightened when I think about or visit my mother. I want my mother to stop belittling me. Wait, let me word it differently. I don't want to feel belittled when my mother criticizes me or screams at me. I want my mother to accept me, but I guess I first have to accept myself and realize that I am not a weak, scared person."

Mrs. Atkins added, "I guess my long-term goal is to have at least a cordial relationship with my mother, but if that's not possible then the goal would be for me to give up the dream of having that kind of relationship. My short-term goals are to be less scared of her and not to let her push me around."

We asked Mrs. Atkins if she thought her mother was aware of how she felt about her or the impact she had on her.

"She must. I think it's very obvious."

We wondered, "It may be obvious, but has she ever heard it directly from you?"

Mrs. Atkins answered, "No, I don't have the nerve. She might scream at me or even hit me."

"When she screams, what do you typically do?"

"I don't like to admit this, but I get so upset that I usually start to cry and leave the room. I don't do that with other people, just with her."

We asked, "Keeping in mind your goals, what would you like to do?"

Mrs. Atkins said, "First, I would like to tell my mother that I want to have a better relationship with her but that I will not allow her to scream at or hit me again."

"What's keeping you from saying that?"

Mrs. Atkins replied, "The thought of her screaming or trying to slap me frightens me." She then smiled.

We asked her what prompted her smile.

"This may sound weird, but my mother is actually a rather frail woman now and I am much bigger than she is. As I'm sitting here I realize that physically she can't hurt me, but I still see her as this powerful woman and myself as this weak child."

We commented, "When we've been following a script for years, it's amazing how frozen our perceptions become. What would you like to do if she tries to slap you?"

Mrs. Atkins smiled again and said, "I've had this image for years—I guess you would call it a new script, except I haven't used it in real life. I imagine my mother screaming and then trying to hit me. I catch her arm, hold it, and firmly say to her, 'You are never to do that again! I am not someone you can abuse!'"

"What do you imagine your mother's response would be if you did that?"

Mrs. Atkins replied, "Sometimes I imagine her looking stunned and apologizing to me, but other times I imagine her screaming more and telling me I shouldn't speak to her like that, and then I fall back into the old script and begin to cry and leave the room."

In an effort to help Mrs. Atkins think of different scripts and different responses, we asked, "What if you tell her how you felt as you imagine yourself doing and she starts to yell at you? Besides running away, what else might you do?"

"I could look her right in the eye and tell her she can scream all she wants, but she will no longer hurt or intimidate me."

"Do you think you can do that?"

Mrs. Atkins thought for a moment and said with some doubt, "I think I can."

"What would help you feel more certain?"

Mrs. Atkins smiled once more and said, "This might sound crazy, but I just have to remind myself that in reality I am bigger than she is."

During the next couple of sessions we rehearsed various scripts and engaged in role-playing to prepare Mrs. Atkins for her new script. She reported involving her husband in the role-playing, much to his delight because he had never been very fond of his mother-in-law and resented how she treated his wife.

Mrs. Atkins noted, "My husband and I switch roles. Sometimes he plays me, sometimes my mom. When he plays me he loves to tell my mother off in language that could not be used in polite company. When he plays my mom and I confront him, he loves to ask for my forgiveness. He's really into this. I think it's been very therapeutic for him. I told him that you should bill his insurance number." Mrs. Atkins's sense of humor served as a strength.

Perhaps if this were a Hollywood movie, we could report that when Mrs. Atkins confronted her mother, her mother apologized and their relationship improved. Although Mrs. Atkins was sensitive "but firm" with her mother, her mother yelled at her for being ungrateful. Mrs. Atkins told her she was not to yell or she would leave. Her mother continued to yell and Mrs. Atkins left. As she did so, her mother screamed, "I don't want to see you anymore. You don't deserve a mother like me."

Mrs. Atkins replied, "You don't know how right you are."

Mrs. Atkins made one more attempt at establishing a more cordial relationship by writing her mother a letter that contained a conciliatory tone. Her mother wrote back, "I don't want to see you again."

Mrs. Atkins said, "It's sad to think that my mother has cut herself off from me and from her grandchildren. I've explained the situation to my kids so that they understand what's going on."

Then she added a revealing comment. "Although I feel sad, I also feel very relieved. I did what I had to do. I reached my goal of not being intimidated by my mother. I realize that my goal of having a better relationship with my mother was beyond my total control because it also involved her making a change."

Mrs. Atkins called us months later to say she had not had any contact with her mother but that all other parts of her life were going very well. "I'm feeling more content and more relaxed, and my husband and kids have commented about the change. That means a lot to me."

"We're Not Giving In—We're Changing Our Script"

As a final example of the sequence involved in changing scripts, let's return to Mr. and Mrs. Savin, the couple whose son, Wade, was performing poorly in school and not acting "responsibly." When they first spoke with us, they had not progressed past Step One, believing, as Mr. Savin asserted, "Why should we be the ones to do something different? It's his problem. I don't want him to feel he can get away with being irresponsible."

We reframed the problem by observing, "Attempting a new approach does not mean giving in, as long as the goal is to help your son be more responsible without your having to continually nag him."

Once they were able to recognize that their script with Wade was bankrupt and that changing this script was not synonymous with giving in, they were open to considering their goals and applying new scripts. A couple of their long-term goals were for Wade to become a more responsible person and for them to have a more pleasant, less tense relationship with him.

We kept these longer-term goals in mind as we considered several short-term goals. One short-term goal was for Wade to complete his homework without being reminded to do so. Another short-term goal was to spend time with him, free of tension. We discussed different scripts that they might adopt to meet these goals. With our input they decided on two main ones to pursue.

The first involved both his schoolwork and home responsibilities. At a calm moment they sat down and designed a new script. They asked him if he thought they were nagging him.

Without hesitation Wade responded, "Yes. I'm glad to see that you finally realize what you've been doing."

Rather than becoming angry as they typically would, they continued with their new script. They said that they did not want to nag him because it was hurting their relationship with him and it wasn't helping him complete his work at school or his responsibilities at home. They then engaged in a problem-solving dialogue with him, asking him what he thought would help the situation.

At first Wade said, "I don't know."

In our sessions with Mr. and Mrs. Savin, they had anticipated this answer from Wade. Thus, they were prepared and said, "That's OK. It may take some time to think of possible solutions."

Mr. Savin said, "Wade looked stunned when we said this. He wasn't prepared for our new script. Even though it was a serious matter, I had to keep from laughing when I saw his expression."

Most important, within a few days Wade actually arrived at a couple of solutions, including doing some of his homework before dinner and posting household responsibilities for each member of the family on the refrigerator. Wade told them that having the responsibilities posted would serve as a reminder so that they would not have to "nag" him. Much to their surprise and delight, he even advised them that if he needed to be reminded they could point to the refrigerator.

To improve their relationship with Wade, Mr. and Mrs. Savin initiated the practice of having a special time each week with him. This special time involved going out to dinner. When one of them took Wade out for dinner, the other parent did the same for his younger sister but at a different restaurant. We often advocate such "special times." This intervention was very successful with Wade, especially when the rule was instituted at Wade's recommendation that any discussion of school was off limits during dinner.

Although there were expected bumps along the road in achieving their goals, Mr. and Mrs. Savin were better prepared for these bumps. When Wade forgot a responsibility, his parents pointed to the refrigerator, a strategy that was successful because it was Wade's idea. When they found themselves getting angry with him, instead of resorting to their old script they kept their goals in mind and asked, "Is what we are doing in accord with our goals or working against these goals?" They found that asking this question served to "keep us on the right track and to stick with our new script."

Mrs. Savin said, "We constantly remind ourselves that if things are to improve, we have to consider what we can do differently. We found that when we were more reasonable, when we did not revert to old patterns, Wade usually responded in a positive way. We had been worried that we would be giving in if we changed, but actually by becoming more flexible we could still remain firm and consistent. And the good news is that Wade has become more responsible and much easier to live with."

Scripts Are Not Cast in Stone

People who have a resilient mindset reflect on what they can do differently when confronted with challenges. The ability to recognize and modify negative scripts serves as a basic foundation for a resilient lifestyle. Think of the exercises we have recommended in this chapter as a guidepost for making desired changes in your life. Reflect on the stories we have shared and on the benefits of searching within oneself for answers to problems. The more we can accept realistic ownership for what transpires in our lives, the more empowered and resilient we will become.

3

Choosing the Path to Become Stress Hardy Rather than Stressed Out

Sam Millis and Gene Newman were in their early thirties and employed by the same high-tech firm in similar managerial positions in research and development. We met them during a consultation. They were both married. Mr. Millis had two young children, while Mr. Newman's wife was expecting their second child. Their positions at work were demanding, filled with deadlines and the need to design, test, and produce new products in a very competitive market. Yet in interviewing these two men confronted by seemingly similar demands, an immediate difference was apparent. Mr. Newman was burdened by a great deal of anxiety at work, while this was not the case with Mr. Millis.

Mr. Newman experienced headaches on a regular basis and had difficulty sleeping. A perceptible anxiety was his constant companion. When the stress intensified, he became impatient and demanding of his staff, often making critical comments. At times, he would question the value of the project he was working on. When the person to whom he reported suggested changes in a project, Mr. Newman would think, "This is the last straw. They keep wanting me to change things. It's one more pressure to deal with. Everyone is so rigid. They won't listen to what I have to say." Not surprisingly, Mr. Newman's distress spilled over to his home environment, causing him to be less responsive to his wife and young daughter.

Mr. Millis shared responsibilities similar to those of Mr. Newman, yet his outlook on work and his level of anxiety were noticeably different. He openly discussed the demands of his job but said, "It's the nature of our work. I expect it and am prepared for it." He added, "I remind myself that what I do makes a difference to this company and in the lives of others."

He went on, "I would be surprised if a week went by without some unexpected modifications in projects. When I start to feel more stressed, I make certain I find ways to deal with it and not let it overwhelm me. If I come across as stressed out or if I become angry with my staff, it only adds to everyone's discomfort. If that happens, we will have trouble finishing our project successfully."

Mr. Millis also observed, "When I come home I quickly change clothes. I like to get in my denims. It may seem funny, but changing from the clothes I wear at work, taking off my tie and getting into my denims, is more than just a change of clothes for me. Once I'm in what I call my 'home clothes,' I feel I'm no longer at work and I can concentrate on my family rather than on the latest work project. I hope that doesn't sound weird."

It didn't sound weird at all. Mr. Millis had discovered effective ways to manage stress.

The Impact of Stress

Mr. Newman and Mr. Millis. Two men with similar jobs but strikingly different outlooks. One was evidently more stressed than the other. But why? In what ways do they differ? Attempting to answer these questions is not merely an academic exercise, because, as we have noted, a basic feature of resilient people is their ability to deal effectively with stress and pressure. Research clearly indicates that a high level of stress is related to psychological and physical problems.

Severe stress is associated with the emergence of depression and anxiety. In one study, subjects who experienced a stressful situation had nearly six times the risk of developing depression within that month. In about a third of the cases, the stress itself was not the cause of the depression; instead experts believe that individuals genetically predisposed to depression may also be more vulnerable to becoming involved in high-stress situations. It was also found that "stress diminishes the quality of life by reducing feelings of pleasure and accomplishment, and relationships are often threatened."[1]

Stress causes and exacerbates a wide spectrum of physical problems, including heart disease, stroke, susceptibility to infections, gastrointestinal difficulties, weight loss or gain, diabetes, pain, and sexual and reproductive dysfunction. Also, people under chronic stress frequently seek relief through drug or alcohol abuse, tobacco use, abnormal eating patterns, or passive activities, such as watching television.

> *The damage these self-destructive habits cause under ordinary circumstances is compounded by the physiologic effects of stress itself. And the cycle is self-perpetuating; a sedentary routine, an unhealthy diet, alcohol abuse, and smoking promote heart disease, interfere with sleep patterns, and lead to increased rather than reduced tension levels.*[2]

Statistics reported by the U.S. Bureau of Labor Statistics, the National Institute for Occupational Safety and Health, and Roper Starch Worldwide Study indicated that job burnout typically attributed to stress was responsible for 40 percent of worker turnover. Three hundred billion dollars ($7,500 per employee) is spent annually in the United States on stress-related compensation claims, diminished productivity, absenteeism from work, health insurance costs, direct medical expenses, and employee turnover.[3] The recognition of the high personal and financial toll of stress was reflected in more than $11 billion spent in 1999 on stress management programs and products.

Stress Hardiness and a Resilient Mindset

It is evident from these statistics that the better equipped we are to manage stress, the more productive, satisfying, healthy, and resilient we will be. The impact that stress has on all aspects of our lives invites the following questions:

- What are the factors that help people to respond to difficult situations in a less stressed way?
- Do people who are less stressed see the world and themselves differently from those who are more vulnerable to stress? If so, what are these differences?
- In what ways do less stressed people respond to events that distinguish them from their more stressed counterparts?

Reflect on how you might answer these questions in relation to Mr. Newman and Mr. Millis. As we noted in Chapter 1, inborn temperament plays a role in how effectively a person copes with pressure. Research related to temperament indicates that some people from birth are predisposed to feeling stress more intensely than others. However, inborn temperament is not the sole factor in determining one's level of stress; many life situations, including interactions with others, contribute to how stress and pressure are experienced and managed.

A person's lifestyle, including exercise, proper diet, and adequate sleep, all influence the effectiveness with which they manage stress. But how do you develop a healthy lifestyle, and what is the mindset that is the foundation of this lifestyle? The research of psychologist Dr. Suzanne Kobasa and her colleagues offers sensible guidelines for addressing these questions.

Dr. Kobasa defined the characteristics of what she called the *stress hardy personality*.[4] Individuals who possess these characteristics experience and respond to seemingly stressful events in a more adaptive, effective way than those who are limited in these characteristics. Given our focus on the concept of mindsets, we prefer to refer to a stress hardy *mindset*. As we noted earlier, we use the word *mindset* to highlight the fact that mindsets can be changed; in contrast, the word *personality* seems to be associated with an entity that is fixed and may be resistant to modification. This is not just an issue of semantics, but rather a reflection of our approach, which is rooted in the values of personal control and empowerment.

Dr. Kobasa outlined three components of stress hardiness. As we describe and provide examples of each component, including those from the lives of Mr. Newman and Mr. Millis, ask yourself, *Do I practice this component in my life? If not, how can I begin to adopt this mindset and make it part of my everyday lifestyle?* Let's examine these three features of the mindset of stress hardy people.

Commitment

Dr. Kobasa described *commitment* as being involved with, rather than alienated from, the many aspects of life. When commitment is present, we possess a sense of purpose that tells us why we are doing what we are doing. We are guided by a vision that provides passion and meaning to our lives and lessens the impact of stress. In essence, we have a reason for waking up each morning and meeting life's challenges. Commitment is not confined to a single area but is evident in our personal relationships, in our work, in our charitable activities, in causes we adopt, and in our religious practices. It is impossible to lead a resilient life devoid of purpose.

In our workshops we often ask questions such as the following:

- What are two or three things that give meaning and purpose to your life?
- What energizes you?
- Do the main activities you engage in give meaning to your life?
- Do you derive satisfaction from each of these activities?

On pages 271–272 in Appendix A, jot down your answers to these questions. Resilient people are those who, even in the face of intense pressure, find meaning in their activities, thereby lessening the pressure to which they might be exposed. Not only do resilient people appreciate what brings meaning and value to their lives but, as we shall discuss in Chapter 6, their actions are in accord with these values. We are more vulnerable to stress if we believe our lives are bereft of purpose or if we fail to follow a path in which we feel that we are being honest and true to our values.

Mr. Sargent, whom we met in Chapter 1, felt stressed because his behavior was not in accord with his priorities or commitments. Although he listed his roles as a husband and as a father as his two top priorities, the time he spent with his wife and children was very limited. Mr. Sargent listed those areas that gave purpose to his life, but his behavior did not reflect what was important to him.

Some people have difficulty identifying or keeping in the forefront of their minds the beliefs or activities that provide meaning, thereby increasing their vulnerability to stress and lessening their capacity for resilience. Lou Bauer, a thirty-eight-year-old high school science teacher, was one of those people.

"I Felt I Had Little Spark Left" Mr. Bauer came in to see us because of "feeling fatigued, having little energy, and becoming more and more irritated at work and at home." The suggestion of a trusted colleague who noted that Mr. Bauer was becoming increasingly "bitter" at school triggered his call to us.

Mr. Bauer told us that this colleague observed that in the teacher's lounge all of his comments were "very negative about the students, about our work conditions, and about our salaries." Mr. Bauer added, "My friend said that I looked very stressed and unhappy and that he was very concerned about me."

We asked Mr. Bauer what he thought.

"I wish I could say my friend is wrong, but I can't. I dislike going to school each morning. I find the students don't seem to care. I get little enjoyment out of teaching. I get a lot of pressure from parents to give their kids good grades so they can get into good colleges, even if the kids don't deserve good grades. I hate to admit this, but I wish I had more years in the system so that I would be eligible to receive a high pension right now."

"How long have you been teaching?" we asked.

"Sixteen years. I got my first teaching job right out of college and then attended college in the evening to get my master's."

"What led you into teaching?"

"I haven't thought about that in a while. I can tell you one of the main things was Miss Lapora. She was my science teacher when I was in the ninth grade. I guess I was goofing off, starting to get involved with kids who didn't like school. I failed one of the first tests she gave. I will never forget that she asked me to come see her and told me that she thought I had much more talent than I was showing and that she was concerned that I was wasting it. She said, 'You have a choice. You can throw away opportunities, or you can decide to succeed. I can't make the choice for you, but if I could I would certainly tell you to take advantage of how smart you are.'"

Mr. Bauer paused and then added, "I was stunned. My first reaction was to politely tell her it was my life to lead. But I didn't say this because I knew by the way she spoke that she really cared about me. I can honestly say that her comment had a major impact on me. It probably came at a critical time. I thought a lot about what she said and I slowly turned things around. I remember at the end of the following year I made the honor roll and she said to me, 'Congratulations—it took a lot of courage to change what you had been doing.' That comment also had a major impact on me."

We asked, "In what way?"

"I remember feeling so proud of what I had accomplished and thinking that I wanted to do for others what she had done for me. I think she was the main reason I went into teaching."

"How was teaching for you when you first started?"

"It seems so long ago. I remember being nervous and excited. I remember thinking I was only a few years older than some of my students, that some of them probably knew more than I did. But I enjoyed it. I felt I was making a difference in the lives of my students. I remember trying to create moments with them similar to what Miss Lapora had created with me."

As Mr. Bauer described the beginning of his career, it was obvious that at one point he had felt a strong passion for his work, one that brought him much satisfaction. During our next few sessions, we focused on what had changed, what had led him to feel bitter and burned out. The discussion prompted the following exchange:

Mr. Bauer said, "Maybe everyone gets burned out if they stay with something too long, especially in the teaching profession."

We said, "We're not certain about that, but what's more important is to determine what you see as leading to your change, your feelings of burnout."

Mr. Bauer continued, "I'm not sure it was any one thing. After a few years I felt I had little spark left. The students just sat there and seemed to lack any interest. And to be honest, I don't think I showed much enthusiasm. Recently I went home and I had a really morbid thought. I thought that if I died in a car accident that day, the students might not even realize I wasn't there the next day or they wouldn't care that I was absent. That really led me to think that it was time to leave teaching."

We then asked another question to focus on the issue of commitment and purpose: "Do you think that any of your students see you in the same way you saw Miss Lapora?"

"I guess you'd have to ask my students."

"But what do you think?"

Mr. Bauer paused and then said, "I would guess none of them see me that way."

We continued, "It might help to look back to figure out what changed. During the first few years of your teaching, do you think any of your students felt about you the same way you felt about Miss Lapora?"

"It's interesting you should bring that up. The other day I was cleaning up some of my files and found some notes and letters that students had sent me from my first few years of teaching. Most were written after they graduated from high school, telling me what a difference I had made in their lives. What a wonderful feeling. I haven't received notes like that in a long time. Actually, when you asked what led me into teaching and I told you about Miss Lapora, I realized that I hadn't thought about her in a long time." As Mr. Bauer said this, feelings of resignation and sadness were pronounced.

A passion for or excitement about one's work or other activities of life cannot always be sustained at a high level. However, it was evident that Mr. Bauer, similar to many people, had lost sight of the meaning of his work.

It had become just another job, and an unhappy one at that. A loss of meaning invites dissatisfaction and stress, but many individuals, instead of reflecting on ways to recapture purpose and meaning, get trapped in a negative script, becoming even more lost and bitter.

One of the main reasons that we ask people to list the priorities in their lives is to initiate a process that we hope will energize them as they reflect on their values. Based on what they list as their priorities (such as family, work, hobbies, or charities), we pose such questions as:

- Why did you go into your profession?
- Why did you become a parent?
- Why did you get married?
- What satisfactions do each of these activities or roles provide you?
- What frustrations have been associated with these activities or roles?
- How do you cope with the frustrations?

Take a moment to ask yourself these questions. Write your answers on pages 272–273 in Appendix A. As you think about what you would list as the priorities in your life, recall your feelings and thoughts about these priorities when they were new to you and how these feelings and thoughts have changed over the years.

We asked Mr. Bauer the following question: "Would you like to feel again what you felt during the first years of teaching?"

Mr. Bauer immediately replied, "Yes, I'm sure if I did I would feel much happier and less stressed. I think I'd also be a better husband and father. I know that I'm bringing my unhappiness into my home."

"What do you think would help you recapture the excitement from your early years of teaching?"

We will share Mr. Bauer's very interesting response and our subsequent interventions with him later in this chapter when we review one of the other components of stress hardiness. Until we do, if you have faced a situation or life crisis similar to Mr. Bauer's, think about how you might answer the last question we posed.

The importance of commitment as an antidote to stress was captured in an article written by the late psychologist Dr. Julius Segal that focused on managing life's struggles.[5] He highlighted the importance of "giving purpose to your pain" and described the response of Eileen Stevens when her twenty-year-old son, Chuck, died as a consequence of a college fraternity hazing incident. Chuck was locked in a car trunk after being instructed to drink bottles of beer, whiskey, and wine. When the trunk was opened, Chuck was unconscious. He never recovered.

Mrs. Stevens said that "tragedy has a way of getting priorities in order" and founded CHUCK (Committee to Halt Useless College Killings). Dr. Segal reported that Mrs. Stevens devoted her time not only to speaking with and writing to hundreds of fraternities across the country but to helping many states pass laws that controlled the types of hazing activities that took her son's life.

Mrs. Stevens observed, "I travel, I speak. I share information. . . . I've channeled my grief in a positive direction."

Dr. Segal also discussed Norwegian psychiatrist Leo Eitinger, a concentration camp survivor. Dr. Eitinger was convinced that it was devotion to a higher cause, "whether another person or a political or religious belief," that provided the energy for many Nazi death camp inmates to survive and go on to lead relatively normal lives.

Dr. Segal emphasized that altruism, an unselfish desire to help others, can minimize stress and pain. He cited the work of psychiatrist Dr. Irvin Yalom finding that a commitment to and compassion for others allows us to deal with adversity. Dr. Yalom observed that "the idea of being a model for others, especially for children, can fill life with meaning until the moment of death." Similarly, psychologist Dr. Lynn Videka-Sherman studied 200 parents nationwide after they had lost a child. She found that depression and stress were significantly less among those parents who reinvested or recommitted their energy to another person or an activity. Some volunteered to help other parents who were facing the death of a child—for example, in such organizations as The Compassionate Friends, a national self-help group that offers support to bereaved parents.

Perhaps one of the most powerful and poignant examples of the importance of commitment or purpose was captured in the words of another Holocaust survivor, the renowned Austrian psychiatrist Dr. Viktor Frankl, developer of a form of psychotherapy known as *logotherapy*, or *meaning therapy*. In his book *Man's Search for Meaning*, Dr. Frankl describes a moment while imprisoned in a concentration camp when he had given up and his will to live had all but disappeared. He recognized that if he were to survive he must discover some purpose to life even within the death camp, some force that would permit him to go on.

The purpose he devised was to imagine himself lecturing after the war about what had transpired in the concentration camps in order to help others understand and appreciate what he and millions of others had experienced. Dr. Frankl confronted unfathomable sadness, pain, and resignation through the act of articulating a goal and image that served to provide meaning to his life. Given the horrors and mass murders of the concentration camps, he could not know with any certainty whether he would survive the camps or die within the next hour. What he knew was that as long as he was alive, he could draw strength from an image of his lecturing in the future. For Dr. Frankl, that image was to become a reality.

As we leave this component of stress hardiness, return to the exercise we suggested earlier, and record your priorities and what brings meaning to your life. Also, ask yourself, *Am I leading a life that reinforces my priorities and values?* Are the activities in which I choose to engage in accord with my priorities and values? If there is too great a discrepancy between your values and behavior or if values have not been well defined, you will be more vulnerable to stress and its many negative concomitants.

Challenge

The second component of a stress hardy mindset is *challenge*. Not surprisingly, stress hardy individuals are those who perceive difficult situations as challenges from which to learn rather than opportunities to feel defeated. It is not always an easy task when faced with adversity to search for the opportunities that may lie ahead as hidden nuggets in the terrain. But not to undertake this search is to continue to experience pessimism and stress.

Interestingly, in the Chinese language the same word is used for "crisis" and "opportunity with danger." The Chinese recognized that difficult situations contain the seeds for growth. We recently heard of a similar definition of crisis: "opportunity riding dangerous winds." To move beyond a crisis outlook to one of opportunity and growth often requires abandoning negative scripts and summoning the courage to author new scripts.

The Fear of Leaving One's Comfort Zone Frank Celester was a fifty-year-old man whose job was being eliminated because of downsizing. He had been with his company for twenty years. He obtained a generous severance package affording him months to search for another position. However, he began to experience intense anxiety and stress. At one point he thought he was having a heart attack. He felt directionless and frightened.

Mr. Celester came to see us. He talked about the shock of losing his job after twenty years and the uncertainty of not knowing what he would do next. His anxiety was heightened by the reality of having two children in high school, one of whom was to begin attending a private college with a hefty tuition within the year. While some level of anxiety was certainly understandable, two things immediately impressed us. The first was how paralyzed and lost Mr. Celester appeared to be. The other was how much he had disliked his job for the past ten years, a job that brought him little satisfaction and much pressure.

After he described his unhappiness at work, we felt that in order for Mr. Celester to move ahead, we should spend some time focusing on the question of why he had remained in a position for ten years that he had disliked so much.

Mr. Celester responded, "I was making a good living. It was scary to think about looking for another job."

As we discussed this further, Mr. Celester acknowledged that several of his colleagues had sought and found other positions and that several years ago one of his former coworkers had invited him to apply for a position in his new company. Mr. Celester said he gave only "fleeting thought" to the invitation. He added, "What's that expression? A bird in the hand is worth two in the bush."

We agreed but wondered, "What if the bird in the hand is not very satisfying and you haven't even considered the possibilities that are in the bush?"

Mr. Celester smiled and said he was not much of a "risk taker." In essence, he preferred to stay in his comfort zone even though this zone was filled with negative feelings and pressure. He said that if his job had not been eliminated, he was certain that he would have remained in the position until retirement. He also acknowledged how stressful the last ten years had been on him and his family because he was so "miserable" at work.

Mr. Celester was encountering something many people experience: an inertia caused by fear of the unknown. But the elimination of his position was a blessing in disguise. It forced him to leave his comfort zone and enter unknown territory. We reframed his situation from one of uncertainty and anxiety to one of opportunity. We considered with him the reasonable steps that he could take in his search for a new job. As he created a list of these steps (such as consulting with an executive search firm, defining more clearly the kind of position he would like to have and was qualified to meet, and developing a résumé) and followed through on them, his anxiety decreased. Each small step reinforced a sense of success. After a few months he had several positions from which to choose and selected the one that best matched his interests, style, and temperament.

Mr. Celester said, "I don't know why I remained in my old job for so long." Returning to the metaphor he used earlier, he explained, "Sometimes you can get too comfortable holding a bird in the hand, even one that you don't like." In a follow-up phone call three months later, Mr. Celester happily reported, "I'm really enjoying my new position and the people I work with. I'm also much more relaxed with my family."

As we noted, an outside factor, the loss of a job, served as the catalyst for Mr. Celester to move forward and turn a seeming crisis into an opportunity. Obviously, one need not wait ten years to change a stressful situation. As Mr. Celester reflected on the previous ten years, he observed, "It was a change that should have been made years ago. I know that given all of my financial responsibilities, I was frightened about leaving my position. But I also realize that I never even considered how I could slowly leave my comfort zone and at the same time not compromise my financial responsibilities. I sacrificed years of possible happiness because I wore blinders and did not permit myself to see opportunities."

The obstacles to changing negative scripts described in Chapter 2 explain why so many people wear blinders, afraid to venture off a path that offers little satisfaction. They feel too anxious or uncertain to venture down new, unchartered paths, instead resigning themselves to unhappiness. You might wish to review the obstacles to changing negative scripts as you reflect on the concept of stress hardiness.

Pursuing One's Dream Mary Clark was forty-eight years old when she came to see us after listening to one of our tapes. Her husband had died suddenly of a heart attack three years prior to her visit with us. She described their marriage as "wonderful," and it was clear that his absence created a large void in her life. She also said that he had provided very well for her and their two children so that finances were not a problem. She had two grown children, a twenty-four-year-old son who was a high school English teacher and a twenty-two-year-old daughter who had recently graduated from college and secured work with a financial firm. Her son and daughter both had their own apartments within an hour of Mrs. Clark's house.

Mrs. Clark characterized her problem as "feeling lost" and not knowing what to do with her life. She jokingly said, "I guess it's like a midlife crisis." She had felt rooted in her roles as a wife and mother, but since her husband's death and her children's moves to their own apartments, she felt "directionless." She kept busy with charitable work for several organizations but found she was less and less satisfied. She added, "I loved my husband very much but I would like to meet someone at this point, not necessarily to remarry but just to go out to eat or to a show."

Given her dissatisfaction with her current situation, we asked Mrs. Clark, "What would you like to do? What do you dream about?"

She answered, "In college I majored in graphic design, and then I worked for two years for an advertising firm before becoming pregnant. After the birth of my first child I made a decision to be a stay-at-home wife and mother."

She continued, "Even when my kids were older and I wasn't needed as a stay-at-home mother, I continued to stay home. I was involved with various volunteer organizations. I can honestly say that I felt content. But since my husband's death and my kids' being on their own, I've had this crazy thought that I might like to resume my graphic design and advertising career."

We wondered, "Why crazy? What stopped you?"

Mrs. Clark offered a litany of reasons, including, "I think I'm too old to begin my career again. The field has changed so much since I last worked in it, especially with the use of computers. I may not have the energy to return to work or to take courses to update my knowledge. I haven't taken a college course in twenty-five years. The whole idea seems stressful and daunting."

She then added a perceptive observation characteristic of others who have backed away from challenges: "One of the main reasons I came in to see you is that the more I run from what I would like to do, the worse I feel." Half-joking, half-serious, she noted, "So I would either like to overcome the obstacles I have to following my dreams or to not feel bad if I continue to run from these dreams."

We smiled and asked, "Which option do you prefer?"

She laughed and said, "If I keep running for too much longer I think I'll become exhausted."

"So it sounds like we should focus on what is required to follow your dream."

The picture that emerged of Mrs. Clark was of a very competent, energetic, caring person who had doubts that she could transfer these attributes to an arena outside her family and personal life. She perceived pursuing a career in advertising and graphic design at her age as overwhelming, prompting doubts and anxieties. Changing her life script was not viewed as a challenge to confront and master but rather as a stress to avoid. However, as Mrs. Clark eloquently noted, if she kept running "she would become exhausted." Also, she would remain dissatisfied and unhappy.

Our work with Mrs. Clark initially focused on assisting her to reframe her dreams and goals as challenges rather than as stresses and to establish realistic steps to reach these goals. Her current mindset was filled with self-doubt, which led her to perceive her goal of returning to the business world as a herculean task equivalent to climbing Mt. Everest.

An effective way of rendering a long-term goal more manageable and less stressful is to divide it into short-term steps. We discussed the steps that could be taken and cast each step as a challenge or hurdle. Mrs. Clark decided that the initial step would be to set up a meeting with an adviser at a local university specializing in working with adults returning to college. The meeting went very well. The adviser was very supportive and encouraging and arranged an interview with a faculty member who specialized in graphic arts. The latter recommended a sequence of several courses that focused on the use of computers in graphic arts.

As Mrs. Clark contemplated the steps that were necessary to realize her goals she described her feelings of insecurity. We empathized with her, noting that it would not be unusual to experience uncertainty and anxiety returning to an activity after a twenty-five-year hiatus. Acknowledging the likelihood of insecurity and considering ways to cope with these feelings helped to transform the experiences into challenges to confront rather than stressful situations to flee.

Mrs. Clark pursued her dream. Much to her surprise, she delighted in learning the new technology associated with her field and found that not all of her "brain cells had disappeared in the past twenty-five years."

Some people might wonder, what if Mrs. Clark couldn't master the computer, or what if she found graphic design and advertising not very satisfying? Our answer would be that there are no guarantees when we follow our dreams. However, it is far more effective to take action to change an unhappy situation than to remain unhappy and passive. When people take action, they are more likely to look for other solutions if the first one proves unsuccessful. Resilient people recognize that they can learn from actions that prove ineffective but they learn little, if anything, by adhering to an unhappy status quo.

A Challenge Leading to a Novel Solution We were impressed with feedback we received from a school social worker who had attended one of our workshops about unmotivated, angry students. During the presentation we described the benefits of (a) providing seemingly resistant youth with opportunities to help others in the school setting and (b) actively involving them in devising solutions to problems they were encountering. Following the workshop, this social worker was asked to develop interventions for a group of high-risk students with behavior and attendance problems.

In her note to us, it was obvious that she transformed what could easily have been a stressful situation (attempting to change the longstanding behavior of a group of at-risk students) into a challenge, a challenge that involved translating some of what she had learned at the workshop into her own creative, successful intervention. She designed a program that enlisted the five students with the poorest attendance and behavior records to join a committee to do "research" on the topic of why students might be reluctant to attend school. The students were informed that their research would be helpful to the school, to parents, and to other students experiencing difficulty attending school.

The students and school social worker developed a questionnaire that was used when interviewing other staff and students. One of the committee's recommendations was to adopt an early-intervention approach and help any first graders who began to demonstrate attendance problems. The committee's work was so impressive that the members were invited to present the findings of their research to members of the administration. In the process, the attendance of the committee members improved significantly, as did their behavior. Given the past history of these five students, other school staff could easily have said, "What's the use? Nothing has helped in the past. Why should we expect something to work now?" This school social worker replaced existing negative thoughts and stress by viewing the situation as a challenge.

The words we use to describe our lives are rooted in and reflect our feelings and thoughts, which then direct our behavior. Words such as *challenge* connote an optimistic, problem-solving outlook. When we define a situation as a challenge we are more likely to confront rather than retreat from that situation, more likely to be flexible and creative, and more likely to learn from rather than feel defeated by setbacks.

Whenever you are faced with a problem that may be stressful, can you discover the realistic opportunities that may reside within the situation? It may help to remember the definition of crisis we offered earlier: an opportunity riding dangerous winds.

Personal Control

The third component of stress hardiness centers on a theme highlighted in Chapter 1, *personal control*. Dr. Kobasa found that people are less stressed when they devote their time and energy to managing situations over which they have some control or influence. A lack of personal control increases the likelihood of emotional and health problems. Unfortunately, as we have already observed, many individuals believe their happiness is rooted in someone else changing first. Such individuals are destined to remain dissatisfied and angry unless they change their perspective. Stress, rather than resilience, will dominate their lives.

The Power of Empowerment   Recognizing what is and is not within one's control is a first step to achieving a sense of personal control. This component of stress hardiness is also intertwined with the theme of negative scripts. Recall that in the last chapter we asked you to list three things in your life that you would like to change and then indicate whether you believe that for each change to occur someone else must change first.

It is not always easy to make this assessment, especially if we are blinded by longstanding assumptions that have not been adequately scrutinized. It is often easier to cast responsibility on others to initiate changes. When they do not change, we become increasingly angry with them. We have frequently heard the excuse we described in Chapter 2 as an obstacle to changing negative scripts: "The other person should change first." Some have added, "I will feel more pressure if I take the first steps to change, especially if the other person doesn't follow with changes." Still others believe that they will be taken advantage of should they modify their approach.

Although we can appreciate these reservations, we believe it is actually empowering to concentrate on what we can do differently rather than to exhaust ourselves in an effort to change others. Also, as we witnessed with Mr. Butler, who wanted his managers to take more responsibility, and Mr. and Mrs. Savin, who wanted their son, Wade, to be more responsible, when we focus on what we can do differently we create an environment that permits other people in our lives to change. In most instances, when we have the courage to modify our *modus operandi* and to adopt a more flexible, realistic approach, others are more willing to change their negative scripts.

Some might argue that this did not occur with Mrs. Atkins. In response to her change, her mother not only remained belligerent but ended their relationship. However, Mrs. Atkins recognized that she had done all that she could to repair the relationship but had no control over her mother's response. Once she could accept this reality, she became less stressed and was able to move on with her life. A sense of failure is not predicated on whether others respond to our changes, but on whether we possess the courage to be honest with ourselves, to pursue actions in concert with our values, and to modify these actions when indicated. These are the characteristics of a resilient mindset.

In his book *A Whack on the Side of the Head*, Roger von Oech offers a powerful example of looking within oneself for change rather than assigning responsibility or blame to others. He writes:

> *Several years ago I did a seminar with the direct sales force of a large pharmaceutical company. Prior to the session, I had the opportunity to talk to the people in the bottom 25% of sales performance. I asked them, "Why aren't you more successful?" They answered with such comments as:*
> *"Our products cost too much."*
> *"I've got a crummy territory."*
> *"I don't get along with my manager."*
> *"The moon is in Sagittarius."*[6]

Mr. von Oech then writes, "What was their problem? They weren't taking responsibility for their own performance. They spent their time creating excuses rather than thinking of innovative sales solutions."

Mr. von Oech contrasted this more negative perspective about personal control with the mindset of successful salespeople. He noted that the latter group said, "If I get turned down by a physician or nurse, I think of a second way to get the business, a third way, and sometimes a fifth way." In essence, the successful group did not wait passively, hoping that factors outside their control would miraculously change. They appreciated that effective change resided within themselves and their proactive behavior.

Changing a Negative Work Environment   Another illustration of the power of empowerment that in some ways is similar to the situation experienced by Mr. Butler occurred when we were consulting with Marjorie Nance, a businesswoman who complained that her office environment was "filled with negativity." She said, "People are quick to tell you what you have done wrong, but almost no one goes out of their way to compliment you when you've done a good job."

We empathized with Ms. Nance but then asked in a caring way, "Do you recall the last time you went out of your way to give special thanks to someone?"

Ms. Nance's response was revealing but not atypical. She said, "Why should I do it for someone else when no one does it for me?" Without being fully aware, she had fallen into the trap of seeking her happiness in the behavior of others rather than asking what she had control over that might begin to change the negative atmosphere in her office.

In our consultation with Ms. Nance, we encouraged her to find opportunities to provide positive feedback to colleagues. We discussed the importance of not becoming discouraged if some of them did not respond enthusiastically to her compliments or if they seemed to suspect her of having an ulterior motive. We emphasized, "You have control over what you say and do, but not over the response of others. However, we have found that when we change our behaviors, it often sets the stage for others to change theirs." In fact, many business leaders have discovered that if they adopt a more positive approach, most of their staff will do the same.

After following our recommendation, Ms. Nance reported that she was witnessing positive changes in her workplace. She stated, "I can't believe how a few small changes on my part resulted in such a positive change. I don't know why I didn't do it sooner."

Many don't "do it sooner" for a variety of reasons, including the self-defeating beliefs that it is the responsibility of others to change first and that it is a sign of weakness if we take the first steps to change an unsatisfactory situation. Nothing could be further from the truth.

Eradicating the Ghosts of the Past In our book *Raising Resilient Children: Fostering Strength, Hope, and Optimism in Your Child,* we described a situation similar to that faced by Mrs. Atkins that we would like to highlight as an example of the empowerment and growth associated with personal control. George and Melinda Larsen, both forty years of age, were referred to us by their family physician for marital difficulties. They were raising two teenaged sons. As we listened to their histories, it was obvious that Mr. Larsen had been rejected at an early age by his father.

"My father was abusive," he said. "He called me a wimp or a sissy because I didn't like to fight. He told me that if I didn't get into a few fights each year, I probably wasn't sticking up for myself."

When we asked about his relationship with his mother, he said, "My mother was afraid of my father. He yelled at her too. But if she would come to my aid, he would tell her she was raising a mama's boy."

Mrs. Larsen listened as her husband spoke. She commented that she had been aware of some of his childhood experiences but that they had never discussed their impact on him.

"On one occasion," Mr. Larsen continued, "when I was eight years old, I was beaten up at school. I don't know what happened; it was just one of those playground things. I told my mother when I came home from school. When my father came home after work, he sent me out to look for this boy and told me not to come home until I had beaten him up. I'm still ashamed at what I did. I found a stick, came up behind the boy, and began hitting him. I had to be pulled away by an adult."

Tears came to Mr. Larsen's eyes as he concluded the story. "The boy's father brought him home and was pretty angry. My father told him to stop complaining, that boys would get into fights. As he closed the door, he told me it was about time I didn't act like a sissy. That's all he said, and then he walked away."

Mr. Larsen explained that he never felt comfortable in any conflict, and although he had desperately desired acceptance from his father, his father never gave it. As a teenager, Mr. Larsen turned to alcohol, probably to dull his psychological pain. On graduating from high school, he moved from one job to the next with regularity.

"When I met my wife," he said, "I finally found someone who could provide the love, acceptance, and support I hadn't known. I found a job I liked, stopped drinking, and got my life together."

During this period, Mr. Larsen's mother died, and he continued to have little contact with his father. As his own sons reached their adolescent years, the normal stresses of raising teenagers awakened much of the pain he had experienced in his relationship with his father. He began to worry that his sons would grow apart from him just as he had done with his father. He turned to alcohol once more to deaden his worries, and as a consequence his interactions with his wife and children were marked by increasing anger. Fortunately, with the support of his wife, he sought our help.

What quickly emerged in our sessions were Mr. Larsen's unresolved feelings toward his father and his realization that he still yearned for his father's acceptance. He resolved to stop drinking. In several family therapy sessions, family members aired their grievances and set solutions in place. Mr. Larsen, however, felt that the only way he could truly remove the burden of his unresolved feelings was to convey to his father how he felt and to see if there was an opportunity for a possible reconciliation.

We discussed ways of expressing his feelings to his father. After much consideration, Mr. Larsen decided to write his father a letter. Although they had maintained minimal communication during the previous fifteen years, Mr. Larsen made an effort to change his script toward his father. He took an active role and assumed personal control to rid himself of the ghosts of his past. The letter was not accusatory or demanding. It explained his feelings and his desire to reestablish a relationship.

We discussed in advance the different ways in which his father might react, such as writing a hostile letter in return or not responding at all. We did not expect what occurred. Mr. Larsen's father ripped his son's letter into small pieces, placed the pieces in an envelope, and mailed them back.

Interestingly, Mr. Larsen was not upset as he recounted this news. We believe he could sense our anger at his father's response. He smiled and stated, "You've often said that you have to focus on what you have control over. I had control over communicating with my father but not his response. I did what I had to do, and now that I know my father's reaction, I can get on with my life and concentrate on making certain I have the best possible relationship with my family."

He added with profound insight, "From the time I was born, he couldn't accept me, couldn't love me. He wanted me to be something I could not be. I used to think it was my fault, but now I realize it wasn't. I can give up the fantasy of being accepted by my father and concentrate on accepting my sons."

Given the support of his wife and his success at work, Mr. Larsen could move ahead once he focused on what he had control over and what he did not. Both would lead more resilient, less stressed lives.

The Revitalization of Mr. Bauer Earlier in this chapter, while considering commitment as a component of stress hardiness, we described our work with Mr. Bauer, a teacher who felt fatigued and burned out with little spark left in his life. Mr. Bauer recalled that his motivation to become a teacher was based on his experiences with Miss Lapora, his ninth grade science teacher. It was evident that in the beginning of his career he was enthusiastic and truly felt he was influencing the lives of his students, just as Miss Lapora had greatly influenced him. However, over the years his enthusiasm had waned and he felt little passion for his work. Given his feelings of burnout, it was difficult for him to interpret his situation as a challenge.

We want to return to Mr. Bauer at this point and highlight our work with him in terms of the theme of personal control. We had asked him, "What do you think would help you to recapture the excitement from your early years of teaching?"

Mr. Bauer's response was revealing. "I think the students and their parents are different these days. Students seem less interested in learning. They seem focused on just getting good grades to get into a prestigious college. Parents put pressure on me to give these good grades, even if the students don't deserve them. Administrators don't seem as involved with us. I remember when I first started teaching, the principal would walk in the halls, come into the staff room, chat with you. Now you rarely see the principal outside of a staff meeting. Is it any wonder that I lost my spark for teaching?"

Mr. Bauer's description of what would renew his passion for teaching was remarkable in that almost everything he described to improve the situation rested on the initiative and behavior of other people. Thoughts about what he could do differently were noticeably absent. This kind of thinking is not unusual when one is feeling pessimistic and fatigued. As we noted, a lack of energy often leads to the belief that things would be better if only the world would change. Obviously, there is some truth to this, but as we have emphasized, if we seek our happiness by waiting for others to change, we may wait for a lifetime.

We shared with Mr. Bauer information about the components of stress hardiness, observing that his prescription for renewing his passion for teaching resided in factors outside his control. We encouraged him to consider actions he could initiate. To facilitate this task, we asked him to think about Miss Lapora and his early days in the teaching profession.

During the next few sessions Mr. Bauer realized that, unlike his behavior in the beginning of his career, he had become lax in developing a closer relationship with his students. He said, "There was a time within the first couple of weeks of school I made it a practice to learn every student's name, even though I had more than 150 students in my different classes. I now realize that as I became less enthusiastic about teaching I let that practice slip. Too many students were anonymous to me. I've made an effort the past few weeks to learn each student's name. I have also begun to say hello to students when I pass them in the hallway. I've already noticed a positive difference."

Mr. Bauer continued, "There are several other things I've done. I mentioned to my students that sometimes the material we are studying can be difficult and that if anyone needs some extra assistance, they should let me know and I will set up a time to meet with them. I wanted to let them know I was available to them, just as I felt Miss Lapora was available to me.

"I also realized how stale some of my teaching had become. I've begun to share with my students why a science experiment can be exciting. Instead of reciting facts and results, I've presented the experiment and asked them to anticipate in advance what they think the results will be, almost like detectives looking for clues. Just asking them to think about the possible results has added some energy to the classroom."

A few weeks later Mr. Bauer said, "I have been thinking a lot about Miss Lapora since I mentioned her to you. It's interesting—she meant so much to me, but I never really thanked her. I think she knew how appreciative I was of what she did for me, but I'm not certain I ever thanked her. So I called my old school and found she was still teaching there. I wrote her a letter."

Mr. Bauer then showed us a copy of the letter he had written. It was very poignant. He thanked Miss Lapora for the "immeasurable way" in which she had helped to direct his life. He described his initial excitement about teaching and shared his dissatisfaction the past few years. He then added, "Thinking about you and your style has rekindled my spirit in teaching. It's interesting how we can fall into such a negative cycle."

A week later Mr. Bauer brought in a letter he had received from Miss Lapora. To say he was beaming would be an understatement. She thanked him for his thoughtfulness in writing and said how much his words meant to her. She ended with the following sentiment: "Letters such as yours are the best antidote when I become discouraged. They remind me why I am doing what I am doing."

Mr. Bauer renewed the energy in his life. He discovered once again the purpose of his work. This discovery may not have occurred had he continued to wait for others to change first. By assuming a more proactive stance Mr. Bauer was able to replace fatigue, cynicism, and stress with optimism and purpose.

Concluding Thoughts: Revisiting Mr. Millis and Mr. Newman

At the beginning of this chapter we described Sam Millis and Gene Newman, two men who had similar responsibilities at the same high-tech firm but were markedly different in terms of the level of stress and anxiety each experienced. We wondered in what ways their outlooks differed to produce such disparate ways of perceiving themselves and their situations. Answers to these questions can be found by applying the framework of stress hardiness. As we apply this concept to the lives of Mr. Millis and Mr. Newman, reflect on your life and the degree to which you follow the precepts related to commitment, challenge, and personal control. Also, consider in what ways you might change your behavior so that a stress hardy mindset becomes a dominant feature in your life.

Mr. Millis appreciated the purpose of his work when he stated, "I remind myself that what I do makes a difference to this company and in the lives of others." He interpreted the demands of his job as a challenge, noting, "It's the nature of our work. I expect it and am prepared for it. I would be surprised if a week went by without unexpected modifications in the project." In addition, Mr. Millis recognized that he could minimize stress by focusing on what he had control over and adopting effective coping strategies, such as changing from his work clothes to his denims the moment he arrived home.

In contrast, Mr. Newman questioned the value of the projects he was working on, minimizing a sense of purpose or commitment. Rather than appreciating the challenges of his work, he interpreted change as an additional burden, noting, "This is the last straw. They keep wanting me to change things. It's one more pressure to deal with." His feeling that events were beyond his control was captured in his statement, "Everyone is so rigid. They won't listen to what I have to say."

Some may question whether, given his mindset, Mr. Newman is destined for a life of dissatisfaction and unhappiness. Our response is, not necessarily, especially because we believe that mindsets are open to change. To accomplish this change Mr. Newman would first have to understand the different components of a stress hardy mindset and determine whether his feelings, thoughts, and behavior were in accord with these components. If they were not, he could engage in the exercises we recommended in this chapter, such as creating a list of his priorities and values, assessing whether he was leading an authentic life in accord with these values, defining what he would like to change in his life, and evaluating the possible changes over which he had control.

We recommend that you use these exercises on an ongoing basis. These activities should not be interpreted as academic exercises with little relevance to our lives. Rather, the attainment of a stress hardy mindset, a mindset that places the spotlight on concepts such as passion, purpose, challenge, and personal control, is one of the most significant steps we can take in discovering and maintaining a resilient lifestyle.

4

Viewing Life
Through the Eyes
of Others

Years ago when I (Bob) was in graduate school, I eagerly awaited a lecture by a prominent visiting mental health professional. I had read two of this man's thought-provoking books about mental health and illness and was prepared for a stimulating discussion. Following the formal presentation, questions and comments were invited from the audience. A psychology professor offered an opinion about the ways in which mental health and illness were defined by society and asked the presenter for his thoughts. While the professor's viewpoint varied somewhat from that of the speaker, the opinion was raised in a respectful, collegial manner. The speaker's response stunned the audience.

"Questions like yours reflect views found in a fascist state. They suggest little regard for civil liberties."

The psychology professor, while startled, remained calm and said, "I don't believe in a fascist state. I asked the question to help clarify the issues you brought up in your talk."

Rather than accept this explanation, the speaker, who ironically had lauded such concepts as respect and individual rights during his presentation, dismissed the professor's comment with the statement, "What you said doesn't help to clarify issues. It shows a lack of understanding of the issues."

The professor, appreciating the intensity and arbitrariness of the speaker's response, did not reply. When the speaker asked for further comments or questions from those in attendance, none were forthcoming. The anger in the room was palpable. Even if the speaker had attempted to elaborate on his position, few, if any, in the audience would have been listening. An atmosphere of learning and discourse had rapidly evaporated.

Not surprisingly, my respect for the speaker dropped significantly. I also wondered why such an intelligent man would respond in this manner. Whatever the reason, it was obvious that the speaker failed to "read" his audience, giving little, if any, consideration to their feelings and reactions. He failed to apply one of the major features of a resilient mindset: *empathy*. In the process, he failed to inform and teach. Instead, his comments triggered anger, disappointment, and resentment. What transpired in that lecture hall in just a few moments illustrates the importance of empathy—or, more specifically, what occurs when seeing through the eyes of others. Let's examine this concept more closely.

The Definition and Role of Empathy

Empathy is popularly defined as the ability or capacity to identify with or vicariously experience the feelings, thoughts, or attitudes of others. It has been associated with such phrases as "walking in another person's shoes" or, as we note, "seeing the world through the eyes of another person."

Empathy significantly influences the quality of our personal and professional lives, especially those activities related to social relationships. Empathy facilitates communication, cooperation, respect, and compassion. It provides the strength to change negative scripts as we seek to enhance our interactions with others. It is not just an essential component of a resilient mindset but is at its very foundation.

In their book *Primal Leadership: Realizing the Power of Emotional Intelligence*, Daniel Goleman, Richard Boyatzis, and Annie McKee capture the significance of empathy:

> *Empathy is the fundamental competence of social awareness. . . . Empathy is the sine qua non of all social effectiveness in working life. Empathetic people are superb at recognizing and meeting the needs of clients, customers, or subordinates. They seem approachable, wanting to hear what people have to say. They listen carefully, picking up what people are truly concerned about, and they respond on the mark.*[1]

As you read this description of empathy, you can appreciate how "off the mark" this prominent lecturer was and the adverse impact his behavior had on his audience.

Questions to Consider

Given the importance we place on empathy in leading a resilient lifestyle, we pose questions and recommend exercises in our clinical practice, consultations, and workshops to encourage people to assess and strengthen their capacity for empathy. Reflect on how you would respond to the following questions. We urge you to consider and write down a thorough response on the worksheet on pages 274–275 in Appendix A to each of these questions before reading further.

- How do I hope other people would describe me?
- How do I interact with these people so that it is likely that they would describe me in this way?
- How would these other people actually describe me?
- How do I interact with these people to cause them to describe me in the ways that they do?
- Is there a significant discrepancy between how I hope people would describe me and how they actually would describe me?
- If there is a discrepancy, how can I change my attitudes and behaviors so that others will begin to describe me in the way I would like to be described?

Answering these questions often arouses strong feelings about past and present actions and relationships with important people. We pose these questions to demonstrate this truth: every time we interact with another person, that person forms words and images to describe us. These words and images play a major role in determining the ways they will interact with us and whether these interactions will be characterized by respect and cooperation or anger and mistrust. Empathic people possess an accurate sense of how they are perceived by others because they possess the ability to place themselves inside the shoes of these others. If they believe their behaviors are prompting other people to see them in ways that they do not wish to be perceived, they make the necessary changes so that their actions are in concert with their values. They assume personal control for what transpires in their lives.

There are still other questions that can be considered to further expand and clarify the concept of empathy. The first three questions we articulated in Chapter 1:

- In anything I say or do, what do I hope to accomplish?
- Am I saying or doing things in a way that others will be most willing to listen and respond to me?
- Am I behaving toward others in the same way that I would like to be treated?
- Think of an instance (from your childhood or adulthood) when someone said something to you that made you feel safe and understood, even if the content of the message could easily have been experienced as critical in nature. What about the communication helped you to feel this way?
- Now think of an instance when someone said something to you that was critical and you felt hurt and misunderstood. What about the communication caused you to feel this way?

A comparison of this last question with the one before it helps to clarify the ways others communicated and interacted with you that led to feelings of cooperation and safety or to anger and hurt. We recommend that you use these experiences to guide your present behaviors.

The exercise of addressing these questions with patience and honesty is intended to serve as a catalyst to examine your mindset and behavior and to alter them when necessary. We encourage you to consider these questions on a daily basis over the coming weeks. We have known individuals who have sought feedback about their behavior from others as they attempted to answer these questions—for example, teachers who asked students to anonymously draw them, describe them, or list what they liked about the class and what should be changed; parents who initiated a discussion with their children about how they acted; and a manager who requested the observations of his employees about his style of leadership.

Failures in Empathy

When you solicit this kind of feedback, you must be careful not to respond to critical comments in an angry way, but rather to reflect on and learn from them. This is not always easy to accomplish, as the following example illustrates.

"Give Me Feedback, but Only If It's Positive"

The head of a department encouraged feedback from those who reported to him. Given his response to their observations, it was evident that the hidden message was, "You can evaluate me as long as the evaluation is positive. If it isn't positive, then there is something wrong with you."

One of his staff wrote a very thoughtful observation, offering positive remarks but also mentioning a practice that resulted in staff feeling angry and intimidated. The practice in question concerned the department head's tendency to respond to questions about his actions, which were often marked by a quality of arbitrariness and impulsivity, by raising personality issues about the individual who provided the feedback. For instance, instead of reflecting on the meaning of the message, he would react with such comments as, "You have difficulty accepting direction," or "You are an insecure person."

The lack of self-awareness, the defensiveness, and the insecurity of this department head were demonstrated in his response to the staff member who mentioned his counterproductive style of analyzing an individual's personality rather than responding to the content of the message. In an ironic way, the reaction of the department head confirmed the concern that the staff member had raised. He sent back a memo accusing the staff member of "having trouble with authority." The staff member decided to respond and asked, "If you request feedback, is there any way it can be offered, especially if it contains ideas for change, without your accusing the person of having trouble with authority?"

The department head's response was disheartening but not unexpected. He wrote, "This is another example of your insubordination, a problem that has existed for a while." When the staff member reviewed the situation with us in consultation, there was no evidence of insubordination or issues with authority. What was at issue was the manager's inability to take the perspective of his staff and learn from this perspective. Goleman, Boyatzis, and McKee would, most likely, describe this department head as producing "dissonance" rather than "resonance." They note, "There are countless kinds of dissonant leaders, who not only lack empathy (and are out of synch with the group) but also transmit emotional tones that resound most often in a negative register."[2]

Back to Mr. Butler

As you are aware from our previous description, Mr. Butler frequently demonstrated a lack of empathy. While his goal was to motivate his managers to develop new ideas, he responded to their efforts with harshness and criticism. If he had asked himself the empathy questions we posed earlier in this chapter, he might have altered his style sooner. For example, we know that he would not want anyone to say to him what he said to his staff when they presented new ideas: "Is this the best you can do? I expect more. We'll never be successful if you keep coming up with these kinds of ideas!"

In addition to the interventions we described in Chapter 2 with Mr. Butler, we engaged him in listing the words he hoped his managers would use to describe him and the words they would actually use. His initial response was, "I don't care how they would describe me as long as they do a good job."

We wondered, "Do you think their job performance might improve if they had a more favorable picture of you?"

"I don't know."

"What do you think?"

Mr. Butler responded, "I suppose so."

"You don't seem certain."

"I'm not sure."

We said, "Because you're not certain, you might want to list the words you would hope they would use to describe you and then ask yourself whether you are relating to them in ways that would prompt them to use those words. If not, ask yourself what you can do differently so that they're more likely to do so."

Mr. Butler was intrigued by this exercise. He came in with a list at the following session. The words he included on his "wish list" were "demanding but supportive," "helpful," "encouraging," "a good teacher," and "clear with expectations."

Mr. Butler was very honest in acknowledging that he knew the words that his managers would use to describe him would not have a favorable quality, a realization that further prompted him to engage in writing the new script we discussed in Chapter 2.

Back to Mrs. Stevens

When we last outlined our intervention with Mrs. Stevens in Chapter 2, she had recognized the extent to which her anger toward her son, Jimmy, was a product of her anger toward her parents and her brother, Al. She believed Al was a very irresponsible adult, in part because her parents had always made excuses for his behavior and demonstrated favoritism toward him.

Mrs. Stevens realized that her comparison of Jimmy with Al, which prompted her to view her son heading down the same counterproductive path in life as her brother, caused her to be increasingly negative toward Jimmy, a negativity rooted in and fueled by anger toward Al and her parents. Her insight into the dynamics operating in her relationship with her son was a major step forward in helping her write a new script. The exercises we described on pages 37–41 also assisted in this process.

We discussed with Mr. and Mrs. Stevens the importance of empathy and appreciating how we are perceived by others. We asked them to reflect on how they hoped Jimmy and their daughter, Sophie, would describe each of them and how they thought their children would actually describe them.

Not surprisingly, given the very positive relationship that Mrs. Stevens had with Sophie, the two lists of words—what she hoped Sophie would say to describe her and the words she believed Sophie would use—were very similar. This was not the case with Jimmy. Although these results were not unexpected in light of the different feelings and thoughts Mrs. Stevens had toward her two children, they represented an important revelation to her.

She said, "In writing the words I hoped that Jimmy and Sophie would use to describe me, I wrote 'loving,' 'available,' 'fair,' 'supportive,' and 'encouraging,' but when I sat down to write the words I thought Jimmy would actually use, they were very different. I think he would say I was a nag, that I didn't really love him, that as far as I was concerned he could do nothing right, that I really didn't like him."

As Mrs. Stevens recited these last words, she began to tear up. She said, "I want the two lists to be closer, just as they are with Sophie."

Mr. Stevens took his wife's hand and, in a caring, supportive way, said, "I think we can both work on the lists becoming closer."

Mrs. Stevens responded, "I don't know why I never thought about the connection between Al and Jimmy before or why I didn't stop to think about how I came across to Jimmy. It's interesting. As I was writing down the words that I thought Jimmy would use to describe me, I thought about the words I would use to describe my parents, especially when I was Jimmy's age, and they weren't very flattering. But I don't think my parents gave much thought to how I saw them, just as I gave little thought to how Jimmy saw me."

In our sessions we focused on Mrs. Stevens's long-term goal of improving her relationship with her son, a major part of which involved distinguishing Jimmy from Al. Mrs. Stevens found it helpful to list the words she hoped Jimmy would use to describe her and to record next to each description one or two short-term goals and subsequent actions she could take that would contribute to his seeing her in a more positive way. As part of this process we also anticipated possible obstacles to achieving these short-term goals.

For example, in her quest to reinforce Jimmy's viewing her as "loving" and "encouraging," Mrs. Stevens set aside a time to be alone with him each night (as she typically did with Sophie) just to play and have fun. We discussed in advance the obstacle that would occur if she used "fun time" to lecture him about responsibilities. She said that a number of times she almost resorted to her old script of criticism, but the fact that we had discussed this in advance helped her to avoid saying anything negative. The time alone with Jimmy remained fun and playful, strengthening their relationship.

Mrs. Stevens also noticed and acknowledged the many ways in which Jimmy was helpful. She found herself complimenting him more for realistic achievements. When he was having difficulty with school, she did not criticize him for not trying hard enough, but instead offered empathic comments such as, "I know some work in school can be tough, but Dad and I are here to help."

When Mrs. Stevens recounted how she had changed her script, she observed, "I'm now speaking with Jimmy the way I would like to be spoken to. It's made a world of difference in our relationship."

"The Worst Child I Have Ever Taught"

A striking example of a failure in empathy occurred at a school conference to discuss Duane, a six-year-old patient of ours who displayed hyperactive and impulsive behaviors. At a conference with Duane's parents, Mr. and Mrs. Vintor, and his teacher, Ms. Alisa Vaughn, the latter began the meeting by asserting, much to our astonishment, "I've been teaching thirteen years, and your child is the worst child I have ever taught."

Not surprisingly, we were all taken aback by this statement. Mr. and Mrs. Vintor became noticeably upset and defensive. Accusations and mistrust flooded the room, washing away any possible positive atmosphere of problem solving and collaboration.

Subsequent to the conference, we spoke briefly to Ms. Vaughn, endeavoring to be empathic in the hope of nurturing a more constructive relationship for the future. We wondered about her opening remark.

"I was just trying to be honest. Too often we downplay students' problems with parents. Not being truthful comes back to haunt us years later when the student continues to have problems. Parents wonder why we weren't honest initially about the severity of their child's problems. I wanted to emphasize to the Vintors that Duane had significant problems."

As you think about Ms. Vaughn's reasons for her opening comments, reflect on two of the questions we posed earlier about reinforcing a more empathic stance and how these questions might have been applied by this teacher to foster a more cooperative relationship with the Vintors: "In the school meeting, what do I hope to accomplish with Mr. and Mrs. Vintor?" and "Am I saying things in a way that will make the Vintors most responsive to hearing my message and working with me?"

It appears that Ms. Vaughn knew her goal: to inform the Vintors of the severity of Duane's problems. However, she neglected to consider whether she was communicating this information in a manner that would encourage Mr. and Mrs. Vintor to listen to what she had to say in order to examine Duane's problems and brainstorm possible solutions in a trusting, respectful atmosphere.

If we were consulting with Ms. Vaughn about a more productive script, we would not advise her to be untruthful with Mr. and Mrs. Vintor, but rather to express her thoughts with greater empathy and compassion. For example, she might have started by saying that she wanted to collaborate with them and then mentioning a couple of Duane's strengths. Next she might have said, "There are several areas that concern me about Duane that I would like to describe, and then we can try to figure out what strategies might work best to help him and how we can all work closely together."

If Ms. Vaughn had introduced the difficulties Duane was having in this way, the Vintors would have been receptive to hearing the seriousness of their son's problems and to working closely with Ms. Vaughn. However, given a past experience in which Ms. Vaughn was criticized for not being more forthcoming about a student's problems, her ability to be empathic was compromised.

The Struggle to Be Empathic

In our workshops, the topic of empathy arouses great interest. When we describe examples in which empathy is absent, such as with Mr. Butler or Mrs. Stevens, the audience wonders how people can be so blind to the impact they have on others. However, when we review the questions and exercises we listed earlier in this chapter to develop empathy, most individuals acknowledge that they rarely think about how their spouse, children, friends, students, or colleagues would describe them. Some can readily recall instances when they said things to others that they would not have wanted said to them. One man summed up what many feel when he declared, "I never really thought about how I come across or how others would describe me. The more I think about it, the more I realize there are changes I have to make."

The more clearly we understand the obstacles to being empathic, the better we can address these obstacles and successfully use the exercises we have described to improve empathy. In the following section we describe four roadblocks to empathy. We then offer guidelines to begin to alter thoughts and behaviors that mediate against being empathic.

Obstacle One: Practicing What You Have Lived

As is apparent in the examples we have offered, it is more difficult to be empathic if one grows up in a home in which parents do not demonstrate empathy. In such homes children are often told how they should feel and think. The validation of feelings is limited, at best. Of course, having empathic parents does not guarantee one will be empathic. Many factors contribute to personality and behavior. However, it is easier to be empathic when we witness the practice of empathy on a daily basis by our parents and other caregivers.

Mr. Butler and Mrs. Stevens, both of whom reported that they had parents who were not empathic, struggled to be more empathic in their relationships with others. Jeremy Taylor provides another vivid example of the impact of past experiences on one's capacity to be empathic.

"I'm Made Out to Be the Bad Guy" Jeremy Taylor, a thirty-six-year-old contractor who specialized in restoring older homes, was married and the father of three children, ages five, seven, and ten. His wife, Janine, also thirty-six years of age, worked part-time as a nurse in a local hospital. The Taylors contacted us because of arguments they were having about raising their children. Most of their disagreements centered around expectations and discipline. We addressed a variety of parenting and marital issues in our sessions, including some directly related to the theme of empathy.

Mr. Taylor said that he felt he had to be the disciplinarian because his wife "let the kids get away with murder." Mrs. Taylor said that she felt she handled things well and expressed concern about her husband's harsh words toward their children. She said, "I think they are actually afraid of him."

Mr. Taylor responded, "Because my wife won't meet her responsibilities to discipline the kids, I'm made out to be the bad guy when I have to step in and set limits."

Mrs. Taylor answered, "I think I do a good job disciplining the kids. They're just kids, and I think Jeremy expects so much from them. If they giggle or tease each other a little at dinnertime he sends them to their rooms. Or he says things that I think are hurtful. The other night when he didn't like something they did, he told our oldest two that they never used their brains. Later that night, our oldest child said, 'Daddy doesn't love me.' She cried and said that all he does is yell at them and never says anything nice."

Mr. Taylor immediately jumped in, "See, this is exactly what I was talking about. I'm made out to be the bad guy because Janine won't discipline the kids. And maybe the reason they don't think I say anything nice is because all of the discipline seems to land on my shoulders. Janine just doesn't have the courage to do what has to be done. She's afraid of everything."

Not surprisingly, Mr. Taylor's comment about his wife's lack of courage was not well received by Mrs. Taylor. She said to us, "You're getting a first-hand look at what upsets me so much about Jeremy. He can say really hurtful things. He says them to the kids and to me. I wish he understood how it felt."

Mr. Taylor responded, "You say it's hurtful. I'm just trying to let you know that you have to be more of a parent and not leave everything to me."

Mrs. Taylor answered, "I just wish you could be more supportive and not say things that hurt so much. I feel when you talk this way to me or the kids, it's just like the way your father speaks to your mother." This last observation was not said with anger but rather with sadness and resignation.

The interaction between Mr. and Mrs. Taylor transpiring in our office was played out repeatedly in their lives. As we worked with the Taylors and listened to the harsh, often demeaning words Mr. Taylor used with his wife and children, we realized that a major part of our intervention would be to nurture empathy. Given the observations of Mrs. Taylor, we also appreciated that Mr. Taylor's anger and lack of empathy were rooted in his experiences with his father.

In one session we asked Mr. Taylor to describe his father.

"He was a good provider. We lived comfortably."

"If we interviewed you when you were a child, perhaps the age of your oldest child now, what might you have said then about your father?"

"It's hard to know how to answer. It's been many years since I've been a kid."

In an attempt to make the question more specific, we asked, "Think of a situation in which you have a happy memory of your father interacting with you and one that was not pleasant. Then think about the words you would use to describe your father in each of these situations."

After reflecting on this question for a few moments, Mr. Taylor's answer was very revealing, especially in light of his current situation with his wife and children. He gravitated to the negative experience first and said, "My father had this habit of always looking for what you had done wrong and then lecturing you about your shortcomings. If I didn't do well in a Little League game or finish a homework assignment, he would always say things like, 'You could do better if you wanted to,' 'You never put in all of your effort,' or 'Do you think you will be successful in life if you don't give your best effort?'"

Mr. Taylor added, "I can remember his saying this when I was seven or eight years old. Can you imagine saying that to such a young kid? It hurt a lot. As I think back, he would say sarcastic things to my mother about her cooking, her weight, just about anything. Boy, the more I think about this, I realize that even his positive remarks weren't so positive. I remember in the third or fourth grade finally getting a good grade on a spelling test, a 90. I missed only two words out of twenty. He didn't really congratulate me. I remember what he said as if it were yesterday: 'Imagine if you could buckle down even more and not fool around, you might be able to get a 100.'"

Mr. Taylor then offered a very revealing comment related to the theme of empathy: "As I'm remembering these things, I wonder if he ever realized how I felt or how my mom or my brother and sister felt."

When people believe they have a message to get across, they often fail to consider how their message is being received by others. Given Mr. Taylor's recollection of his childhood and the question he raised about whether his father recognized the negativity of his words, we were able to enter into a fruitful dialogue about the words Mr. Taylor used with his wife and children. For the first time, he could clearly comprehend and appreciate how his behavior was modeled after his father's even though he had never liked what his father said.

As we noted in Chapter 2, we are often unaware of negative scripts, especially if they are all we know. Mr. Taylor did not possess models to contrast with his father. He witnessed far too few instances of empathy, of considering the viewpoints of others, and of asking whether the ways in which one said or did things increased the probability that others would feel understood and supported.

Mr. Taylor was able to benefit from the exercises we presented, especially in the context of a therapeutic relationship. He became increasingly sensitive to examining whether he would want anyone to say to him what he said to his family. This task was facilitated as he recalled his own childhood experiences. He also learned that although he did not have models of empathy when he was a child, it was never too late to develop greater empathy as an adult. An added benefit was Mr. Taylor's report that he was successfully applying what he termed the "empathy questions" not only at home, but at work as well.

Obstacle Two: Harboring Disappointment or Anger

At many of our workshops, we ask participants to raise their hands if they consider themselves to be empathic. Although at first there is some hesitancy, after a few brave souls have the courage to raise their hands the vast majority of those in attendance follow suit. It is not unusual to hear people say,

"I'm empathic. I always attempt to understand the point of view of my spouse, children, parents, friends, and coworkers."

However, while most of us judge ourselves to be empathic, empathy is more evident when the behavior and attitudes of others suit our own preferences. For instance, it is easier for managers to be empathic with their staff when the latter follow through on the wishes of the manager. It is easier for parents to be empathic toward their children when the children listen to what the parents say, meet their responsibilities, finish their homework without being reminded, get good grades, and say "hello," "please," and "thank you" to others without being prodded to do so.

It is much more challenging to be empathic when the actions of friends, relatives, and colleagues don't meet our expectations. Anger and disappointment have an insidious way of lessening empathy and blinding us to the negative impact our words and actions might have. When angry or disappointed, we seldom pause to reflect on the questions we raised earlier in this chapter, such as, *How would this other person describe me right now as I am yelling at him?* Typically, at such moments our main goal is to get our point across. We often fail to consider the question, *Am I saying or doing things in a way that this other person will be most willing to listen and respond to me?*

Obstacle Three: Making Assumptions About the Motives of Others

We witnessed the negative impact of anger and disappointment on empathy in Mr. Butler's interaction with his managers, Mrs. Stevens's relationship with her son, and Ms. Vaughn's comments to Mr. and Mrs. Vintor. Ruth Petrie, a forty-two-year-old woman, encountered similar difficulties. She came to see us because of what she called "a general unhappiness with my life." Her sadness was immediately evident as she described frustration with her two children, ongoing arguments with her husband, and dissatisfaction at work. She was in the marketing field and felt that she had been passed over for advancement in favor of "people who were less qualified than I am." She also noted, "I think some people are born with lucky lives. They have happy marriages, children who listen to them, and colleagues who appreciate them." One may interpret her comments about lucky lives in terms of her not feeling a sense of personal control, a situation that could easily contribute to stress and anger.

As we worked with Mrs. Petrie, we quickly became aware of her angry assumptions about the motives of others, assumptions that served as obstacles to developing empathy and more satisfying relationships. One vivid example concerned an interaction with her two children, fifteen-year-old Sean and thirteen-year-old Vicky. She characterized her children as "lazy" and "selfish" and offered an example of how they are expected to clean their rooms on Saturday.

She observed, "When I was a child I wouldn't think of going out to play unless my room was clean and I had done my chores. Yet I have to constantly remind my kids to do so. They're so lazy and selfish."

"What do you mean by the words *lazy* and *selfish*?" we asked.

She responded, "I think they just don't care about me. They only care about themselves. They don't realize how hard I work so we can live in a nice house and have nice things. We couldn't live this way on my husband's salary alone."

We asked how she reacted to her children's failure to clean their rooms.

She answered, "When they don't help out and do what's expected I get very angry. When they didn't have their rooms cleaned last Saturday, I told them that they were ungrateful and didn't appreciate all that I do for them. I also told them that they cared more about being with their friends than helping out at home."

We wondered what happened.

Mrs. Petrie said, "You would think they would clean their rooms. Instead they got into an argument about how controlling I was. Can you believe that? I wouldn't be controlling if they would just do what's expected. So I told them, 'I'll show you what controlling is, you're both grounded for the weekend.' They finally did clean their rooms, but they haven't said more than a couple of words to me the past few days. I know they're really angry."

As you read this account, you can understand Mrs. Petrie's frustration. But, unfortunately, her response to her children represented an ongoing negative script that was fueled in part by her lack of empathy. Perhaps at one point she had been more empathic, but empathy can easily become a casualty of anger.

In our intervention with Mrs. Petrie we focused on two related areas that are integral components of a resilient mindset: personal control and empathy. Mrs. Petrie tended to perceive occurrences in her life as beyond her control, attributing the success of others to good luck and her own misfortunes to bad luck. Her lack of personal control was also manifested in her tendency to demand that others change their behaviors without her taking any responsibility to change her own. A vicious circle was in full operation. As she grew more frustrated and angry with others, including her children and husband, her ability to be empathic was weakened. With each new assault on empathy, her assumptions about her children's behavior became more negative. She then acted in ways that exacerbated the situation, which further fueled her anger.

Similar to the interventions we described in Chapter 2 with Mr. Butler, Mrs. Atkins, and Mr. and Mrs. Savin, we tried to help Mrs. Petrie appreciate the way her tendency to see others as lucky and to blame others for her unhappiness was actually reinforcing the very feelings of distress that she wished to end. We helped her define what she did and did not have control over, specifically examining her relationship with and empathy toward her children and the assumptions she made about their behavior.

During one session we had her list the words she hoped her children would use to describe her and the words they would actually use. In the former list she included "loving," "caring," "available," "good provider," and "supportive."

When considering the words they would actually use, she said, "I don't think they would be very positive."

"What might they be?"

"I would guess they would say that I'm a nag, always on their back, nothing is good enough, I don't let them have fun."

In a caring way we asked, "How accurate would that be?"

At first, Mrs. Petrie contended that it might seem accurate to her children but that if she came across this way it was because of their irresponsible, lazy behavior. However, she quickly caught herself and said, "That's putting the blame on them and not looking at what I can do differently."

We agreed.

Once Mrs. Petrie was able to accept ownership for her actions and question the assumptions she held about the motives of her children's behavior, the shackles of a negative script were broken and she was free to reflect on what she could do to change. An important step in the process was to reframe the problem. Rather than wondering how she could make her children become "less lazy and less selfish," a question that contained negative assumptions about the motives of their behavior and increased her annoyance, she began to ask, "How can I change my behavior so that my children will not only become more responsible and cooperative but, just as important, begin to describe me using those words that I hope they would use?"

Guided by these questions, Mrs. Petrie, together with her husband, discussed with their children the responsibilities that each member of the household had. Mrs. Petrie shared honestly with her children her observation that she had been a "nag" and that she found herself thinking of them as "lazy." She said that in considering the situation she did not think they were lazy, but rather that there was too much negativity in the household, which made it difficult for family members to be cooperative and to meet responsibilities.

In a very skilled manner Mrs. Petrie turned her typical nagging format into a problem-solving dialogue as the family considered the responsibilities in the household that had to be met, how to delegate these responsibilities fairly, and ways to remind each other should a family member forget to do a task. This latter step is important to minimize reminders being equated with nagging.

As the situation improved at home, including her relationship with her husband, Mrs. Petrie applied the same principles and exercises related to personal control and empathy to her work environment. She recognized how sorry she felt for herself because she was not "born lucky," and that the so-called luck she envied was usually earned rather than mysteriously granted.

At one point she told us, "When I was passed over for a promotion I assumed that it was a result of people not liking my honesty when I told them what I felt was wrong. When I didn't get a promotion I became even angrier and I'm certain it came across to my colleagues. But then I thought about the questions you raised about how I would like to be described, how I would actually be described, and how I might act so that I would be described in more favorable terms. I realized that the way I was behaving guaranteed people would use less than flattering words to describe me."

Equipped with this new insight, Mrs. Petrie made an effort to change her behavior. She began to compliment her colleagues. When offering feedback, she was guided by the question, *Am I saying or doing things in a way that others will be most willing to listen and respond to me?* She told us, "It seems like such a simple, commonsense question. I'm not sure why we don't think about it all the time." It may seem simple and common sense, but when anger dominates our lives, even sensible questions are cast aside.

Obstacle Four: Fearing That If You're Too Empathic People Will Take Advantage of You

One of the most common reservations we hear about empathy in our seminars and clinical work is that if you are too empathic people will take advantage of you. Parents voice this concern about their children, employers about employees, husbands about wives, and wives about husbands—the list is endless.

At one of our workshops about family relationships, a man said, "When I start thinking about how my kids feel when I discipline them, I begin to feel sorry for them. I don't want them to be distressed, so I back down. If I didn't think so much about how they feel, I could be firmer."

At another workshop, a woman in a managerial position observed, "My secretary is very competent in most areas, but there are a couple of areas that require improvement. However, when I discuss these areas with her she becomes upset and feels I am very critical of her work. As you mentioned, I try to be empathic and put myself in her shoes. Because I don't want her to feel bad, I find that I'm hesitant to give her feedback about areas that need improvement. I think being empathic is actually an obstacle to being more honest and leaves you open to being taken advantage of."

At another seminar a man worried that if he were too empathic his business would suffer. He contended, "If I stop to think about how I come across to my employees and how they would describe me, I think it would keep me from acting decisively. I would second-guess every decision I made, wondering how everyone else felt about it." He then offered an interesting analysis. "They aren't motivated to do what I tell them to do now. Imagine what would happen if I were less decisive."

At our parenting workshops, these sentiments are voiced repeatedly by mothers and fathers who fear that empathy will result in their failure to set limits and use consequences, leading them to raise "spoiled" children.

It is unfortunate that many individuals confuse empathy with giving in, not being true to one's feelings, or not being decisive or honest. If anything, we believe that empathy provides a vital foundation for increased honesty and decisiveness, and becoming a more effective leader and disciplinarian.

Empathic people do not refrain from giving others feedback or from setting appropriate limits, but rather, as Mr. Butler and Mr. and Mrs. Savin discovered, they do so in a way in which these others will be most likely to listen and respond positively to what they have to say.

In the brief interaction we had at the seminar with the man who worried that he would compromise his decisiveness if he considered how his employees would describe him, we shared an alternative view. We guessed that if he began to reflect on how his message was being received by his employees he would not compromise his effectiveness as a leader, but rather enhance his influence. We said, "Leaders are more effective when they communicate in ways that resonate with those they are leading. This is best done when leaders consider how they and their message are being received."

The same approach is true when we set limits for others, a task that is very relevant in the parenting process. As we noted in our book *Raising Resilient Children*, we can be empathic and yet disapprove of what our children do. We can validate our children's feelings and beliefs but not necessarily agree with them. We can set limits and consequences even if our children do not embrace our actions with enthusiasm. For example, twelve-year-old Julie told her parents they were unfair for not permitting her to hang out at the mall with her friends.

Instead of responding angrily or lecturing Julie about the perils of hanging out in a mall, they began with empathy, validating her feelings. They said, "We know that you think we are not being fair, and we know that unless we said you could go, you would still think we were not being fair. We're sorry about that, but we don't feel comfortable with a twelve-year-old hanging out at the mall all afternoon."

While Julie did not thank her parents for setting this limit, the fact that they were empathic and validated her feelings made it easier for her to listen to what they had to say. Thus, being empathic did not result in giving in or spoiling, but rather in setting limits in a more constructive manner.

Goleman, Boyatzis, and McKee directly address the confusion of empathy with indecisiveness and weakness in their description of effective leadership qualities. They write:

> But empathy . . . doesn't mean a kind of "I'm okay, you're okay" mushi-
> ness. It doesn't mean that leaders would adopt other people's emotions as
> their own and try to please everybody. That would be a nightmare—it
> would make action impossible. Rather, empathy means taking employees'

feelings into thoughtful consideration and then making intelligent decisions that work those feelings into the response.[3]

While the authors address empathy in terms of leadership attributes, their words are applicable to each of our interactions. Empathy provides a basic foundation for more satisfying, successful relationships in all spheres of our lives.

Becoming an Empathic Person

Although the word *empathy* appears to have gained an increasing presence in our lexicon in recent years, it should not be misinterpreted as a fad or flavor-of-the-month concept. We believe that it deserves a central place in our daily existence. Once we have gained greater awareness about the beliefs or obstacles that work against empathy, we can focus our time and energy to dismantle these roadblocks and continue on the journey to nurture empathy. The following are several guidelines that will facilitate this journey.

Guideline One: Exercise Empathy

The process of developing and practicing empathy is a lifetime journey. It requires concentration and exercise. Just as daily physical exercise improves our stamina and strength, so too do regular "empathy exercises" nurture our ability to be more empathic. What may prove difficult to achieve at first becomes less burdensome as we become emotionally stronger. We must continue the process yet recognize that there may be setbacks along the way. Keep in mind that we have all experienced fatigue some days that affects our ability to jog as many miles or complete as many sit-ups or push-ups as the previous day. However, if a basic foundation has been established for proper exercise and diet, in most instances we will return to a higher level the next day.

In concentrating on empathy, return again and again to answer the following questions we posed at the beginning of this chapter:

- How do I hope other people would describe me?
- How do I interact with these people so that it is likely that they would describe me in this way?
- How would these other people actually describe me?
- How do I interact with these people to cause them to describe me in the ways that they do?

- Is there a significant discrepancy between how I hope people would describe me and how they actually would describe me?
- If there is a discrepancy, how can I change my attitudes and behaviors so that others will begin to describe me in the way I would like to be described?

"You're Strong-Willed! No, You Are!" Max and June Harris came to see us for marital counseling at the recommendation of Mrs. Harris's physician. They had been married for eighteen years and had one daughter, age fifteen. Mr. Harris was an engineer and Mrs. Harris was an attorney. In our first meeting they both described themselves as "strong-willed."

Mrs. Harris said, "We both like to have our own way. The final straw, and what brought us in, was that I wanted to go on a winter vacation skiing, while my husband wanted to go to a warmer climate for relaxation. It was going to be a family vacation, so I asked my daughter what she wanted to do. Maybe she had an opinion but didn't want to get into the middle of an argument, so she said whatever we decided was fine with her. I think that sometimes she's more even-tempered and wiser than either of us."

Mrs. Harris continued, "Max and I sat down to discuss things, and within a minute he was calling me strong-willed and stubborn. He said I never compromised, which is not true. If anyone is stubborn, it's Max."

Mr. Harris interrupted, "Whatever June wants, she gets. She grew up in a home where her parents placed her on a pedestal, where she was given whatever she wanted, and she expects the same now. Well, I'm tired of giving in."

Mrs. Harris jumped in, "You giving in? I'm the one who gives in. And I'm tired of your always saying I was put on a pedestal."

Interruptions abounded for the next few minutes. We asked, "Is this a typical conversation in your house?"

Mr. Harris answered, "Yes, but *conversation* may be too polite a word. *Yelling* may be a better description. I used to give in, but not anymore."

The interruptions flared up again when Mrs. Harris blurted, "You giving in? I can't believe you would say that. I'm the one who gives in because you're always so stubborn. I call him 'no compromise Max.' He's always trying to control me."

We could devote many pages to our intervention with Mr. and Mrs. Harris, but wish to focus on those features related to empathy. As we gained a more comprehensive picture of their relationship, we learned that issues of control and stubbornness had marked their marriage for years. However, they acknowledged that the problem had intensified over the past few years, sadly noting that their daughter had said, "It's not fun to live with you. You fight all the time." Each placed the responsibility for the intensification of the problems on the other, another example of the negative impact of not assuming personal control.

We took note of the negative words Mr. and Mrs. Harris used to describe each other, words that all but guaranteed a further deterioration in their relationship. As we often do, we asked them to think back to when they first met and to the beginning of their marriage. They said problems existed even then, but they were more willing to compromise. They now reinterpreted the early compromises not as a product of negotiation but rather as "giving in" to the demands of the other.

We wondered, "What has kept you together, even with all of these problems?"

Mr. Harris smiled and said, "I think June would agree. We had a very strong physical attraction to each other."

We glanced at Mrs. Harris and she said, "I would agree. I thought Max was a very attractive and a very funny man. I still think he's very attractive and he can still be funny. If he would only be less stubborn."

Mr. Harris responded, "Except for the part about being stubborn, that's a really nice compliment. I still find June very physically attractive."

In terms of our therapeutic activities, it was reassuring to observe this playfulness and to hear a few complimentary descriptions. Even if they had not voiced these positive comments, we still would have encouraged them to write answers to the following:

- What words do you hope your spouse would use to describe you?
- What words do you think your spouse would actually use?
- Why do you think your spouse would use these words? (We wanted them to consider how their words and actions affect the other.)
- What is it that you, not your spouse, can do differently?
- What is an example in your relationship that would lead your spouse to describe you with the words you would like to hear? (By examining the "exception to the rule," we learn what may help to turn these exceptions into the rule.)

Mr. and Mrs. Harris were very motivated to participate in these empathy exercises. We have worked with individuals who are less inclined to do so, either because they feel the other person should change first, they believe the situation is beyond repair, or their anger is very intense. In such instances additional therapeutic work is necessary to bring people to the point of engaging in these exercises.

The lists that Mr. and Mrs. Harris generated independently were remarkably similar. They reassured us that they had in fact written these descriptions without consulting each other. As they compared lists, Mr. Harris said, "After living together for so many years, I guess a couple can even start to think alike."

Each hoped the other would use the following words to describe them: "fair," "open-minded," "humorous," "considerate," "supportive" and "helpful." Each said the other would probably use the words that had been highlighted during our sessions, including "strong-willed," "inflexible," "stubborn." As part of the exercise, we also requested that they write down the words they would use to describe each other. Because we witnessed some playful exchanges between them, we were not surprised to find several positive words mixed in with the negative.

This exercise served as a catalyst for Mr. and Mrs. Harris to consider the impact their words and behavior had on each other. It also prompted them to begin to change those words and actions that were not in concert with how they hoped to be described.

We wish to emphasize that even if you do not request specific feedback from other people, such as through these recommended exercises, you can still keep these empathy questions in the forefront of your thinking. They can be applied in every relationship.

Guideline Two: Use Your Experience as a Guide

Reflecting on current and past experiences is an excellent resource to nurture empathy. The following questions, similar to the ones that we listed earlier in this chapter, help in this process:

- Think of an instance (from childhood or adulthood) when someone said or did something that helped you feel comfortable or secure or understood.
- What was it that this person said or did?
- Think of an instance (from childhood or adulthood) when someone said or did something that made you feel uncomfortable or insecure

or misunderstood. What about this person's behavior caused you to feel this way?

- Do you use your experiences to guide what you do in your current relationships? If so, what are one or two examples?

These questions are intended to be thought provoking and helpful. Yet many people fail to use this resource, instead becoming entangled in a negative script. For example, numerous parents have reported saying to themselves, "I promised I would never say this to my own children because I didn't like it when my parents said it to me. Yet I find myself saying it to them."

We encourage you to take the time to jot down on page 276 in Appendix A one or two positive and one or two negative interactions you had in the past with other people, together with your feelings and reactions. Then consider whether in your current relationships you are treating others the way you would like to be treated. Stated somewhat differently, keep in mind that in your current interactions you are creating memories for others. What do you want the content of these memories to be?

Guideline Three: Put Empathy into Practice Every Day

The exercises we have suggested in this chapter have as a basic goal developing personal action plans for change. Mr. Bauer's memories of Miss Lapora provided a source of information and strength in his quest to rediscover his passion for teaching. Mr. Butler's negative memories of his father and his consideration of the ways he was perceived by his managers were significant steps in the process of positive change and leading a more resilient life. Mr. and Mrs. Savin altered their approach to their son, Wade, when they recognized how negatively they came across. Mr. and Mrs. Harris could move beyond pejorative descriptions and constant bickering when they considered how they hoped their spouse would describe them and how their spouse would actually describe them.

Empathy must guide the actions we take. Warren Parsons spoke with us about his strained relationship with his fourteen-year-old son, Jay. When we asked him to describe his parents and how he thought they would have described him when he was Jay's age, he squirmed and became noticeably uncomfortable.

"I never really thought of that question before."

We responded, "If you can't think of an answer right now, think about it for our next meeting."

At our next session, Mr. Parsons said, "Those questions triggered a lot of emotions." He explained that as he thought about how he would describe his own father, the words that came to mind were "inflexible, overly demanding, rarely positive, and a poor listener who always had to be right and who could never say 'I love you.'" He added, "When I was Jay's age, I think my father would have described me as 'bullheaded, inflexible, won't take no for an answer.'"

With much emotion, Mr. Parsons continued, "What dawned on me was that history was repeating itself in my family. I would describe Jay the very same way that my father would have described me, and I bet Jay would use the same words to describe me that I used to describe my father. I don't want history to repeat itself any longer."

Mr. Parsons's ability to be empathic, to place himself in his shoes as a youth as well as in the shoes of his son and his father, was pivotal in changing negative scripts and nurturing the seeds of resilience in his family.

Concluding Thoughts

In our personal and professional lives, empathy serves as a necessary ingredient to maximize the development of satisfying relationships. As we will discuss in greater detail in Chapter 7, our emotional connections with our children, spouse, colleagues, students, and friends will be stunted if empathy is absent. Empathy allows us to exercise compassion and deal with interpersonal conflict effectively and constructively. We must actively seek to refine and fortify our empathic skills and be aware of the roadblocks that may arise. If we are successful, not only will our lives be enriched, but we will also enrich the lives of others.

5

Communicating
Effectively

The shelves of bookstores are lined with works about effective communication. Bestsellers examine the communication styles of men and women, with at least one author attributing these differences to the planet of origin of each gender! Other authors investigate the impact of effective communication on leadership and on managerial, parenting, or teaching skills. If one measure of the importance of a topic is the number of articles and books devoted to it, then communication rates near the top. Deservedly so.

Communication themes dominate our clinical practice and seminars. At one of our workshops a man half-jokingly asserted, "My communication skills are excellent. If only the people I interact with could improve theirs, I would be much happier." At a parenting seminar a mother ruefully wondered, "Is being monosyllabic a condition of adolescence?" Similarly, another parent observed, "I *am* communicating, but my child is not!" One of our favorite quotes is that of a woman who contended, "In terms of communicating with my husband, I don't think he's from another planet. Another galaxy would be more accurate." In response, her husband, who had a puzzled expression, shrugged his shoulders and said, "What do you mean by that?"

Communication and a Resilient Mindset

We deliberately placed this chapter about communication immediately after the chapter about empathy because of the close association between these two components of a resilient mindset. It is difficult to communicate effectively if we lack empathy. If we neglect to consider the perspective of others, then our words and actions will often miss their mark, as was illustrated with several examples in Chapter 4.

Communication plays a pivotal role in leading a resilient lifestyle. People possessing effective communication skills are able to express their thoughts and feelings clearly and diplomatically; listen closely to what others are saying; articulate expectations, goals, and values; solve problems; and resolve, rather than fuel, conflicts. Similar to the questions and exercises we recommended to nurture empathy, we believe that our communication with others should be guided by the following questions:

- What goal am I attempting to achieve in this communication?
- Am I saying or doing things in a manner in which others will be most responsive to what I have to say?
- Would I want anyone to speak to me the way I speak to others?
- How would others describe me as I communicate with them?
- What makes it easiest for me to listen to what others have to say?
- What do others say or do that turns me off and keeps me from listening to their message?
- Even if I disagree with someone, do I at least validate his or her point of view?

These questions must be answered thoughtfully. Jot down your initial thoughts on pages 276–278 in Appendix A. Within your answers lie the explanations for success or failure in all walks of life. We suggest you consider these questions and your answers during the next week, month, and year. In this way, your answers will become part of a process to assist you to become more effective in your communication skills and interpersonal relations. Doing this will reinforce a resilient mindset. If we fail to reflect on these and related questions, we may face a situation similar to that of Joshua Semper.

"I Don't Think What I'm Saying or Doing Is Unreasonable"

Joshua Semper, thirty-one years of age, worked in the business office of an agency providing services for the elderly. He came to see us at the recommendation of his brother because he was confused about whether he wanted to remain in his current job, especially in light of a recent negative evaluation by his supervisor. He noted that an additional source of stress and anger in his life was that Amy, his girlfriend of more than a year, had told him that she was ending their relationship because "he had such difficulty expressing his feelings."

We asked Mr. Semper to tell us more about the struggles he faced at work and in his relationship with his girlfriend.

"My supervisor said that I was not a 'team player,' whatever that means."

"Did you ask him what that means?"

"Yeah. He told me that I was rubbing people the wrong way, that sometimes I say things that irritate my colleagues. It's weird. My girlfriend tells me that I have trouble expressing my feelings but my boss tells me I express my feelings too directly. Go figure!"

Although Mr. Semper perceived the remarks of his girlfriend and his supervisor as contradictory, we assumed that there might be a common thread in the problems he was experiencing at work and in his relationship with Amy. We considered both to reflect difficulties with communication, most likely triggered by feelings of anger and a lack of empathy. As we gathered additional information, we found this to be the case.

We asked, "What did you think when your supervisor said you were rubbing people the wrong way?"

"I thought he wasn't being fair."

"Did you say anything?"

"Yeah. I asked him for specific examples."

"Was he able to give you any?"

"Yeah, but I didn't agree. He said that I come across as 'bossy,' telling people what to do rather than working with them. He also said that I get loud and argumentative when I disagree with someone. If I do get loud, it's when I feel people aren't listening to me. He said I wasn't a team player, but I told him I think it's these other people I work with who aren't team players."

As you may recognize, these comments capture several issues linked to a failure to develop a resilient mindset, most notably those pertaining to personal control, empathy, and communication.

Mr. Semper continued, "I told my boss that I thought his evaluation wasn't accurate, that I try to be a team player. He said I should watch the way I say things to people. He said that when I disagree with someone, I tend to come across as sarcastic. He also said that I very seldom give people positive feedback. I told him I don't think that's accurate. He said I should think about what he said."

"As you think about what your supervisor said, do you feel there are things you can say or do differently?" We wondered whether Mr. Semper was able to accept in even a small part his supervisor's feedback and whether he could entertain some responsibility for change and, if so, how he thought he might change.

"I'm not certain. I guess part of the problem is that I don't think what I'm saying or doing is unreasonable."

We replied, "That's something we can discuss further. But because you brought up problems you were having with your girlfriend, it might help to examine that relationship." We returned to his comment about his girlfriend to assess any similar behaviors in his personal and professional life that might highlight more clearly his patterns of relating to and communicating with others.

"Amy and I had been going together for a little more than a year. I really like her. I thought we had a very good relationship, but about a month ago, just when I thought things were getting more serious, she said something that surprised me. She said that I almost never told her how much I cared about her. I told her I did care about her, and she asked why didn't I ever tell her. She also said that when something seemed to be bothering me and she asked what was wrong, I always told her it was nothing and then I wouldn't talk about it."

"What do you think about what she said?"

"I told her that she should know I cared about her and that maybe the problem was that she was insecure. I also said that the reason I didn't like to talk about things that were bothering me was that whenever I said anything she would begin to ask me more and more questions about it. I told her that she was never satisfied with my answers. That just got her more angry, and that's when she said she wanted to end our relationship."

"Were you surprised by her reaction?"

"To be honest, I was. But maybe it's for the best. She seemed to be looking for problems where none existed."

One need not have an advanced degree in psychology to realize that Mr. Semper's communication style was not in concert with a resilient mindset. Earlier we noted that individuals with effective communication skills are able to express their thoughts and feelings with clarity and diplomacy, attend to the verbal and nonverbal messages of others, define and solve problems, and resolve rather than intensify conflicts. Although we did not know Mr. Semper's supervisor or girlfriend, based on our initial conversation with him it appeared that Mr. Semper communicated in a fashion that derailed problem solving and increased tension. Similar to the department head in the last chapter who reacted to less than positive feedback by accusing staff of "insubordination" or "having problems with authority," Mr. Semper effectively closed off discussion by criticizing others and failing to reflect on his contribution to problems.

Mr. Semper needed assistance to change his style of communication. We will describe our interventions with him later in this chapter.

Obstacles to Successful Communication

Three key obstacles operate to prevent people from communicating effectively. Given the close relationship between empathy and communication, you will notice that these obstacles are similar to those we've described for empathy.

Obstacle One: Being Trapped by Models from the Past

Positive and negative experiences from our childhood shape our current behavior. If we grew up in a home where parents and other adults did not communicate effectively, where feelings and thoughts either were not expressed or were expressed in an atmosphere of hostility and anger, where feelings were not validated, but rather ridiculed or ignored, it is more difficult, but not impossible, to develop effective communication skills. The struggles of Mr. Parsons and Mr. Taylor (Chapter 4) to be empathic and communicate constructively with their families bear witness to the adverse consequences of a childhood taking place in a home devoid of meaningful communication.

"I'm Beginning to Sound Just Like My Mother" Jessica Caldwell, a twenty-eight-year-old administrative assistant at a local university, came to see us for what she described as "a general malaise about life." She was unhappy at work, reported having few friends, and noted that she was becoming "increasingly irritable and angry." While the problem was not new, she said that it was becoming more pronounced.

In our first session she described feeling unhappy and angry and then offered an intriguing observation: "I'm beginning to sound just like my mother." The moment she uttered these words her eyes filled with tears.

She continued, "I get upset thinking about what I just said. The last person I want to sound like is my mother."

We asked her to explain.

Ms. Caldwell said her parents divorced when she was a toddler and her father moved to another part of the country. She had little contact with him and had not been in touch with him since she was a teenager. She didn't know where he lived or even if he were still alive. She added, "I really don't care."

She then recounted memories of her childhood. "My mother was a single mom who worked as a secretary in a law office. I know that she didn't have an easy life, but that was no excuse for how negative she was. Nothing I did was ever good enough for her. She always criticized me. She would say angry things like, 'You look so much like your father,' or 'Why don't you have the discipline to lose a few pounds?' or 'How come Jane and Nancy [two neighbors and classmates of Ms. Caldwell's] seem to have so many friends and you don't?'"

Ms. Caldwell paused for a few seconds. She resumed, "I can honestly say that the only compliments I ever received from my mother always had a negative tone. When I went on a diet and lost fifteen pounds, I tried on a new dress. Instead of telling me how good I looked or congratulating me on losing the weight, she said, 'It's about time you lost that weight.' She was a bitter woman."

"How do you think her bitterness affected you, especially because you said you thought you were beginning to sound just like her?"

"As I look back I realize how much I wanted her to accept me, to say something nice about me, but I can't remember her ever doing so. I always felt that I was a burden to her and that I constantly reminded her of my father, which was not a very good thing because she detested him. It's difficult to feel good about yourself growing up in such an atmosphere. I know one of my strongest feelings was insecurity. I was always questioning how smart I was, what I could accomplish, how pretty I looked."

We wondered, "How has this background affected you today?"

"The sad thing is that I'm twenty-eight years old and I still struggle with self-esteem and I find that I have become a pretty negative person, just like my mother. The other day a coworker who had difficulty learning a new computer program finally learned it. I said, 'I told you it wouldn't be hard to learn.' The problem was that the way I said it was really in a negative tone, almost like, 'Listen to me, I know what's best for you.' I didn't really mean it that way. That's exactly how I felt my mother constantly spoke with me."

"With hindsight, what would you have liked to have said to this coworker?" We asked this because Ms. Caldwell seemed trapped adhering to a negative script and we wanted to open up possibilities for the creation of new scripts.

"I just wish I would have smiled and said something like, 'Nice job' or 'Congratulations.' I know it would have meant a lot to her. I could tell right away how hurt she felt. She had worked hard to learn that program, and all I could do was give her a backhanded compliment. I spoke in my mother's voice. I never liked my mother's voice, but here I was using it. I don't want to be my mother."

Ms. Caldwell's psychological pain was very evident. Once again, tears came to her eyes as she said, "Sometimes I feel I can't compliment people because I never learned how to do it. Doesn't that sound silly, that you have to learn how to compliment?"

We said it didn't sound silly and we empathized with Ms. Caldwell's distress. Without searching for positives in a Pollyanna fashion, we observed that she already had taken steps to improve. We emphasized that her awareness of her negative script and her willingness to demonstrate empathy by placing herself in the shoes of her coworker were positive signs.

"But they seem to be such obvious signs."

"They may seem obvious to you, but they are not to a lot of people."

"But how do I change? I know that if I could get rid of my mother's negative attitude, I would be less unhappy and it would be easier for me to express more positive feelings."

We framed her question in a different way: "Rather than first trying to get rid of a negative attitude so you can then become more positive, it may help to consider and begin to say or do positive things. Even if these positive gestures seem a little forced or artificial at first, it may lead to a more positive attitude. Then the more positive you feel, the easier it will be to continue to say or do positive things. Also, there will be less time for negative comments."

This approach is in accord with the steps we described in Chapter 2 for changing negative scripts. It is similar to what Bill O'Hanlon advocates in his book *Do One Thing Different*: by saying or doing one thing differently you can begin to change attitudes and open new, more promising doors.

During the next few months our sessions with Ms. Caldwell focused on rehearsing and role-playing positive communications. As part of our interventions we asked her to observe other people's communications, especially those she believed demonstrated a more positive attitude. We developed short- and long-term goals for reinforcing healthy communications, including such gestures as greeting people with a smile in the morning and searching for one moment to say something positive. At first glance these may sound like simple steps, but changing lifelong communication patterns that are rooted in the behaviors of our first models consumes much time and energy and typically is most successful when taken in small steps.

At one point in our work with Ms. Caldwell, she described a colleague at work, Bobbi, whom she admired. "Bobbi has a way of saying things that makes you feel good. She is genuine. The other day I noticed she complimented one of our colleagues. The colleague appreciated what Bobbi said, but I also noticed something else. Bobbi seemed to enjoy offering the compliment. It was as if giving the compliment lifted Bobbi's spirits. It seemed such a simple thing to do, yet it has always been so difficult for me."

She added, "I keep thinking about some of the questions you asked me. I realize that I wouldn't want anyone to speak to me the way I am speaking to other people. I didn't like it when my mother spoke to me that way, so why should I talk the same way to someone else?"

Ms. Caldwell had struggled for years with obstacles that compromised the nurturance of a resilient mindset—negative scripts, a feeling of being unloved, problems with empathy, and a communication style tinged with bitterness and anger. As she embarked on the journey to remove these obstacles, she could replace her "mother's voice" with her own. In studying Bobbi's positive approach, she attended more vigilantly to her own verbal and nonverbal communications. Consequently, her attitude and outlook improved. A positive cycle was set in motion as her communications prompted positive feedback from others that reinforced the changes she was making.

One Evening, a Lifelong Lesson Our interventions with Ms. Caldwell, as well as her observations of Bobbi and others, helped her to learn more effective communication skills at the age of twenty-eight. Many learn these skills with less effort at an earlier age when exposed to nurturing adults whose communication is characterized by empathy, respect, and kindness.

The influence of positive models at any age was vividly captured in a story told to us by Stacy Lamsted, a forty-four-year-old mother of two teenaged girls. Mrs. Lamsted came to see us about doing some volunteer work in an inpatient program for children and adolescents with emotional and behavioral problems.

Mrs. Lamsted was a warm, personable woman with a lovely sense of humor. For the past several years she and her husband had taken in foster children with the encouragement and support of her daughters. At one point, our conversation with Mrs. Lamsted led us to inquire what was the briefest stay of a foster child in their home.

"It was Angie. She was fifteen years old. I wouldn't really call her a foster child because she was only with us overnight. Even though she was with us such a brief time, she said she learned a lifelong lesson from us. Actually, I think I learned a lifelong lesson from her."

"That's quite a statement."

"I know, but it's true. I'd love to tell you what happened. Angie was removed from an abusive home. The emergency shelter for teenagers in our town was at capacity. A caseworker called me and asked whether Angie could stay overnight with us until a placement could be found the next day. She came over, and I will never forget that night."

"What happened?"

"I should preface this by saying that my husband and I and my daughters have a very loving relationship. We all tend to be calm and soft-spoken. A friend once jokingly asked me, 'What is your family really like when no one else is around?' I told her, 'What you see is what you get.' Unfortunately, we were not calm the evening Angie came over. My older daughter, Nina, and I got into an argument. At this point I don't even remember what it was about, but we actually were yelling at each other. All I could think of was that Angie was just rescued from an abusive home and ends up in a home where there is screaming and yelling. Nina and I finally ended the argument, but I felt terrible that Angie had to hear us yelling at each other.

"Angie left the next morning. A couple of weeks later I spoke with her caseworker, who called to thank me for taking Angie in for the evening. This caseworker said, 'Angie can't stop talking about the night she spent at your house.' The moment the caseworker said this I felt miserable again and I began to apologize. I said, 'I really feel terrible about what happened. We're usually such a calm family. I'm sure Angie must have wondered why you were sending her from one abusive home to another.' The caseworker laughed, which surprised me."

Mrs. Lamsted continued, "I asked the caseworker why she was laughing, and she answered that it was because I was actually apologizing for something positive that had happened. She said Angie kept talking about how the evening she spent at our house taught her something. It was the first time in her life that she observed family members argue and then resolve the argument. The caseworker said that all Angie had ever experienced when her family argued were insults, yelling, pushing, and shoving. Angie told the caseworker she was amazed when Nina and I kissed good night after the argument. She had never seen anything like that before."

We observed, "That's a very powerful story."

Mrs. Lamsted said, "I think so too. Looking at my own life, plus having two kids of my own and having taken in several foster children, I know that a change of attitude usually takes time. I don't know how long lasting the impact will be on Angie of seeing me and Nina argue and then make up, but I think it may be something she will remember for a long time. I may be fooling myself, but based on what the caseworker said, I think the night Angie spent with us provided her with some hope. She saw that people could argue, end the argument, and then express love toward each other. She had never witnessed that before."

Mrs. Lamsted smiled and added, "Not that I'm recommending the way to offer hope to kids who are hopeless is to have them witness yelling between a mother and daughter, but in this instance it seemed to help. I guess I learned that even brief experiences coming at a particular point can begin to change the ways we perceive things and communicate with other people."

Mrs. Lamsted's observations were very perceptive. While our behavior and communication skills are shaped in great part by the home in which we grow up, later experiences can modify the impact of these early experiences. We are not doomed to speak in the voices of our first models, especially when these voices are negative and angry.

Obstacle Two: Harboring Disappointment, Anger, or Frustration

If we could write an ideal script, it might contain the following action: when we become angry or upset, an automatic system would elicit our most advanced communication abilities to help defuse our emotions and direct our attention to a search for effective solutions. Possessing this system would minimize anger, bitterness, and power struggles.

Unfortunately, it is precisely when we are disappointed, angry, and frustrated that our communication skills, which are interwoven with other resiliency skills such as empathy, conveying love and appreciation, and problem solving, are appreciably weakened. The angry communication that follows often exacerbates, rather than resolves, a problem situation. This pattern was apparent with Mr. and Mrs. Harris, Mrs. Petrie, and Mrs. Stevens.

As we have often noted, it is much easier to be empathic and to communicate most effectively when we are with people who agree with us and behave in ways that we find acceptable. It is a much greater challenge to listen actively and respectfully and express our thoughts and feelings with calmness and clarity when we are upset, annoyed, and irritated.

A Marriage on the Brink of Collapse Lisa and Alex Dembar, both in their early thirties, came to see us about marital problems. They had been married for two years and had known each other for about four. We asked them how we might be of help.

Mr. Dembar began. "I must be honest. I don't think we would need to come in for marital counseling if Lisa wouldn't withdraw and refuse to communicate when we have a disagreement. It drives me crazy. We can be having a great discussion for an hour, and then when we begin to disagree, she says she doesn't want to talk anymore, and she doesn't. A perfect example was last night. We were having what I thought was a pleasant conversation about some redecorating we want to do in our house. Then we disagreed about whether to put in new cabinets or look into staining the old ones. It's much less expensive to stain the old ones. Because we were spending a lot of money on other things, I said I thought it would be best to stain the old ones because that would make them look new. She immediately accused me of being a penny-pincher. I said I was just trying to be realistic in terms of our finances. The next thing I know, Lisa refuses to talk. She just clams up."

We glanced at Mrs. Dembar, who, not surprisingly, had an angry expression on her face. After a moment she responded, "Alex is right. We communicate very well when we agree, but what that really means is we communicate well when I go along with him, because he feels his opinion is the right opinion. He's one of the most opinionated people you'll ever meet. Because he feels he's always right, when you don't agree with Alex he can keep badgering you until you either give in or just want to get away from the situation."

Mr. Dembar jumped in and said, "If you feel that way, why don't you discuss it with me instead of withdrawing and becoming silent?"

"Because if I try to discuss anything you disagree with, you devalue my viewpoint, so I feel it's better if I say nothing. Sometimes I think our marriage is on the brink of collapse."

This pattern of communication is not atypical, especially when anger enters the scene. Anger and frustration eclipse any semblance of a rational discussion. Instead, people fail to listen to each other. They interrupt each other to offer their own views, views that are often laced with negative assumptions. They fail to ask the questions we posed earlier, such as:

- What goal am I attempting to achieve in this communication?
- Am I saying or doing things in a manner in which others will be most responsive to what I have to say?
- Would I want anyone to speak to me the way I speak to others?
- How would others describe me as I communicate with them?
- What makes it easiest for me to listen to what others have to say?
- What do others say or do that turns me off and keeps me from listening to their message?
- Even if I disagree with someone, do I at least validate his or her point of view?

As you read the interaction that transpired between Mr. and Mrs. Dembar in their first session with us, do you think they considered how the other person perceived their message or how comments such as "She just clams up" or "He's one of the most opinionated people you'll ever meet" were certain to arouse strong emotions and derail a problem-solving attitude? It is easier to consider the questions we posed to guide effective communication when anger and frustration are absent. However, it is even more vital to keep these questions in the forefront when anger permeates a situation.

We asked the Dembars to examine their communication style, especially when disagreement and anger were present. Initially both cast blame on the other for the difficulties in their interaction. Mr. Dembar repeatedly said that his wife refused to speak with him when she didn't agree with his point of view. In turn, she responded that her husband really didn't listen to her because he believed any position that differed from his was incorrect.

On a positive note, they agreed that they wanted the situation to improve. For this to happen, we knew that we had to encourage them to change their mindsets and counterproductive style of communicating. To promote the notion of personal control, we asked both to consider what they could do differently. We attempted to facilitate this task in several ways. We requested that they not say things to each other that they would not want said to them. We asked them to think about how their words and actions were experienced by the other. We especially addressed Mr. Dembar's tendency to use words that devalued his wife's opinion and Mrs. Dembar's tendency to hurl similar words back at him.

We reviewed what Mrs. Dembar began to call "guidelines" for better communication. For instance, if Mr. Dembar said something that was demeaning, rather than become silent she was to say to him that she felt his remark was hurtful. Another guideline was that even if Mr. Dembar disagreed with his wife's point of view, he was at least to acknowledge and validate it rather than summarily dismiss it. Although these guidelines might seem like minor interventions, as we have often discovered in our clinical activities, seemingly minor changes can produce significant results. Making these small changes began to lessen the frustration and anger that had permeated Mr. and Mrs. Dembar's relationship.

Obstacle Three: Losing Sight of How Best to Achieve Your Goals

Although this obstacle is contained within the previous obstacles, we believe, given its importance, that it deserves special mention. It is directly linked to the first two questions that we asked in this chapter:

- What goal am I attempting to achieve in this communication?
- Am I saying or doing things in a manner in which others will be most responsive to what I have to say?

If we lose sight of our goals and how best to achieve these goals, then our communication is likely to suffer from a lack of direction or be compromised by anger and frustration.

We have illustrated this obstacle on many occasions. Mrs. Petrie wanted her children to be more responsible, but the manner in which she communicated to them worked against this goal. Mr. and Mrs. Savin experienced a similar situation with their son, Wade. Ms. Vaughn wished to communicate to Mr. and Mrs. Vintor the severity of their son's problems, but she, too, lost sight of the goal by clouding her communication with the very negative statement, "I've been teaching thirteen years, and your child is the worst child I have ever taught."

When our goals are ambiguous and poorly defined, it is difficult to communicate effectively. However, even when goals are well defined, if we express our feelings and thoughts in ways that preclude others from joining our efforts, then the best-defined goals will remain unfulfilled.

Take a moment to think about two or three goals you have that involve changes you would like to see occur in your life and consider how well you have articulated these goals. Once they are clearly defined, jot them down on page 278 in Appendix A. Reflect on what you have done or plan to do to accomplish these goals. Next, think about whether your past communications or your planned communications have moved you or will move you toward reaching these goals. This is one of the most important exercises you can undertake to replace ineffective forms of communication with productive ones.

Strengthening Our Communication Skills

Just as obstacles exist for successful communication, steps exist that can be taken to nurture this component. As you undertake to strengthen your communication skills, remember that the reinforcement of any feature of a resilient mindset involves a process that takes time, reflection, patience, and effort. Each small step contributes to reaching your goals. Also, think of setbacks as opportunities for improving your approach.

Step One: Practice, and Then Practice Some More

In the last chapter we noted that just as exercises exist to improve our physical well-being, so too exercises exist to improve our ability to be empathic. The same is true when one considers the skills necessary to communicate effectively. An initial step is to return on a regular basis to the questions we posed earlier in this chapter. The more these questions become part of your mindset, the better equipped you will be to make the necessary changes in your behavior to improve your capacity for resilience.

As we witnessed, Mr. and Mrs. Dembar adopted guidelines that they practiced consistently to improve their styles of communicating and their marriage. Ms. Caldwell rehearsed and role-played new scripts until they became increasingly refined and comfortable. In addition, she assumed the role of what she labeled "a social skills investigator" as she observed the interactions and communications of individuals whom she judged to exhibit excellent communication abilities. Her favorite target was her colleague Bobbi; without attempting to become a clone of Bobbi or to copy Bobbi's behavior in a robotic fashion, she applied and practiced what she learned from her in a way that was in concert with her personality.

Back to Mr. Semper When we left our discussion of Mr. Semper, he was experiencing difficulties at work because of what his supervisor described as his failure to be a team player and his tendency to be loud and argumentative. In addition, his girlfriend, Amy, had recently ended their relationship, contending that he rarely communicated that he cared for her and that he withdrew from discussing things that were bothering him. Exacerbating the problem was Mr. Semper's difficulty assuming personal control or responsibility for these issues, instead arguing that Amy was "insecure," that "she seemed to be looking for problems where none existed," and that it was his coworkers who failed to be team players. He closed off discussion by casting blame on others.

Not surprisingly, as we have learned in our roles as clinicians, consultants, and educators, if we are to help others improve their communication skills, we must practice and strengthen our own. Thus, when considering our interventions with Mr. Semper we asked the same questions of ourselves that we ask others: "What do we hope to achieve, and how do we communicate with Mr. Semper to maximize the likelihood that he will hear what we have to say and cooperate with us rather than feel he is being criticized?"

We began with empathy by acknowledging the stress he was feeling at work and in his relationship with Amy. We recognized that if we were to create an atmosphere in which Mr. Semper could begin to examine his current beliefs and communication style, we would have to minimize his perception that we didn't appreciate or understand his perspective.

We said, "It's difficult when we feel people don't understand us or even blame us for things. We can understand why you would feel annoyed when your supervisor says that you're not a team player and that you come across as bossy when you feel that it's your coworkers who aren't team players. Also, it's easy to understand why you were frustrated when Amy said you don't tell her you care about her when you feel you are showing that feeling."

Mr. Semper concurred, "It's very frustrating."

We continued, "We're not certain you will agree with what we have to say, but because your supervisor and Amy are not here and we can't really change them, it might be helpful to look at what you have control over, what you can change." Advising people in advance that they might disagree with our viewpoint actually helps them to be less defensive and more open to what we say. Also, empathizing with Mr. Semper about his frustration increased the likelihood that he would reflect on how he might change (specifically, assume greater personal control).

Even with what we considered to be empathic comments, Mr. Semper replied, "Are you saying I'm to blame? I already said that I don't think what I said or did is unreasonable."

"No, we're not blaming you at all, and we regret if it came across that way. When people are upset by certain situations, what we have actually found helpful is to encourage them to look at what steps they might take to change the situation. Sometimes as they change, other people may also begin to change."

Mr. Semper replied, "I think I've done just about everything I can. Maybe it's time for my supervisor and Amy to change. Maybe I shouldn't even bring up Amy, because I think that our relationship is over."

"Sometimes it seems like we've exhausted all the things we can do, but perhaps there are some things we haven't thought about."

"Like what?"

This was an excellent opportunity for us to introduce questions for Mr. Semper to consider in an attempt to reinforce empathy and effective communication. We encouraged him to continue his dialogue with his supervisor and to gather examples of times that he comes across as loud or argumentative.

Several sessions later, Mr. Semper said, "It's funny—just talking in here about the way I come across made me think more about it. At a meeting at work I noticed that I began to raise my voice when I disagreed with Harry, one of my coworkers. I noticed something else. When I got angry I didn't really listen to what Harry had to say. Instead, all I could think of was what I was going to say next."

"It sounds as if you're doing quite a good job observing the way you communicate with others."

"I'm trying to. What helps is that I think my colleagues are listening more closely to what I have to say. Not that they agree with me, but they seem to be listening more closely."

"We think people are more likely to listen to us when they feel we are making an effort to change."

At a subsequent session Mr. Semper came in looking sad. We asked whether anything had happened.

"I've been thinking a lot about Amy. I guess I never stopped thinking of her. You know, she was right when she said I really didn't tell her how much I cared about her. Maybe it's a male thing."

As Mr. Semper said this, he looked at us. We didn't say anything.

"OK, it's not a male thing, it's a Joshua Semper thing. Or maybe I should say it used to be a Joshua Semper thing. I'm trying to change."

"Why the sad look when you came in?"

"I hadn't spoken with Amy in months. I called to apologize for some of the things I said to her—that she was insecure and that I didn't like to answer things because when I did she would just ask me more questions."

"What was her reaction?"

"She seemed pleasantly surprised and thanked me for calling. But what made me sad is that she told me she's very seriously involved with another guy. I wished her well. When I got off the phone I felt that I had let a wonderful relationship slip through my hands."

"We can understand why you would feel that way. But we also think it took a lot of courage to call Amy and apologize to her."

Mr. Semper said, "Maybe, but I did have an ulterior motive. I wanted to see if she was still available. If she was, I would have asked about getting together again."

"You may have had an ulterior motive, but we're not certain you could have made that call several months ago."

Mr. Semper smiled. "Did anyone ever tell you that you have a way of asking questions and saying things that prompts people to think about what they are doing? You never ordered me to think about the questions you raised to help me communicate better, but you encouraged me in a non-threatening way to do so. You may not realize it, but when I sit here with you I notice the way you say things. It's been very helpful."

As Mr. Semper said this, we thought about Ms. Caldwell's description of a "social skills investigator."

We responded, "Thanks for the feedback. You really are observant." In a humorous way, we added, "It's a good thing we practice what we preach."

Mr. Semper laughed.

On a more serious note, we said, "It would have been great if Amy was still available. What we're going to say now isn't going to magically ease some of the pain you feel, but we think it's important to say. We're certain that you will use what you learned from your relationship with Amy with other women you meet in the future."

"I appreciate your saying that."

It was evident that Mr. Semper was diligently practicing more effective communication skills and that he was using the questions we raised to facilitate this process.

Step Two: Become an Active Listener

When we discuss communication, many people immediately ask us what they can do to express themselves more effectively. It is as if they perceive the art of communication as synonymous with the words we utter. While expressive language is a major component of communication, we must begin, as author Stephen Covey reminds us, by ensuring that we understand before seeking to be understood. It is difficult, if not impossible, to engage in effective communication if we fail to listen to and understand what others have to say.

To be an active listener implies that you attempt to understand the verbal and nonverbal messages being conveyed by others; that you perceive the feelings, thoughts, and beliefs they are communicating; and that you do not permit your agenda or preconceived assumptions about their motives to undermine your ability to appreciate what they are attempting to communicate. Active listening also involves the recognition that unspoken messages or meanings are typically conveyed along with the spoken word. Active listening involves an effort to understand these meanings before seeking to be understood.

Recall the trials and tribulations of Mr. and Mrs. Dembar. Active listening was a lost commodity in their relationship. Subtly or not so subtly, they failed to listen, assuming they were right and their spouse was wrong. They interrupted each other, presumed negative motives, and cast blame toward each other. Active listeners do not interrupt or muddy communication with negative assumptions. Instead, they listen and ask, "What is this person trying to say?" It was only after Mr. and Mrs. Dembar were able to incorporate guidelines for effective communication into their daily interactions that active listening became an important ingredient of their relationship. As it assumed greater importance, their communication problems lessened.

During the next few weeks and months, notice your behavior and ask yourself:

- Do I attempt to understand before being understood?
- Do I encourage expressions of feelings and thoughts from significant others in my life, or do I say and do things that discourage communication?
- Do I model effective communication by listening to what others have to say?

If the answer to any of these is negative, ask yourself what is one small thing you can change in the process of becoming an active listener.

Step Three: Validate; Let Others Know They Have Been Heard

Although it is extremely important, it isn't enough to just listen. We must also learn to validate what others are saying and confirm that they have been heard. Validation does not imply that we agree with the views of other people, but simply that we acknowledge and respect their perspective.

I (Bob) learned the importance of validation early in my training. A nine-year-old patient told me that he felt he was "dumb and ugly." Wishing to be supportive, I said what might easily be understood as an encouraging remark: "But you're not."

The child looked at me and angrily responded, "Do you listen to people?"

Not only had I failed to listen actively, but in my attempt to be reassuring I failed to validate what this child had said. People do not want to be told what they should feel, especially after they have told you something different. What might I have said instead that would have been both validating and encouraging?

One possibility is, "I'm glad you can tell me how you feel. I know you feel dumb and ugly. I want to let you know that while you may feel that way, I have a different view. I hope it's something we can talk about."

Or, depending on the situation, one can establish a problem-solving task by saying, "I'm glad you can tell me how you feel. I know you feel dumb and ugly. Would you like to figure out what would help you not to have those feelings?"

A similar situation occurred with fifteen-year-old Rachel when she commented at the beginning of a family therapy session that she felt depressed. Rachel's mother, Mrs. Sterling, said, "But there's no reason for you to be depressed. We give you everything you need, and we are a loving family."

Although Mrs. Sterling's intention was to relieve Rachel's sadness, her own apparent anxiety prompted a response that led Rachel to become more withdrawn. Imagine Rachel's response if Mrs. Sterling had said, "I know you feel very unhappy. I wish you didn't, but I know you do. That's why we're here to talk with a therapist and figure out how all of us can be happier and get along better."

We would surmise that if Mrs. Sterling had responded in this way, Rachel would not have withdrawn, but instead would have been more willing to engage in conversation.

A failure of validation was apparent in the interactions between Mr. and Mrs. Pace, whom we described in Chapter 1. When Mrs. Pace said, "To be honest, I've been feeling pretty depressed for the past year," Mr. Pace answered, "But Andrea, there's no reason for you to be depressed. We have a nice home and good jobs, and we go on great vacations. You're just letting yourself get depressed."

At that moment, anger, frustration, and sadness permeated the room and there was little opportunity for constructive communication.

One of the most certain ways to derail communication is to neglect to validate, whether it is in the form of a department head accusing a staff member of insubordination for disagreeing with him, or a mother desperately wishing to remove the sadness dominating her daughter's life by questioning why her daughter should feel depressed, or a man judging his girlfriend to be "insecure" when she shares her feeling with him that he has not expressed how much he cares about her.

Step Four: Live by the Golden Rule

We want and expect others to treat us with fairness and respect, to listen to what we have to say, and to communicate with calmness and clarity. As we have seen, this is easier said than done. Anger, frustration, and inflexibility render the so-called Golden Rule inoperative. The Golden Rule is rooted in our ability to be empathic and is a cornerstone of living resiliently.

In this chapter, as in Chapter 4, we have highlighted many instances of failures to treat others as we would like to be treated, a situation that weighs heavily on effective communication. It is for this reason that we recommend your communication be guided by reflecting on the questions we listed earlier, including:

- Would I want anyone to speak to me the way I speak to others?
- How would others describe me as I communicate with them?
- What makes it easiest for me to listen to what others have to say?
- What do others say or do that turns me off and keeps me from listening to their message?

These and similar questions were catalysts in helping Mr. Parsons, whom we met in the last chapter, begin to change the way in which he communicated with and related to his son Jay. Mr. Parsons realized that his father had communicated with him in the same way he communicated with Jay. Most important, Mr. Parsons did not like the way his father treated him, yet he was doing the same to his son. With this recognition, it was not surprising that Mr. Parsons lamented, "What dawned on me was that history was repeating itself in my family. . . . I don't want history to repeat itself any longer."

To keep negative history from repeating itself, let's examine the third and fourth questions we just listed and make them even more specific. How would you answer the following?

Think of one interaction you had as a child and another as an adult that you would classify as containing positive communications—that is, interactions in which you felt validated and respected. What did the other person or people say or do that helped you to feel this way? What was your reaction?

Think of one interaction you had as a child and another as an adult that you would classify as containing negative communications—that is, interactions in which you felt a lack of validation and respect. What did the other person or people say or do that made you feel this way? What was your reaction?

Use these memories to guide your current behavior and communication.

Step Five: Avoid All-or-None Statements

This suggestion could be placed within other steps, but given the frequency with which all-or-none statements appear in our daily lives, we believe it deserves its own place. What do we mean by *all-or-none statements*? They are pronouncements that almost guarantee the rupture of effective communication. They are typically cast in exaggerated, polarized terms. Our two favorites contain the words *always* and *never*; there is nothing inherently wrong with these words, except when uttered in the following fashion:

- You are always inconsiderate!
- You never help out!
- You always find mean things to say!
- You never think about my feelings!
- You always think of yourself first!

Children and adolescents often feel bombarded by *always* and *never* phrases, such as:

- You never clean your room.
- You always forget to hang up your towel.
- You always have to be reminded to do things.
- You never take out the garbage.
- You're never considerate.

We're certain you can add to this list. It is endless.

In one of our workshops, a woman asked, "Well, what if it's true? What if your husband never helps out or never says nice things to you?"

We are not suggesting that these kinds of comments may not have a kernel of truth, but rather that they are experienced as accusatory exaggerations that limit productive communication and problem solving. Voicing these kinds of sentiments, even if they are true, does little to resolve conflicts.

See what happens when you remove negative all-or-none words or phrases from your vocabulary. You may be very surprised by the results.

Step Six: Serve as a Model of Honesty, Integrity, and Dignity

It is a sad commentary that in the past few years accounts of dishonesty have become so prevalent. People in the public eye—politicians, business leaders, clergy, coaches, and athletes—have lied in the courts, on their business ledgers, on their résumés, and about supplements they are taking to increase their physical prowess. Some argue that the problem was just as prevalent in the past but the media was less invasive and more forgiving. We find little solace in that argument.

In many respects it matters little whether a lack of honesty and integrity was more or less frequent in years gone by. When people are dishonest, when their communications hide or bend the truth, a truly resilient lifestyle is difficult to achieve. We are not talking about the occasional "white lie" that most people have told, although for some these lies certainly accumulate and may become part of a pattern of dishonesty. We are most concerned about individuals who use communication to deceive, manipulate, or hurt others.

At one of our workshops a man asked whether one can be "too honest." We wondered what he meant.

He said, "Some people may ask your opinion about how they look or about a project they have completed. What if they don't look good, or what if the project they have completed is subpar? You don't want to hurt their feelings."

We have heard this kind of question on numerous occasions. The question highlights the important role that empathy and effective communication play when providing feedback. Although it may not be easy, we believe we can find ways to express our feelings honestly without offending the other person.

When we ask people at our workshops or consultations to think about a time they received feedback that could have been experienced as critical but was not, almost everyone can provide an example. When we ask what permitted them to accept the communication in a nondefensive way, we frequently hear such comments as:

- I know this person cares about me because she has gone out of her way to give me positive feedback.
- This person is respectful and listens to what I have to say.
- This person is honest; what you see is what you get.

We can also think of occasions when we interact with someone whose feedback is experienced in an accusatory way, someone we don't trust, someone who we feel is always holding back information. To work in an environment in which dishonesty and half-truths are the norm rather than the exception is to work in an environment in which effective communication and any semblance of trust have been severely blunted.

As we are writing this chapter, recent news has been consumed with the testimony of high-level executives with large severance packages from their bankrupt companies pleading innocence of any knowledge of the deceptions that were occurring under their guard. How many of us believe their protestations? At a conference we once attended someone said, "You can only sell your reputation one time. Once it's sold, it's sold. It is difficult for anyone to trust anything you say after that."

The question of honesty is frequently posed in our parenting workshops. Parents sometimes are not as forthright with their children as they should be. While we are not recommending that parents discuss issues that are beyond a child's emotional or cognitive capabilities or that are highly personal, the fact is that children are extremely astute at recognizing when parents hide things from them or bend the truth. Parents often do this to protect their children, but there is a danger of going too far. Parents and other caregivers must use their best judgment in what to share or not share; in making that decision, parents must be careful not to err on the side of fostering a cloak of secrecy in the household.

We have found that if our communications about difficult situations are handled with sensitivity, children become less anxious and are more resilient. It is when secrecy pervades the home that children may be robbed of opportunities to ask questions and to express and manage their anxieties with greater comfort. They are also robbed of opportunities to become better communicators.

Step Seven: Make Humor an Essential Part of Your Communication

In multiple studies around the world, humor has repeatedly been found to help individuals cope with adversity. It has been found to be a vital component of a resilient mindset. Humor is often an excellent way of changing a negative script or defusing a difficult situation. Obviously, humor should not be used when we are uncertain about how it will be received by others. If we use humor while angry, it is likely to be experienced as sarcasm. However, if used judiciously, humor helps people to be more playful, less anxious, less defensive, and more open to our communications.

Dr. Steve Sainsbury, in an article titled, "Stress in the Workplace: Five Great Ways to De-Stress," listed humor as the first strategy. He noted, "The ability to find humor in stressful situations can dramatically lighten everyone's load. For example, while suturing a patient, I routinely tell jokes and ask them to do the same. By the time the procedure is completed, we have laughed and smiled together with a minimum of tension."[1]

At one of our school consultations a teacher told us that the staff room at her school had become a place to "moan, groan, and complain." She said that these communications did not serve to let off steam, but rather reinforced a negative attitude.

She added, "All we do is talk about uncooperative kids and uncooperative parents. A few of us realized that we felt worse rather than better after spending time in the staff room. We recognized that we had to lighten things up because everything was so oppressive. No one was having any fun."

With the input and support of several colleagues, they decided to try an "experiment" that was agreed to by the entire staff (this teacher said that she felt some went along to indulge her). On two designated days a week no one could utter a negative comment in the staff room; in addition, on those two days staff would take turns bringing in a cartoon to hang up. The staff also agreed that if anyone offered a negative statement in the staff room during the two designated "positive days," the guilty party would be assessed a fifty-cent fine.

Their experiment yielded very encouraging results. Cartoons began to appear even on the three "off" days. Before long a third positive communication day was added, and the negativity on the two remaining days was markedly reduced. The teacher added, "People walked in and out of the staff room with smiles on their faces. I wonder what the students thought was going on."

We wish these kinds of experiments were always as successful as the one that transpired in this school. However, if they are not attempted, positive changes will not occur.

Resilient people know how and when to use humor in their communications. It is a feature to which we should all attend.

Communication: A Cornerstone of Resilience

To say we all communicate is equivalent to saying we all breathe. It is a vital function of our existence. Communication can bring people together or divide them forever. It can promote love and compassion or reinforce anger and mistrust. Communication can build a foundation either to solve problems or to exacerbate conflicts in our personal and professional lives. Effective communication is easier for some people, especially if they have had the benefit of adequate models from whom to learn. For others, effective communication is a struggle often filled with obstacles and disappointments. Whether a struggle or not, if we are to be resilient, it is an area of our lives requiring time and energy.

6

Accepting Oneself and Others

The humor of comedians Rodney Dangerfield, Woody Allen, and Richard Lewis is rooted in self-deprecating jokes—jokes that capture the struggle to be accepted and to accept oneself. Dangerfield's one-liners come spewing out at a rapid pace interspersed with his well-known phrase, "I get no respect." In his inimitable style he describes this lack of respect as originating at the beginning of his life. "I was so ugly as a kid that when my mother saw me, she diapered my face instead of my bottom." The laughter of the audience typically reflects the content's relevance to their lives. Humor far removed from our personal experience rarely evokes the intensity of laughter that "hits home." Humor pertaining to respect and acceptance, which are core issues for all of us, hits home. Such humor will prompt laughter with one major exception: if, in hitting home, it touches our most vulnerable areas too directly. When that occurs, strong feelings are triggered that have little to do with laughter. The distinction between a joke that elicits laughter and one that occasions pain may be tenuous, especially when the material relates to self-acceptance.

"My Therapist Dozed Off"

A mixture of humor and pathos was evident when we saw Luke Larimer in therapy. He had previously been in therapy with another clinician. When we asked why he had left the first clinician, Mr. Larimer stated, "I have major issues with self-esteem. I never felt accepted by my father. He often told me I was unsuccessful and that I would not be a very interesting person unless I expanded my horizons. I was never quite certain what he meant by 'expanding my horizons.' Even as a kid I knew he was disappointed with me and saw me as a boring person who didn't read much and never really knew what to say in front of people. Can you imagine your own father seeing you as a boring, unsuccessful person?

"After years of feeling miserable about myself, I finally found the courage to see a therapist. During one of our first sessions my therapist dozed off while I was talking. I couldn't believe it. At first I thought he closed his eyes because he was thinking about what I was saying. But then he began to snore. It was like a scene out of a Woody Allen movie. I woke him up and he apologized. Would you believe it, two weeks later he fell asleep again. As I listened to his snoring, all I could think of was my father telling me I was boring. Imagine a therapist falling asleep on you. It made me feel even worse."

Mr. Larimer displayed a sense of humor when he noted, "And to add insult to injury, he charged me full price for the session. The least he could have done was to have given me a discount since he wasn't working for part of the session." Needless to say, we made certain we remained very alert during every session with Mr. Larimer. He faced another problem, one that is often associated with feeling a lack of respect and acceptance: he felt criticized and blamed for the problem.

He poignantly observed, "From an early age I felt there was something wrong with me, that I was a weak person, that I had a character flaw. My father and others would constantly tell me to speak up, to read more, to be sociable. I was told that I could change if I really wanted to. I think it's bad enough to not like some of your behavior. It's even worse when people criticize you and then you begin to criticize yourself."

Once again humor accompanied with obvious pain prompted Mr. Larimer to say, "If my life was made into a movie and I was on trial for my behavior, not only would I play myself, I would also play the prosecuting attorney. I'm not certain we could find someone to be a defense attorney. I think a guilty verdict would come in very quickly."

Acceptance and Resilience

If we are to nurture a resilient mindset, we must learn to accept ourselves as well as others. Acceptance involves possessing realistic expectations and goals, recognizing and identifying our feelings, managing our feelings constructively, defining our strengths and vulnerabilities, and leading a balanced life in which our behaviors are in concert with our values and goals. When acceptance is missing in life, as it was in Mr. Larimer's, we experience increased stress, tension, and dissatisfaction and are far removed from enjoying the benefits of a resilient life.

Questions for Reflection

Think about the following questions and exercises related to the themes of acceptance and leading a resilient lifestyle. You can write your answers on pages 278–280 of Appendix A.

- What words would you use to describe the person you would like to be, or your ideal self?
- What words would you actually use to describe yourself?
- How far apart are the words you would use to describe your ideal self and the words you would use to describe your actual self?
- Describe a time in your life when you believe you came closest to your ideal self. What occurred in this situation that made you feel this way?
- Describe a time in your life when you felt far removed from your ideal self. What occurred in this situation that made you feel this way? What, if anything, did you do to change the situation?
- List two or three goals or expectations that are a priority. For each goal or expectation, list one or two activities in which you engage to achieve that goal. Are there expectations you have for yourself that may be unrealistic?
- List three values or priorities in your life that are of greatest importance to you.
- Is the way in which you conduct your life in accord with these values and priorities?

These questions cannot be answered in a moment. Rather, we encourage you to think about them during the next few days, weeks, months, and even years and to use your answers as a guide to achieving a more resilient, authentic life. As you read about the issues that confronted Mark Holland and Lenore Gateman in their struggles to develop realistic expectations and learn to accept themselves, you may find it helpful to apply the questions we outlined to their situation.

"I Feel I'm Caught in a Rat Race and There's No Escape"

Mark Holland, a forty-six-year-old financial analyst, came to see us for a consultation. He described himself as feeling "overwhelmed." He had been married to Amanda for sixteen years and they had a fourteen-year-old daughter and an eleven-year-old son. He contacted us after attending one of our presentations about raising resilient children.

"I came to your lecture because I wanted to learn new ways to be a better father and help my kids become more confident and resilient. But I think I also came to figure out whether I'm a resilient person. I'm not sure I am. I've always wished I could be more confident, but I seem to have constant doubts about my abilities and how successful I am. I'm not happy with work and I don't feel very energetic. Also, I know I've grown more distant from my wife and I haven't been as available to my kids as I would like to be. I feel I've let my family down."

With a sad expression, Mr. Holland added, "I feel I'm caught in a rat race and there's no escape."

We asked Mr. Holland to explain this last statement.

"I've always wanted to be a good provider for my family and to be able to live the good life. Right now I'm not certain I'm a good provider or living the good life."

"What do you mean by the 'good life'?"

"I guess the American dream. You know, having a nice house in a nice neighborhood, being able to provide for your kids, going on nice vacations."

"You don't feel you have these things?"

"On the surface it looks like I have them, but I think I've sacrificed too much. I often work seven days a week and have little time for my family. Some of my colleagues at work who earn as much as I do still seem to have time to do things they like. I don't. Most people looking at my life would probably say that I'm successful and have provided well for my family, but I struggle day to day to keep my head above water."

As you read Mr. Holland's words, think about how he might answer our questions about goals and expectations and the degree to which he believes he is leading his life in accord with his values and priorities.

Mr. Holland continued, "I remember when my wife and I first met. I knew Amanda for two years before we got married. We would talk about many things, like the kind of home we would have and what our life would be like. She was in the human resources field, and we talked about her leaving work when we had kids because she wasn't that happy at work anyway. She left work a few months before our daughter was born and stayed home for the next few years. But she went back to work shortly after our son was born, primarily because of our financial needs. That was ten years ago and she's been working ever since. She said she liked her new job, but I know it was a strain. I feel that if I could have been a better provider she wouldn't have had to work."

As Mr. Holland described his distress, it wasn't clear whether the pressure to provide more for his family was coming from his wife, from his self-imposed goals, or from a combination of the two. It also wasn't clear how realistic his expectations were for his stated role of being the "provider" in his family. To help answer these questions, we asked, "Have you and your wife discussed your feeling that you are caught in a rat race?"

"We really haven't talked that much about it. Actually, I never told her I feel caught in a rat race, but she probably recognizes I do. She has said that she feels my work has become all-consuming and that we have less time together and that I have less time for the kids. I tell her that given our lifestyle, I have to work as hard as I do."

"What does your wife say?"

"She says that we should sit down and look at our lifestyle to see whether there are things we can cut back on. I remind her that it was mainly her idea that we live in an upscale neighborhood. Most of our neighbors are wealthier than we are, and whether we want to or not, we really do have to keep up with the Joneses. I don't want my kids to feel deprived in comparison to their friends. That's one of the reasons Amanda has to work."

We asked, "We're not clear. It sounds as if your wife feels you're spending too many hours working. But does your wife wish she didn't have to work?"

"Not at this time. When our kids were younger, it was more difficult and we had to juggle schedules. But now that they're older, it's a little easier. Things can still get hectic at times. It seems we're always on the run with little time to relax. Just driving our kids to their games and attending their games or other activities requires a lot of coordination. Amanda is more available to do this than I am. I enjoy spending time with my kids, but I just can't seem to find the time to do so."

We responded, "From what you've said, you're feeling a lot of pressure to provide. Why haven't you talked with Amanda about feeling trapped in a rat race, especially since she's said that she feels you're not available to her or the kids and she suggested that the two of you examine your lifestyle?"

Mr. Holland thought for a moment and said, "It's what I mentioned before. We wouldn't be able to lead the life we have if I didn't work the hours I do."

"To lead that kind of life seems very important to you."

Mr. Holland's response to our comment was very revealing and vividly captured the extent to which ghosts from one's past can affect our current thoughts, feelings, and behavior.

"It is. I want to be a good provider. When I was eleven years old my father's business failed and he filed for bankruptcy. He and my mother fought all the time about his bad decisions. I think he was so embarrassed by his business failure that he stopped speaking with his friends. Before the business failed we had planned to move into a bigger house, but we never did. I know that always hurt my dad. A year after he filed for bankruptcy, he committed suicide. Things were very tough for my mom, my younger sister, and me. We really struggled. I know that my dad felt he had let us down, and I remember thinking I would never want to let my family down. For years I was very angry with my dad for what he had done, even though I can now understand how desperate he must have been."

"Losing a father to suicide must have been very difficult."

"It was. I know that he felt he let us down and he couldn't deal with that feeling."

"Do you feel you've let your family down?"

"In one way, no, because we have a nice house in a nice neighborhood and I make a decent salary; but in another way, yes, because I'm not around as much as I would like and my wife has to work full-time. I wish my salary could be more than it is."

We decided to return to the question of Mrs. Holland wanting to examine their lifestyle because we felt this could be the necessary starting point for improving the existing situation. "It sounds as if your wife wants to discuss what's going on in the family, but you don't."

"I don't, because I don't think there is much we can do to change things."

"Yet you came in to see us. You said you were feeling overwhelmed and caught in a rat race with no escape. What were you hoping to get from your consultation with us?" We asked this to assess whether Mr. Holland thought there might be some room for improvement.

"I'm not sure what I expected. I have been feeling so much pressure that I felt I needed to talk with a therapist."

Mr. Holland was struggling with what appeared to be unrealistic expectations as a husband and father, expectations rooted in great part in his father's history. Not only was he experiencing pressure about providing for his family, but his stress was aggravated by living a life that was not in accord with his values. He wished to be a good husband and father but did not make the time to do so. In addition, his experience of being caught in a rat race with no escape suggested that he felt little personal control for change, another factor intensifying his stress and interfering with his comfort in communicating with his wife about their current situation and possible options for change. These features of his mindset were powerful forces interfering with achieving a resilient, satisfying life.

We will return to Mr. Holland later in this chapter. Until we do, consider the steps that he might take to change his negative script. Another way of posing this question: think about what you might say or do if you were his therapist or friend to strengthen a resilient mindset.

"She Reminds Me of Myself, and I Hate That!"

Lenore Gateman, thirty-seven, was very distressed when she called to make an appointment to discuss her relationship with her nine-year-old daughter, Emily. Ms. Gateman never married Emily's father, whom she described as "an irresponsible person who has not contributed to Emily's care and does not visit her." Ms. Gateman worked as a secretary in a local public school, a job that offered a vacation and holiday schedule that paralleled Emily's.

Ms. Gateman immediately said that she was concerned about Emily's shyness. "Emily is a sweet child, but she is so quiet and cautious. She is afraid of her own shadow. She won't call anyone on the phone. Even if friends call, she has trouble speaking with them. When people say hello to her she usually looks down and might whisper 'Hi' to them. Her teacher doesn't seem concerned. She said that Emily is more reserved than other kids her age but that she seems to have friends and is doing well. She says that while Emily might not volunteer to answer a question, when she is called on she seems comfortable."

"So Emily's teacher really doesn't have concerns about her, but you do."

"Yes, but she doesn't see all that I see as Emily's mother."

"What are your biggest worries?"

"That Emily will never learn to assert herself, that she will lose friends because she is shy, and that she will be taken advantage of because she won't stand up for herself."

As Ms. Gateman said this, a look of pain was etched on her face. We empathically said, "Emily's behavior is very stressful for you."

"Very. And you know what makes things worse? I blame myself a lot. She reminds me of myself, and I hate that. When I was a kid I was very shy, I think more than Emily is. I remember growing up having dreams of being able to say hello to people or answering a question in class without shaking. I remember how painful it was for me and I promised myself that if I ever had a child, my child would be outgoing and not scared. But Emily is shy, just like I was. It doesn't help matters when my mother compares Emily to me. I actually remember thinking when Emily was an infant that if she was outgoing and popular it would be a sign that I was a good mother.

"When I was growing up I felt like a coward. Then when Emily came along I had expectations that she would be different from me, that she would have no problem speaking with others, but she hasn't met those expectations. And the less she met my expectations, the more I encouraged her, or perhaps I should say the more I badgered her, to talk with others— but that also backfired."

"What do you mean?"

"The more I encouraged her to speak with others, the more upset she became. At one point, she said she wished I wouldn't ask her about speaking to other people because it just made her feel worse. I thought I was just trying to help, but I know that she thought I was very disappointed with her—and the truth is that I was. But I was more disappointed with myself. I was disappointed in how miserable I was making Emily feel. I thought I should have been able to do something to help her be more sociable, but instead anything I said made her crawl farther into a shell."

As we quickly discovered, Ms. Gateman was very self-critical. Her anxiety and unrealistic expectations prompted her to say things to Emily that added to her daughter's distress; in the process she portrayed herself and Emily as what she labeled "emotional cripples." To justify this powerful label she tended to downplay any opposing positive views, such as those offered by Emily's teacher.

Given Ms. Gateman's job at school, we assumed that her responsibilities required her to engage in many interactions with staff and parents of students at the school. To begin the process of modifying her negative self-image and helping her accept herself and Emily, we decided to focus on their strengths.

"The phrase *emotional cripples* is a strong one. We know that's how you feel, even though you wish you didn't. Sometimes it's helpful to learn from situations that seem at odds with our usual behavior. Are there times you haven't felt so negative about yourself?" This tactic falls under the umbrella of the "exception rule" and is used to encourage people to consider and learn from situations that differ from their usual behavior.

Ms. Gateman said, "I'm not sure."

"In your job, do you have to interact with a lot of people?"

"Yes, but there's another secretary who handles most of the people coming in."

"But when you have to do it, how do you feel speaking with them?"

"It's OK, but I still wish I could feel more at ease."

"But it's easier for you now than when you were a kid?"

"Yes, much easier, but some of the pain and embarrassment is always there, although it is under better control. I never liked who I was growing up and, to be honest, often I still don't like who I am—and now I'm taking it out on Emily. I find it hard not to want to change the behaviors I see in Emily that I dislike in myself, but when I try to do it, I know that what I'm saying is hurting her even though I'm trying to be helpful. I love her so much—I can't understand why I keep saying things that are hurtful."

"We can tell that you love her and you want her to be happy. We have to figure out the best ways for you to help her."

During the next few months our sessions with Ms. Gateman focused on helping her develop realistic expectations for herself and Emily, a task that included identifying and accepting positive aspects of their functioning, becoming more empathic, and learning that characteristics of cautiousness and shyness are not caused by "bad mothering" but are typically part of a child's inborn temperament.

Ms. Gateman was able to apply her positive experiences from work as a foundation for strengthening her parenting role. She acknowledged that while she still had some problems relating with others, she had "come a long way from her childhood" and was much more comfortable with people now. She said that what really helped was that when she first began her job at the school she was fortunate to work for school administrators and another secretary who were very supportive. "I think they sensed I was shy and went out of their way to say hello to me and to give me a lot of positive feedback about my work. It was one of the first times I can remember receiving so many compliments."

We asked Ms. Gateman to consider how she might use these memories from her job to enhance her relationship with Emily. To facilitate this task, we also suggested that she consider several of the questions we posed in earlier chapters and at the beginning of this chapter. She was especially interested in answering the following questions:

- How would I hope Emily would describe me?
- How would Emily actually describe me?
- Am I saying things in a way that Emily will be most responsive to what I have to say?
- Would I want anyone to speak to me the way I am speaking to Emily?
- What words would I use to describe my ideal self?
- What words would I use to describe my actual self?

In reflecting on her job experiences and these questions, Ms. Gateman began one of our sessions by noting, "I learned a lot from thinking about the questions you asked. I wished I had thought about them years ago. I would hope that Emily described me as loving, caring, and supportive. Maybe she would say that sometimes I'm like that, but I know that when I harp about her being shy and withdrawn, she would probably say I'm disappointed in her and that I don't accept her. I know that if at work my boss would have said, 'What's wrong with you? You really have to be less shy and more outgoing!' it would have made me feel embarrassed, angry, and upset. Yet I say similar things to Emily.

"I also thought about my ideal self and the expectations I have for myself, especially as a mother. That was an eye-opener! Maybe I shouldn't have been surprised, but I found myself writing down the same words that I hoped Emily would use to describe me. I also wrote down 'outgoing, self-assured, confident, competent.' As I wrote those words, I realized that at work I was closer to my ideal self than at home, even though there was room for improvement at work. At home—and this was not easy to admit, but I was trying to be as honest as possible—I described myself as 'uptight, irritable, overly critical, and negative.' I actually had a tough time thinking of positive words to describe myself at home."

"Why do you think that's so?"

"I did a lot of thinking about it. I'm not certain I can explain it clearly, so please let me know if what I'm going to say makes any sense to you."

"We will."

"I realize I have very high expectations for myself as a mother. I think there's added pressure being a single parent and also having a mother who can be critical of the way I mother Emily. I know that if Emily didn't have any problems, it would make me feel like I am a good mother and a good person. Not only does Emily end up having problems, but they're the same kinds of problems I struggled with. It was like a double blow. It made me more frustrated and anxious and I began to become more critical of Emily. What she needed was my support. What she got was my anger. Is it clear what I'm trying to say?"

"It's very clear. We're very impressed with your insight."

"I appreciate your saying that." Ms. Gateman smiled and added, "Now, I have to figure out what to do to change."

We noted, "You've already taken important steps by honestly answering the questions we asked you to think about."

In our subsequent meetings, we examined the expectations that Ms. Gateman held for herself and for Emily. Ms. Gateman recognized that certain expectations and beliefs were unrealistic and causing her undue stress, such as assuming that she was to blame for Emily's shyness or that if Emily were more outgoing it would imply that she was a good mother. Once Ms. Gateman could question her expectations and modify those that were unreasonable, her anxiety diminished and it became easier for her to relate to Emily with increased empathy.

As we have suggested to other parents of shy, cautious children, Ms. Gateman began to validate Emily's feelings and offer hope for the future. For example, she told Emily how much she loved her and that she knew it was not always easy for Emily to say hello to people she didn't know. Ms. Gateman shared with Emily her own struggles with this issue and said that maybe together they could figure out what might help Emily to be less hesitant. Emily voiced curiosity about her mother's social fears as a child and what helped her to become more outgoing. Ms. Gateman told Emily about the support she experienced at work and emphasized that change takes time. Possessing newly acquired reasonable goals and expectations permitted Ms. Gateman to accept herself and Emily with greater comfort.

Ms. Gateman reported in one of our final sessions, "Emily has found my new approach very reassuring. I could see that she immediately became less anxious. I must admit that I have also become less anxious. And there's something else, which is hard to describe. For the first time in my role as a mother, I felt more confident and comfortable. For the first time I felt I was doing the right thing. For the first time I felt I was finally accepting Emily for who she was."

As Ms. Gateman shared this insight, tears filled her eyes. It was an emotional moment, one that served as the foundation for continued growth. Ms. Gateman had come to appreciate that self-acceptance is not synonymous with liking everything about oneself, but rather recognizing that we all have our strong and weak points and we must learn to treat ourselves with dignity and respect. When a climate of self-respect is established, it is easier to identify and change those features of our thinking, feeling, and behaving that are contrary to our values. In contrast, when a lack of self-respect dominates our lives, self-defeating and self-demeaning behaviors, rather than self-examination and positive change, are the likely outcomes.

Paths to Self-Acceptance

When we first met Mr. Holland and Ms. Gateman they were burdened by unrealistic expectations and a lack of self-acceptance that compromised the formation of a resilient mindset and lifestyle. In the process of change each embarked on a path with the challenge to identify and examine the expectations they held, expectations that exerted a strong influence on their lives and their sense of happiness. This path requires taking three steps. Though interrelated, these steps are presented separately to highlight each. This will help you gain a precise picture of the factors that contribute to acceptance of oneself and others.

Step One: Recognize Your Feelings, Thoughts, and Coping Style

Our feelings and thoughts direct our behavior and the ways we cope. In turn, our behavior influences our feelings and thoughts. If we do not take time to identify and reflect on our emotions and beliefs, we are vulnerable not only to acting impulsively but to perpetuating the negative cycles existing in our lives.

The ability to identify and recognize our feelings and thoughts parallels researchers Goleman, Boyatzis, and McKee's description of one of the main components of emotional intelligence: self-awareness. As we shall see, their conceptualization of self-awareness also embraces several of the other steps we describe for attaining acceptance. They note:

> *Simply put, self-awareness means having a deep understanding of one's emotions, as well as one's strengths and limitations and one's values and motives. People with strong self-awareness are realistic—neither overly self-critical nor naively hopeful. Rather they are honest with themselves about themselves. . . . Self-aware leaders also understand their values, goals, and dreams.*[1]

On the surface, one might wonder, "Aren't most people aware of the emotions they experience and of their strengths, vulnerabilities, and values?" While some are, many are not. As we noted in Chapter 2, many individuals adhere to self-defeating scripts, projecting their anger and frustration outward, waiting for others to change. We have observed many people wearing blinders when it comes to recognizing their emotions, understanding what triggers these emotions, and sensing how they are perceived by others.

We have provided many examples of people constrained by their emotional blinders, many of whom may not realize the extent to which these blinders have constricted their views. Ms. Gateman's concern for her daughter was compromised by her inability to appreciate the full extent of the anger she experienced toward herself and her mother. Mrs. Stevens overreacted to her son, Jimmy, not realizing that her response was triggered by the comparisons she made between Jimmy and her brother, Al. Mr. Butler was unaware that his behavior toward his managers was very negative and had an adverse impact on them; consequently, he blamed them for the difficulties occurring in his company without examining his contribution to the overall negative climate at work. The department head who accused staff of insubordination when they attempted to give him feedback was unable to appreciate how his own sense of vulnerability precluded him from truly hearing what his staff was saying; instead, reflection and thoughtfulness were eclipsed by impulsivity and defensiveness.

To assist with the task of assessing your self-awareness, consider how you would answer the following questions. You can write your answers on pages 280–281 of Appendix A.

- Are there certain feelings you experience more often than others?
- In what situations do these feelings typically occur?
- Make a list of different feelings you experience, such as happiness, sadness, anger, or anxiety.
- Next to each feeling, describe one or two specific situations that prompted you to feel that way.
- When you experienced the feeling in question, how did you show or deal with it?

This last question will help you to understand the ways you cope with feelings. To become even more specific, we ask:

- Describe a couple of times when you felt you did not handle your feelings very effectively. What happened? Why do you think it happened? Did it lead to changes in how you handled these feelings the next time they occurred?
- Describe a couple of times when you felt you handled your feelings effectively, especially feelings such as anger and frustration. What helped you to handle these feelings effectively?

We have found that the very task of considering these questions strengthens our capacity for self-reflection. The importance of this skill is captured by Goleman, Boyatzis, and McKee when they emphasize:

Perhaps the most telling (though least visible) sign of self-awareness is a propensity for self-reflection and thoughtfulness. Self-aware people typically find time to reflect quietly, often off by themselves, which allows them to think things over rather than act impulsively.[2]

"I Hate It When You Try to Control Me" Millie and Dave Andover came to see us about marital problems. They were both forty years of age. Mr. Andover was a manufacturer's representative and his wife was a salesperson in a large department store. They had two teenage sons. The event that precipitated their seeking assistance was Mrs. Andover telling her husband that she planned to leave him if their marital strife continued.

Mrs. Andover emphasized, "I'm tired of Dave's yelling at me all the time. If you disagree with him, he gets angry and sarcastic. He talks to you and looks at you as if you were the village idiot."

Almost as if to confirm what his wife had said but seemingly not aware he was doing so, Mr. Andover looked at her with scorn and said, "I don't get angry. I just try to talk with you so that you understand what I'm trying to say. I don't know why you can't listen more closely in the first place. Also, you're always telling me what to do as though I have no mind of my own. I hate it when you try to control me. You try to do the same thing with our sons."

Mrs. Andover responded, "At least Dave isn't trying to put on a front. What you just heard is what I hear all the time. This is exactly what upsets me. I dislike his put-downs and his yelling. He keeps telling me I'm trying to control him. He thinks anytime you disagree with him you're trying to control him."

Although our work with the Andovers touched on many issues, for the purpose of this section we want to highlight the interventions that dealt specifically with self-awareness.

At a subsequent session, after Mr. Andover accused his wife several times of trying to control him, we asked him to provide us with some examples of what he meant.

Mr. Andover answered, "There are many. She decides where we go out to eat. She decides where we go on vacation. She decides how to discipline the kids. She tells me what I should wear. Do I have to go on?"

Mrs. Andover looked aghast. She said, "I should just learn not to suggest things. He assumes any suggestion is trying to control him. If he asks where we should go to eat and I suggest a place, it seems that within a minute he tells me that he's always giving in to me. I have to take some of the responsibility for this. I don't know why I keep offering suggestions, because I know he will accuse me of trying to control him. In terms of the kids, I never disagree with Dave about discipline in front of them, but he certainly does with me. I'll talk with him privately, and I keep hearing that I always get my way."

We recognize that it takes "two to tango" in marital conflicts. This statement is not intended to assign blame, but to recognize that each partner in a marriage contributes to some extent to each interaction. While Mrs. Andover at least wondered why she continued "offering suggestions" when she could predict that it would lead to accusations of being "controlling," Mr. Andover didn't even consider his contribution to marital strife, quickly casting responsibility for this strife on his wife's shoulders.

We shared with them the notion of negative scripts and wondered what sustained their pattern of relating. Similar to Mr. and Mrs. Manter, the couple we described in Chapter 1, Mr. and Mrs. Andover fell into a routine in which each believed the other was responsible for their marital conflict and should take the initiative to make the first changes.

We saw the Andovers in marital counseling for a year. What emerged as we explored their backgrounds was a portrait of two individuals with limited self-awareness of the forces that maintained their behaviors. Mrs. Andover had struggled since her childhood with intense feelings of low self-esteem. She recalled verbal abuse directed her way with regularity by her parents. She described her parents as "two unhappy people in a miserable marriage. I was their only child and I desperately wanted to be accepted by them. I would try to please them, but they never complimented me. They both died in the past three years and went to their graves without saying anything positive to me."

We wondered how she thought her experiences with her parents had affected her marriage. Her initial answer might seem surprising: "I never thought about that." As clinicians, we do not subscribe to the view that one has to understand all facets of one's past to change negative scripts, but we do believe that an appreciation of certain patterns can reveal with greater clarity the emotions and thoughts that dominate our current lives. Yet we have worked with many people like Mrs. Andover who possess little insight into their feelings and actions.

During our counseling sessions Mrs. Andover learned that her relationship with her husband contained many of the same features as her relationship with her parents. However, she also learned that behind her anger was a strong need to feel loved and accepted. Just as she had yearned for acceptance from her parents, she wanted acceptance and respect from her husband, to the point that she was willing to tolerate his verbal abuse for many years. In our therapeutic work she became aware of her desperate search for acceptance and the ways in which she coped in an attempt to achieve this goal.

Mr. Andover also brought into the marriage many feelings from his past he was not aware of. His parents divorced when he was six years old. After the divorce his mother moved back to her home state, two thousand miles away from his father. He did not see his father often but had fond memories of him. Unfortunately, three years after the divorce, his father was killed in an automobile accident.

His memory of his mother was not very flattering: "She was the kind of person who always knew what was best for you. Nothing I could do was right. My grades weren't good enough, the girls I dated weren't good enough, the shows I watched on TV weren't good shows, the music I listened to wasn't good music. And when I didn't follow her directions she would try to control me with her martyr act."

"Martyr act?"

"Yeah. She would tell me how much she had sacrificed for me and how ungrateful I was."

"What did you do when she said this?"

"When I was young, I would apologize. But as I got to be a teenager I knew she was trying to control me, so I said nothing."

"What were you feeling?"

"I just remember feeling disgusted with her. To this day I have very little to do with her. Whenever I see her, she's still trying to control me, telling me what to do."

"You've used the word *control* a great deal."

"Yeah, I felt it was a big part of my mother's behavior."

We asked Mr. Andover a question similar to the one we posed for Mrs. Andover. "How do you think your relationship with your mother has affected your relationship with your wife?"

"I think I married someone like my mother."

Upon hearing this, Mrs. Andover asked with a hurt and angry tone, "Why would you say something like that?"

Mr. Andover responded, "Because I feel it's true. I guess I never realized how often I used the word *control* to describe my mother, and I would use the same word to describe how I feel you try to treat me."

"I don't feel I'm trying to control you."

"Well I do!"

Mrs. Andover then said something that jolted her husband: "I think you see anything I do as an attempt to control you. If trying to win your respect is controlling, then I guess I'm guilty. I feel you're so sensitive to being controlled that you read control into everything I do."

Mr. Andover looked as if he were ready to disagree, but he halted what he was going to say and remained silent. We looked at him, and after a few moments we said, "It looks like something is on your mind."

"I just need some time to think."

The session was nearly over and we said, "If you like, we can talk more about it next time."

At the next session, Mr. Andover said something very profound: "This isn't easy for me to say, but I never realized how angry I've continued to be with my mother. I really thought I had put that behind me, but I haven't. I think when I married Millie, I was conditioned to seeing almost anything she did as trying to control me. I think I've taken out on Millie what I couldn't take out on my mother."

Not every couple can develop the self-awareness displayed by the Andovers, although it did take them time to do so. With their new insights, they were able to begin to examine and accept their feelings. This acceptance permitted them to change those behaviors that were interfering with their marriage and to establish a more satisfying, resilient life. As we have written several times in previous chapters, what might appear to be obvious patterns of behavior to others may not be so to the people trapped by these behaviors. Once the blinders are removed, a broader perspective, with increased opportunities, becomes available.

Before we leave this section, we would like to repeat the questions and exercises we posed earlier, questions that we encourage you to reflect on to increase self-awareness. Self-awareness is a vital part of self-acceptance and a resilient mindset.

- Are there certain feelings you experience more often than others?
- In what situations do these feelings typically occur?
- Make a list of different feelings you experience, such as happiness, sadness, anger, or anxiety.
- Next to each feeling, describe one or two specific situations that prompted you to feel that way.
- When you experienced the feeling in question, how did you show or deal with it?
- Describe a couple of times when you felt you did not handle your feelings very effectively. What happened? Why do you think it

happened? Did it lead to changes in how you handled these feelings the next time they occurred?

- Describe a couple of times when you felt you handled your feelings effectively, especially feelings such as anger and frustration. What helped you to handle these feelings effectively?

Step Two: Define Realistic Expectations and Goals for Yourself and Others

In our book *Raising Resilient Children*, we emphasized that one of the most important parenting tasks in nurturing a resilient mindset in our children is to define realistic expectations and goals for them. We offered many examples of parents who struggled to accept their children for who they were rather than what parents wanted them to be. In such instances, parents often set the bar too high; the result was disappointment, frustration, and anger. Not only were family relationships weakened, but so too was the development of resilience.

Establishing realistic expectations and goals for oneself is not confined to the parenting role; it is a lifelong task and an integral component of pursuing a resilient lifestyle. An obvious question that arises in our workshops and clinical practice is, "What are *realistic* expectations and goals?" Life might be easier if we could provide one simple answer, but one simple answer does not exist. We advise parents that, given the different temperament and learning styles of each child from birth, what is a realistic expectation for one child may not be realistic for another. The same principle applies to adults.

Specifically, when parents ask us how to determine realistic expectations, we respond, "First tell us about your child, and then we can provide an intelligent view of appropriate goals and expectations." When adults ask us how to determine realistic expectations for themselves, we offer a similar answer: "Let's examine your strengths, vulnerabilities, and interests, and then we can begin to define realistic goals and expectations for any situation. Once you have defined your goals, you can regularly assess whether your expectations have been set too high or too low and make appropriate modifications. No goals are set in stone; rather, they are open to change."

To assist people to clarify the word *realistic* when considering the expectations they hold, we suggest engaging in the following exercise.

- List two or three activities that you enjoy doing.
- How frequently do you engage in these activities?
- List several areas that you believe represent your strengths.
- How important are these strengths in terms of your daily routine? As we will discuss in greater detail in Chapter 9, if people perceive their strengths as being unrelated to their daily functioning, they are unlikely to feel competent and successful.
- List several areas that you believe represent your vulnerabilities or areas of weakness.
- How important are these vulnerabilities in terms of your daily routine?
- What steps have you taken to strengthen those vulnerabilities that affect your daily living?
- List three or four short-term or long-term expectations or goals you have for yourself.
- How do these goals relate to what you perceive to be your strengths and weaknesses?
- Next to each goal, list what steps you have taken to achieve that goal.
- What expectations about yourself or others have you modified in the past year?
- What led you to modify these expectations?
- When you do not achieve a goal, what do you usually do? Think of a specific example.

As you may surmise, these questions revolve around assessing your strengths and weaknesses, accepting them, deciding how they become part of your goals and expectations, and developing a plan of action to achieve or modify these goals. We want to emphasize that acceptance does not imply adhering to an unhappy status quo. Rather, it suggests that you possess the insight and courage to say to yourself, *This is who I am now. If there are things that dissatisfy me about myself, I have the ability to establish goals and decide on a plan of action to make the necessary changes.* This may seem like a straightforward, commonsense statement, but we have worked with many individuals whose inability to accept themselves generates intense self-doubt, self-loathing, and defensiveness, traits that mediate against taking steps toward assuming a resilient life.

Larry Whitaker, the man we described in Chapter 2, illustrates the negative impact of unrealistic goals. He was overweight and suffered from high blood pressure and high cholesterol. His physician advised him that unless he undertook an exercise and diet regimen, he was placing himself at risk for a stroke or heart attack. Intellectually, he knew he had to make changes in his lifestyle, but had been unsuccessful in the past, which generated even more distress.

He told us, "I think the cure is worse than the disease. I actually feel worse when I try to change because I always seem to have difficulty following through, and then I feel like a real failure. Sometimes I feel like I am tackling Mt. Everest without the best training or equipment. I'm doomed to failure after I climb just a few steps."

Mr. Whitaker's attempts to change were permeated by an air of desperation that resulted in unrealistic goals, expectations, and actions. He was trapped in a script that read, "Major change must take place quickly, or I am a failure." This kind of negative self-evaluation led him to retreat from the challenge to assume a healthier style of living rather than considering more reasonable expectations.

We helped Mr. Whitaker create an appropriate exercise and diet program with clear, specific, achievable short-term goals. The seemingly simple plan of beginning with a mile rather than five-mile walk (Mr. Whitaker's original goal) and adding a half-mile every couple of weeks led to success. We also suggested that Mr. Whitaker meet with a nutritionist, a recommendation that had been made in the past but not pursued. A sensible, realistic diet was instituted, much different from the starvation diets Mr. Whitaker had previously tried, diets that led to dramatic weight loss followed by dramatic weight gain.

Returning to Mr. Holland When we left Mr. Holland earlier in this chapter, we asked you to consider what steps he might take to change his negative script or, if you were his therapist or friend, what you might do to help him nurture a resilient mindset.

Mr. Holland had offered the observation, "I feel I'm caught in a rat race and there's no escape." He emphasized his desire to provide a "good life" for his family, but sadly observed that in his efforts to do so, he was spending less and less time with his wife and two children and that he was feeling increasingly stressed. We learned that a pivotal event in his life was his father's suicide when he was twelve years old, a year after his father's business had failed and he had filed for bankruptcy.

Mr. Holland added, "My dad felt he had let us down, and I remember thinking I would never want to let my family down." When we asked if he felt he had let his family down, he answered that in terms of providing a nice house in a nice neighborhood he had not, but in terms of being available to them he had because he worked long hours. Several times he mentioned that he regretted that his wife had to work full-time. Mrs. Holland had suggested that she and her husband sit down to examine their lifestyle and see what they might be able to change. Mr. Holland was hesitant to do so because he believed there was no way to decrease the hours he was required to work.

In listening to Mr. Holland's account of his past and current life, it was evident that unrealistic expectations about being a good provider, fueled in great part by the unfortunate circumstances of his father's life, were weighing him down. His sense of being trapped contributed to his pessimism and belief that things could not improve; thus he did not see the possible benefit of discussing the situation with his wife. We also believed that it would be very difficult for him to acknowledge to his wife his sense of failure.

In considering possible interventions, we felt that it was necessary to modify his expectations and goals. To accomplish this, we had to help him escape from the rat race and experience a sense of personal control over the events in his life. We recognized that this process would be facilitated by the active participation of his wife. So we discussed with Mr. Holland having his wife join his sessions with us; after an initial hesitation, he agreed.

Mrs. Holland said she was very pleased to come in with her husband and that she had been concerned for the past few years about the stress he was experiencing.

We began, "Your husband has mentioned that you wanted to discuss the family's lifestyle and see what could be changed."

"I have, but Mark seems hesitant to do so. He keeps saying that we decided to live in a nice home in a wealthy neighborhood and that this is the price we have to pay. He also feels that because he hasn't been as good a provider as he should have been it has become necessary for me to work full-time. When the kids were younger it was more difficult for me to work full-time, and even now we have to juggle things occasionally to drive them places and attend their activities. But, to be honest, I enjoy working and would want to do so even if Mark earned twice as much."

Mrs. Holland paused and said with much feeling and perceptiveness, "The kids and I love Mark, and it's upsetting to see him feel that he has failed and that he has to work more and more hours to provide for us. If this continues, I'm concerned his health and his relationship with me and the kids will suffer. I wish Mark could realize that he is a wonderful, loving person, but I think that he has unrealistic expectations of what it means to be a good husband and father."

Mr. Holland responded, "I know Amanda feels that I have unrealistic expectations, but if I try to cut back I don't think we can live the lifestyle we have been living. I would love to have more time with my family. I don't find it fun working as many hours as I do. But I wonder how happy Amanda and the kids would be if we had to give some things up, like the house."

"Mark, I don't think we have to give up the house. Maybe we have to give up some things, but what good is it if, in trying to provide for us, your health deteriorates and you have no time for us?" Mrs. Holland said this with caring and concern.

We asked, "What do you think about what your wife just said?"

Mr. Holland answered, "I don't know." He became silent and then, with obvious emotion, said, "I saw what happened to my father when he couldn't provide, when his business failed. I don't want that to happen to me and my family."

Mrs. Holland looked at us and said, "I know that Mark is haunted by what happened to his father. I can only imagine how difficult it must have been. But I think his worry that he will fail just like his father's business failed is becoming more and more consuming. I just feel that if Mark and I sat down and if he didn't feel he was failing me and the kids, we could arrive at some sensible, realistic solutions."

"I know Amanda thinks there are solutions to this problem, but I'm not certain."

We said, "You may be uncertain, but is there anything to lose in discussing possible solutions?"

"I guess not."

To facilitate their discussion we asked them to keep in mind the questions we posed on page 144 about articulating one's strengths and vulnerabilities and assessing one's expectations and goals in relation to these strengths and vulnerabilities.

Although initially he had been pessimistic about the possibility of extricating himself from the "rat race," once he began the process with his wife of searching for a more resilient lifestyle he was highly motivated to find solutions. He used our questions to help him define his interests, strengths, and vulnerabilities. While he listed reading, playing sports with his kids, going out to eat with his wife, and fixing his car as interests and strengths, he discovered that he spent little, if any, time on these activities. He listed as a "significant" vulnerability his difficulty leading a "balanced life."

During the following year, Mr. and Mrs. Holland initiated several important changes. They belonged to a local country club that "cost thousands of dollars," yet the family rarely used its facilities, so they dropped their membership. Both of their children attended private schools, but their eleven-year-old son asked about going to the local public school for his middle and high school years because most of his friends went to the public school. Their daughter wanted to continue in private school. Mr. Holland initially had reservations about his son attending a public school, although it had an excellent reputation. Similar to other situations, Mr. Holland perceived his children attending private school as an indication that he was a good provider—another unrealistic expectation that he changed.

Mrs. Holland's support, encouragement, and suggestions permitted Mr. Holland to modify his expectations, routine, and schedule, and in the process he lessened his anxiety and stress. Their changes did not require them to give up their house. Most important, as Mr. Holland discovered, it is difficult to lead a resilient life if one is burdened by unrealistic expectations that contribute to a lack of self-acceptance.

Step Three: Live in Concert with Your Values

If we are to accept ourselves, we must live a life that reinforces and resonates with our values. Shakespeare captured this belief in *Hamlet* when Polonius uttered the well-known lines:

This above all: to thine ownself be true,
And it must follow, as the night the day,
Thou canst not be false to any man.

We have worked with many people whose lifestyle is not in concert with their values and priorities. At some point this lack of harmony or denial of one's values will take its toll in the form of stress and pressure. This was vividly reflected in Mr. Holland's life when his stated priority of spending time with his wife and children was overshadowed by his lack of availability.

We observed a similar pattern with Ross Sargent in Chapter 1 that led to anxiety, diminished sexual interest, and "a constant feeling of tiredness." We requested that he make a list of what was important to him. He wrote, "My role as a husband, my role as a father to my three children, my health, my church, and success at work." While "success at work" was listed fifth, his work consumed almost all of his time and attention. As we noted in Chapter 1, the time spent with his wife was limited, he often left for work before his children were awake and came home after they were asleep, and when he came home he was typically so exhausted that all he did was eat a quick meal by himself and go to bed. He no longer engaged in any exercise, ate a poor diet, and had gained twenty-five pounds in the previous eighteen months. He rarely attended church, although when he did he reported feeling a certain comfort.

He observed with sadness, "If you looked at my life it would be obvious that most of it is spent at work, yet I feel little satisfaction at work, even when things go well."

The discrepancy between Mr. Sargent's priorities and his behavior was striking, just as it was with Mr. Holland. However, some people experience stress without recognizing that one of the factors contributing to their dissatisfaction is that they are not leading an authentic life.

To evaluate whether your values and priorities are consonant with your actions, it might help to engage in the exercise we recommended for Mr. Sargent as well as many other individuals:

- Make a list of four or five roles or activities that you believe are most important to you.
- Next, evaluate whether your behavior is in concert with your priorities.

When completing this exercise, many people recognize for the first time the discrepancy between their values and behavior. Some may attempt to rationalize this discrepancy. Mr. Holland contended that his lack of availability was the result of his desire to be a good provider, which he couldn't do unless he worked long hours. As we witnessed, rationalizations often fall prey to increased stress and unhappiness. Ms. Gateman provides another example. Although being a loving mother was a high priority, she interacted with her daughter Emily in a negative way, unable to accept Emily's cautious and shy nature. Ms. Gateman's psychological pain at treating her daughter with a lack of empathy was pronounced.

Sometimes it takes misfortune and tragedy to make us aware of what is truly important. On the afternoon of September 11, 2001, few people, if any, thought about staying at the office to finish a report or to close a business deal. Most desired one thing: to come home as quickly as possible to be with loved ones, to hug them, hold them tight, and kiss them. Some, especially the courageous rescue workers, could not be at home; it was left for them to perform in ways that were in accord with our most noble values involving dignity, honesty, and respect for ourselves and others. True self-acceptance can take place only when we follow such values.

Concluding Thoughts

Self-acceptance is a cornerstone of attaining a resilient lifestyle. In the absence of self-acceptance, it is difficult to accept others. Self-acceptance is associated with self-esteem and dignity. The achievement of self-acceptance is a lifelong process involving an ongoing, honest evaluation of our strengths and vulnerabilities; of our goals and expectations; of whether we are involved in activities that bring us satisfaction, contentment, and joy; and of whether we are living our life in accord with our basic values.

The process of nurturing self-acceptance is filled with many challenges requiring time and energy. However, to avoid these challenges is to invite a life filled with dissatisfaction and failure; a life lacking in honesty, integrity, and self-respect; a life that limits realistic dreams and accomplishments. Meeting the challenges involved in self-acceptance is indeed great. But consider the consequences if these challenges remain unmet.

7

Making Connections and Displaying Compassion

There are many sorrows in today's world! These sorrows are due to hunger, to dislodging, to all kinds of illness. I am convinced that the greatest of all sorrows is to feel alone, to feel unwanted, deprived of all affection. It consists in not having anyone. . . . May we all be instruments of peace, of love, and of compassion.

MOTHER TERESA

At the conclusion of a workshop we offered about resilience, three women in their mid-forties approached the podium to speak with us. One of them pointed to the woman in the middle and said, "Meg is one of the most resilient people you will ever meet. She practices everything you mentioned in your talk about living a resilient life."

Meg smiled and we noticed that the woman who said this was holding one of Meg's hands while the third woman was holding Meg's other hand.

"We would love to hear more," we replied.

The woman who had started the conversation enthusiastically said, "Meg has been through a lot in the past few years. Her husband died of cancer three years ago. She has three sons. Her oldest son died eighteen months ago in a car accident. And you wouldn't know it from how she looks now, but right after her son's death Meg was diagnosed with breast cancer. Thank heavens her cancer is in remission. But with all she has been through, Meg has a wonderful outlook. There have been many tears the past few years, but her smile and positive attitude are contagious. She got us involved in charity events to raise money to find a cure for cancer. It's hard to say no to Meg."

Meg thanked her friend and said, "There's a lot to live for."

Since she seemed open to talking about what had transpired in her life, we asked Meg, "With all you've been through, what's helped you to maintain such a positive outlook?"

Without hesitating, Meg said, "I have two other wonderful children. We've cried together and we've supported each other. I feel blessed having them. I have a wonderful family. Then there's my faith, which is very comforting to me. Also, the charity work has been very important to me. I was really interested during your talk when you mentioned that one of the things that helps us to be resilient is to make a positive difference in the lives of others."

Meg then smiled and added, "Last, but not least, is that I have received incredible love and support from friends, as you can tell from the two friends standing next to me. I could really relate to your emphasis about the importance of our connections to others in helping us deal with adversity and becoming resilient."

When Meg finished saying this, the third woman observed, "What we may give to Meg, we get back tenfold from her kindness and friendship."

What transpired next was very moving. Meg hugged both of her friends, and as she left she hugged us and said, "Thank you."

Most likely, we will never see Meg again, but even in our brief interaction with her she enriched our lives. Her smile, her focus on connections, and her positive attitude in the face of great adversity and loss left an indelible impression.

Connections in the Lives of Children

In *Raising Resilient Children* we described a basic ingredient in nurturing hope and resilience in our children as the presence of at least one adult who communicates to a child, through words and actions, "I believe in you and I will stand by you." As we noted in the Preface, the late Dr. Julius Segal referred to that person as a *charismatic adult*, an adult from whom a child "gathers strength." The power of one adult to change the life of a child must never be underestimated.

Segal's ideas are supported by studies of adults with childhood histories of risk, including abuse, neglect, and school failure. Researchers found that a number of these at-risk individuals had risen above the hardship they encountered. They had overcome significant challenges and were now leading successful, satisfying personal and professional lives. One of the most important factors these resilient individuals cited as helping them to become successful was having at least one adult who cared about and loved them when they were children.

The educational literature has reported that students are less likely to drop out of school or to engage in violent behavior if they believe that there is even one adult in the school who knows and cares about them. When we interviewed students between the ages of five and eighteen and asked them what helps them to feel welcome in school, the two most prevalent answers were "being greeted by name in the morning" and "having a teacher smile at me."

In the report *Early Warning, Timely Response: A Guide to Safe Schools*, the authors noted:

> *Research shows that a positive relationship with an adult who is available to provide support when needed is one of the most critical factors in preventing student violence. . . . Some children need help overcoming feelings of isolation and support in developing connections to others. Effective schools make sure that opportunities exist for adults to spend quality, personal time with children. Effective schools also foster positive student interpersonal relations—they encourage students to help each other and to feel comfortable assisting others in getting help when needed.*[1]

It is evident that the presence of a charismatic adult is a necessary condition for children to become optimistic and resilient. In the absence of a connection with at least one adult who demonstrates unconditional acceptance and love, it is highly unlikely that children will develop a resilient mindset.

Connections in the Lives of Adults: "Don't Adults Need Charismatic Adults?"

During a workshop we described the significance of a charismatic adult in a child's life. A member of the audience asked what appeared to be a rhetorical question, albeit one of great importance: "Don't adults need charismatic adults in order to be resilient?"

Our answer was a resounding "yes." Regardless of our age or how secure and confident we feel, if we are to strengthen and maintain our optimism and resilience it is essential that we interact with people who accept us and from whom we gather strength. While some adults, given their feelings of vulnerability, may require this support more than others, we all thrive on its presence.

We would like to pose an additional question: Is our own resilience nurtured when we serve as charismatic adults to others? We would not hesitate to answer affirmatively to this question as well. If we are to nurture and maintain meaningful, emotionally satisfying connections and lead a resilient lifestyle, it is equally important for us to serve as and be in the company of charismatic adults. We will discuss the benefits of serving as a charismatic adult later in the chapter. First, we examine in greater detail the concept of connections and its relationship to resilience.

The Qualities of Connectedness: A Life Force

There are different features and degrees of connectedness. The connectedness that we associate with resilience in adults involves a mutual give and take; a high level of trust, caring, and openness; and a sense of security and safety. When discussing the power of connections to foster resilience, we are not referring to relationships characterized by negative qualities, such as an overabundance of neediness or dependence, of manipulation, or of a lack of empathy and compassion. These negative connections might be best understood as examples of angry, alienated people, such as we witnessed in Mrs. Atkins's relationship with her mother and Mr. Larson's relationship with his father.

Our good friend and colleague Dr. Ned Hallowell has written extensively about the theme of connections. In his book *Connect: 12 Vital Ties That Open Your Heart, Lengthen Your Life, and Deepen Your Soul*, Dr. Hallowell eloquently expands the definition of connections beyond interpersonal relationships, reminding us of its multifaceted expression. While connections with others has received the greatest attention among mental health clinicians and researchers, it is important to remember that other forms of connections exist. Dr. Hallowell writes:

What is connection or what I sometimes called connectedness*? It is a feeling of being a part of something larger than yourself. This something may* *be a friendship, a marriage, a team, a school, a company, an activity you love, a country, even a set of ideals, like the Bill of Rights, or a belief system, like a religion.*[2]

Dr. Hallowell offers ample evidence of the healing power of connections, citing, for example, a study conducted by Dr. David Spiegel with a group of women faced with terminal breast cancer. Half of the women in the study met on a regular basis to share stories of their lives, while the other half did not meet. The half that met as a group lived, on average, twice as long as those who did not.

Dr. Hallowell also describes an extensive study in which Dr. Lisa Berkman followed the lives of 7,000 residents of Alameda County, California, for nine years. Dr. Berkman and her colleagues interviewed these residents to assess the degree to which they were or were not connected. The researchers identified whether people were married or lived alone, the extent of contact they had with friends and relatives, whether they were members of a church or religious organization, and to what degree they participated in voluntary organizations and groups.

Dr. Berkman then examined each person's risk of dying during this nine-year period in light of the data collected. She found that the most isolated people were three times more likely to die in that nine-year period than those with stronger social connections. One might question whether there was another, overriding variable that influenced these results more than the level of one's relationships. However, this was not found to be the case.

The protective nature of connections was demonstrated to operate at all ages. People in the study ranged in age from thirty to sixty-nine. The highly connected people lived longer within every age group. Even when such health risks as smoking, obesity, alcohol use, poverty, a lack of reliance on health services, and poor health at the start of the study were taken into consideration, those people with strong social ties lived significantly longer than those who lacked such ties. Dr. Hallowell writes:

To gain the benefits of connection, it didn't matter what kind of connection a person had. For example, you could live alone, but have frequent contact with friends or relatives, and be protected. Or you could belong to various voluntary organizations, but not participate in any religious activity, and still be protected. Or your connection could come from church and family, but not from any volunteer organization, and you would still be protected. The key to gaining the benefits of connection was to have several kinds of connection, but the kinds could vary from one person to the next.[3]

Data collected by Drs. Spiegel and Berkman support our assertion that connections provide one of the building blocks of a resilient life, a life filled with both physical and emotional well-being.

Connections in the Workplace

In the past decade there has been increased recognition of the influence of connections not only in our personal lives but in our professional and business lives as well. Daniel Goleman and his colleagues have described the importance of emotional intelligence, empathy, and social skills in the workplace. Similarly, James Kouzes and Barry Posner have highlighted the significance of connections and interpersonal relations in the business world. For example, they describe research sponsored by the Center for Creative Leadership (CCL) in Colorado Springs. In one study the CCL examined factors that appeared to be most critical for success for the top three positions in large organizations. Interestingly, and perhaps surprisingly to some, one's relationship with subordinates was found to be the factor most associated with success.

In another study, the CCL examined the variables that distinguished highest-performing managers from lowest-performing managers. Kouzes and Posner noted that the popular belief about managers is that they have a high need to express control. However, in the CCL study, the single factor that differentiated the highest- and lowest-performing managers was *affection*, both expressed and desired. Kouzes and Posner contend:

> *Contrary to the myth of the cold-hearted boss who cares very little about people's feelings, the highest-performing managers show more warmth and fondness toward others than do the bottom 25 percent. They get closer to people, and they're significantly more open to sharing thoughts and feelings than their lower-performing counterparts. Now these managers were not without their rational sides. . . . It's just that these (rational) factors didn't explain why managers were high performers.*[4]

Kouzes and Posner also observed that one of the most intriguing findings of this CCL study was not only that higher-performing managers provided more affection and positive feedback, but that they also desired affection.

They concluded that "the evidence tells us that expressing affection is important to success, *and* we have high needs for it."[5]

The writings and research of these authors and others confirm the importance of emotional intelligence, interpersonal skills, and affection within the work environment, and they resonate with our assertion that a major force in promoting resilience involves the connections we develop and maintain in all areas of our lives. This was certainly apparent with Mr. Butler and Ms. Caldwell, whom we described earlier; they found success at work only when they discovered ways of connecting with their managers and colleagues. In contrast, the department head who dismissed the negative feedback of others by accusing them of "insubordination" did not display effective leadership because his behavior prompted disconnections with those who reported to him. This department head would do well to follow the words of Irwin Federman, a former chief executive officer and now a venture capitalist. Kouzes and Posner offer the following quote from Federman:

> *You don't love someone because of who they are; you love them because of the way they make you feel. This axiom applies equally in the company setting. . . . Conventional wisdom has it that management is not a popularity contest. . . . I contend, however, that all things being equal, we will work harder and more effectively for people we like. And we like them in direct proportion to how they make us feel.*[6]

Powerful thoughts to reflect on!

Questions to Consider

Similar to our approach in earlier chapters, we believe that answering some questions can guide us in assessing the quality of connections in our lives. While these questions overlap, they help provide a comprehensive perspective of our relationships, especially in terms of the concept of a charismatic adult. Consider how you might answer the following, jotting down your answers on pages 284–287 of Appendix A.

- Who were the charismatic adults in your life when you were a child or adolescent?
- What are two or three examples of what these charismatic adults said or did that caused you to consider them to be charismatic adults?

- When you were a child or adolescent, were there people who interacted with you in ways that were contrary to the qualities of charismatic adults?
- What did these people say or do that disqualified them from being considered charismatic adults?
- Who are the charismatic adults in your life today?
- What are the things they say or do that make them charismatic adults?
- What people would list you as a charismatic adult in their lives?
- What do you say or do that would prompt them to call you a charismatic adult?
- Are there any people who would say that your behavior toward them is contrary to your being a charismatic adult? If so, what would lead them to believe this?
- If you were encountering some personal difficulties, who are the two or three people you would turn to for help, and why would you feel comfortable turning to them?
- Who are the people you would not turn to, and why wouldn't you turn to them?
- Who would turn to you for help and support? Why would they do so?
- Who would not turn to you for help and support? Why wouldn't they?
- As you think about the quality of your relationships, what are one or two things you might change to feel more connected to others?
- How would you like friends, relatives, and colleagues to describe you?
- Are you interacting with them in ways that would lead them to describe you this way?
- If not, what must you change?

Missed Opportunities: The Pain of Loss, the Fear of Connections

These kinds of questions helped Bea Walton examine her life, priorities, and relationships. Ms. Walton was a thirty-five-year-old manager of a successful real estate company. She had never been married. She called us following several episodes of "strong feelings of sadness that would remain for days." The first occurred after she visited a coworker who had just given birth to her first child. What Ms. Walton remembered most from the visit was her colleague "looking so happy, especially when she was nursing the baby."

Another episode of sadness followed shortly after she met with a couple who were in their fifties. They were interested in selling the home they had lived in for more than twenty-five years. They told Ms. Walton that they had enjoyed living in their house, especially because their three children had grown up in it. However, at this point in their lives they felt they did not need as much space and were interested in selling the house and buying a condominium. Ms. Walton recalled, "As they walked around showing me the house, they were holding hands, and they even became a little teary as they showed me the rooms in which their kids had grown up. They said that they had some wonderful memories that would always stay with them."

The third episode occurred on what would have been Ms. Walton's mother's sixty-fifth birthday. Her mother had died eighteen months earlier of breast cancer. Her father died of cancer when Ms. Walton was only seven years old. Ms. Walton said, "I missed and still miss my father so much. It was painful to see my mother so sad after he died. She seemed depressed for so long, and there was nothing I could do to cheer her up."

Her mother remarried when Ms. Walton was twelve years old to a divorced man with no children. Ms. Walton recalled, "He was wonderful to my mom and to me. It was an adjustment for me to have a man in the house, a man I felt was taking my father's place. But then I came to accept and love him, especially when I saw how much happier my mother seemed after she married him."

Unfortunately, a week after Ms. Walton's mother and stepfather celebrated their fifteenth wedding anniversary, he died suddenly of a heart attack. "After he died, my mother just seemed to go through the motions of living her life. She rarely smiled. I could tell how much she missed him."

Ms. Walton added, "I felt very sad on my mom's birthday. I kept wishing she was alive and I could hug her and wish her happy birthday. I also kept thinking of my father and stepfather and how much I missed them."

After Ms. Walton described the three events that triggered her sadness, we asked whether she saw any connections among these situations.

"I'm not certain. As I told you about all three, I felt very sad telling you about them. I'm really not sure what the connection might be."

We said, "It's something we can try to figure out."

Because our initial impression was that all three of the incidents appeared to center on issues of closeness or loss (a mother and her infant, a couple fondly recalling happy memories of their family as they held hands, and the death of her mother, father, and stepfather), we thought it might be helpful to focus on Ms. Walton's relationships with family, friends, and colleagues. We asked her to tell us more about her relationships.

Ms. Walton said she had a brother who was two years older. "My brother and I were close growing up, but he lives 2,500 miles away and it's not easy to see him and his wife and two kids. They used to visit once a year to see my mom, but now that she's gone I'm not sure they'll come as often. And I'm so busy at work that I don't know how often I can visit them."

Ms. Walton described having a couple of "really close friends" from childhood, but added, "They're both married with kids, and it's harder for us to get together. When we do get together, I sometimes feel like the odd girl out because they often talk about their husbands and kids and I'm not married."

We asked about her relationships with men.

"I've had two serious relationships. I dated the same guy in college for three years. We met during the first week of our freshman year. I think I really loved him, but at the beginning of our senior year he started to talk about getting married after we graduated. I felt we were too young, and he broke up with me. Maybe I should have married him, but I felt we were both too young. I also went with a guy for a couple of years when I was around thirty. We actually met at the gym that we both belonged to. He was really very nice and attractive and had a good job. I enjoyed being with him."

"What happened?"

"After two years, he began to talk about marriage. I just wasn't certain he was the right person for me. He said he loved me and would give me time to figure out where I wanted the relationship to go. A couple of months later he asked again about marriage. I still felt uncertain. He was still very understanding. But when he asked me about six months later if I was ready to make a commitment and I said I wasn't, he said it would probably be best for us to end our relationship because it didn't seem to be heading anywhere. I agreed. I heard from a mutual friend that a few months after we broke up he began seeing someone else and married her a year later."

Ms. Walton paused and said, "I forgot to tell you about a fourth incident that left me feeling very sad. It involved the guy I just told you about, and it happened about three months ago. I bumped into him and his wife, and they had a toddler who was adorable. I often thought that it might feel awkward if I saw him again—but I didn't really feel awkward, just sad."

"What were you thinking when you saw him with his wife and child?"

"That I could have been his wife and that could have been my child."

"When you thought that, was there anything else that crossed your mind?"

Ms. Walton responded, "Missed opportunities. I think I was really too young to make a commitment with the guy I dated in college, but I'm not sure why I was so unsure with this other guy. He was really wonderful. I've usually read that men are the ones who have difficulty with commitment, but maybe it's a problem for some women as well, especially me."

"What do you see as your problems with commitment?"

"I don't know."

"Maybe thinking of the situations you told us about might help us to understand what the problems might be."

Ms. Walton paused for a little while and then responded, "When I saw my colleague holding her infant and the couple selling their house, I wasn't certain why I should feel sad seeing people being so intimate. I know that a mother holding a newborn is a different kind of relationship than a couple who has been married many years, but both made me sad. That really seems crazy, because they were such warm situations."

"Yet each led you to feel sad. Why do you think you felt that way?"

"I'm not certain. It's more obvious to me why I was sad on the day that my mother would have turned sixty-five. I miss her. And in thinking about her, I miss my dad and stepfather."

As we listened, we thought that the connection among the four situations was a theme of loss, both loss of loved ones through death and loss of missed opportunities for greater intimacy. The sense of missed opportunities was heightened when in the presence of people who had experienced or were experiencing intimacy (the middle-aged couple reminiscing about their life and children, a coworker holding a newborn, a former boyfriend with a wife and child).

To help Ms. Walton to appreciate these common themes, we presented her with the questions we listed earlier in this chapter. In the following session Ms. Walton told us that she had spent many hours thinking about these questions. She said, "I was amazed by how emotional I became thinking about them."

We wondered, "In what way?"

"When I thought about the charismatic adults in my life today, I first thought of some friends but realized that they weren't really friends, just acquaintances. I'm not sure that I could identify anyone as a charismatic adult. The last charismatic adult I can think of was my mom. And then I thought about who would say I was their charismatic adult. I don't think anyone would list me as a charismatic adult." As Ms. Walton said this, tears came to her eyes.

"We can see that thinking about these questions is emotional."

"Very. The questions hit home. They showed me how alone I feel and how scared I am."

"Scared?"

"That I will remain all alone. I don't want that to happen. I don't know why it has."

During the next few sessions Ms. Walton focused on her feelings of being alone. She recognized that the sadness she experienced when in the presence of intimacy was in response to her distress about "lost opportunities" and her yearning for more intimate relations. Our interventions with Ms. Walton were guided by the goals of helping her to understand the basis of the script that kept her from making commitments and to author a new, more satisfying script that reinforced connections.

As Ms. Walton reflected on the obstacles that resulted in what she interpreted as a "fear of commitment," she came to the following very perceptive conclusion: "I hope this doesn't sound like pop psychology, but as much as I want to get close to other people and to get married, I'm really scared. I remember how sad my mom was when she lost both my dad and stepfather. I actually remember thinking after my dad died that it hurts when you lose someone you love so much. I think I began to feel that you won't feel as sad if you don't get too close to people, because people you love may leave you."

Ms. Walton smiled and repeated, "I hope that doesn't sound like some pat formula straight out of a pop psychology book."

We said we didn't think so. Ms. Walton continued, "But the fact that I've gotten so sad when I've seen how close other people are to each other tells me that I have to change my assumptions and improve my relationships."

Ms. Walton's increasing insight into the roots of her sadness, as well as her wish not to "be all alone," served as the catalyst for change. We encouraged her to define short- and long-term goals. Her long-term goals included "ongoing friendships" as well as "marriage and perhaps motherhood." To achieve these long-term goals, Ms. Walton articulated such short-term goals as

- renewing and maintaining contact with her two close friends from college, even though they were married,
- making at least one trip a year to visit her brother and his family, and
- working as a volunteer for a charitable organization both to meet new people and to help others. (She even joked, "Who knows, an eligible bachelor may have the same motivation.")

We also prepared her for the possible anxiety that might be evoked should she enter into a more intimate relationship. By anticipating this anxiety she would be better prepared to deal with it constructively rather than fleeing from the relationship.

Once this plan was put into action, we kept in touch with Ms. Walton on the phone and in regular follow-up meetings every month or two for a couple of years. During that time she nurtured her connections with others. She dated one man for about three months but soon felt they had little in common. Unlike the serious relationship she ended when she was thirty years old because of her fear of making a commitment, she ended the current relationship recognizing that she and this man shared few interests.

However, a few months later she happily reported that she had met a man whom she "truly enjoyed." She laughed as she told us, "And guess where I met him? Doing volunteer work." She called again to say that they had gotten engaged. She added, "I saved the list of questions you had asked me when I first started seeing you. I looked at them closely for the first time in months. I can honestly say that I feel Ray (her fiancé) is a charismatic adult for me and I think he would say that I am for him." They were married a year later.

Guidelines for Nurturing Connectedness

Ms. Walton's difficulties with close relationships burdened her for years, finally culminating in periods of intense sadness. In one sense, the breakthrough of these painful feelings was beneficial because they served as the impetus for her to seek help. In our experience, many people struggle with achieving a satisfying sense of connectedness. When connections are absent or negative, it is more difficult to pursue a resilient lifestyle. The following are five guidelines that will help you strengthen your feelings of connectedness.

Guideline One: Make Connectedness a Top Priority in Your Life

As we previously reported, especially in Chapter 6, when we ask people to list their priorities they typically place their relationships with family and friends at the top of the list. Yet, as we witnessed with Mr. Holland, Mr. Sargent, Ms. Gateman, Mrs. Stevens, and many others, their behaviors did not reflect an adherence to their priorities. Busy schedules or unresolved issues from the past become roadblocks to achieving connections. Far too often, activities and relationships that we deem most important are relegated to the background. At times it takes a tragedy or a crisis for people to act in accord with their priorities.

The greeting card industry is very cognizant of the extent to which people fail to appreciate loved ones, especially spouses. A number of years ago, I (Bob) was preparing a presentation about men and family relations. By coincidence, in the midst of preparing this talk, I went to buy an anniversary card for my wife. I was struck as never before (perhaps because I was preparing a presentation that focused on family relationships) by the sentiment expressed in the opening few lines of many cards. Most began with an apology to one's spouse for not saying often enough "I love you" or for not displaying affection or spending enough time together. I quickly determined that the apologetic anniversary cards outnumbered those that did not voice regrets.

I bought a few of these cards to read at the beginning of my presentation. Many in the audience laughed when I jokingly said, "I think the greeting card industry is engaged in a plot to keep men from expressing affection to their spouses so that they will feel guilty and purchase apologetic cards." However, a more reflective atmosphere emerged when I asked, "How many of us need these cards?" I then posed questions similar to the ones we raised in this and the last chapter, such as:

- List two or three values or priorities in your life that are of greatest importance to you. Is the way in which you conduct your life in accord with these values and priorities?

- What people would list you as a charismatic adult in their lives?
- Who are the charismatic adults in your life?

A refreshment break followed my talk. Several members of the audience immediately approached me to discuss my presentation and the questions I had raised. One man asked, "Can I buy one of the anniversary cards you read? I know that this might sound funny given what you talked about, but I just realized that tomorrow is my anniversary. I plan to leave this conference a little early to buy my wife a present. One of your cards will certainly help." I donated the card to this man in hopes of saving his marriage. To this day, I am not certain whether he was kidding. However, I sensed that while a modicum of humor may have been present, the man was being honest.

This incident reminded us of the summary of a study reported in a popular magazine years ago. A researcher from Germany asked five thousand German husbands and wives how often they talked with each other. He found that after two years of marriage, most couples managed two or three minutes of chat during breakfast, not more than twenty minutes during dinner, and a few more minutes in bed. By the sixth year, those numbers were down to ten minutes a day. It was sadly noted that "a state of almost total speechlessness" was reached by the eighth year of marriage.

When we reported this study at one of our workshops, couples in the audience laughed. When we next asked them to think about how much time they spent communicating, the laughter soon subsided and several couples glanced uneasily at each other.

With the content of the apologetic greeting cards and the study conducted with German couples in mind, return once more to the questions we raised earlier in this chapter (pages 157–158) before you continue to the next guidepost. Especially consider the last series of questions:

- How would you like friends, relatives, and colleagues to describe you?
- Are you interacting with them in ways that would lead them to describe you this way?
- If not, what must you change?

It is helpful for you to think not only about your answers to these questions, but also their implications. What changes must you undertake in your lifestyle to nurture more satisfying relationships and a resilient mindset?

Guideline Two: Remember That Connections Come in Many Forms

Our main focus in this chapter is interpersonal relationships. However, as noted earlier, connectedness can be expressed in a variety of ways. In addition to our relationship with others, we can feel connected to a cause, a town, a school, a religion, a job, a belief system, a sports team, or a pet.

To lead a balanced, resilient life, we should not restrict our connections to one source, but instead must embrace several. We purposefully selected the word *balanced* to emphasize that as we reflect on our priorities, we must ensure that our connections are not deposited in one place. We recognize that some connections warrant more time and energy than others. Parents of a newborn child will spend a great deal of their time caring for and connecting with their infant, often pushing aside connections to other people or activities until their child is older. Similarly, people beginning a new job may focus their energy on learning the requirements of their job and interacting with their coworkers. However, even if we direct more energy at certain times of our lives into particular relationships and activities, we must guard against letting other important connections slip into the background.

Here are some additional questions for you to ponder:

- Where are your current connections located? How well balanced are they?
- Who are five people in your life with whom you feel most connected? In what ways do you feel connected to each?
- What do you do to express this feeling of connectedness and keep it alive?
- In addition to your relationship with people, what are three other things in your life with which you feel connected—that is, areas of your life that are important to you and provide you with a sense of connectedness and belonging?
- In what ways are you involved with these areas?

We have offered numerous examples of individuals who have enriched their connections in different areas of their life. For instance, Mr. Bauer, the science teacher who had lost his enthusiasm for his profession, revived his initial commitment to his profession by reminding himself of why he had entered teaching. He thought of the impact that one of his teachers, Miss Lapora, had on him. Consequently, in thinking about her, he began to reconnect not only with the purpose of his career but with his students as well. He also reconnected with Miss Lapora.

Ms. Clark, following the sudden death of her husband, returned to college to pursue a career in graphic design and advertising. She redirected time and energy to begin a journey into a new phase of her life. In our discussion in Chapter 3 of the importance of commitment in lessening stress, we learned of individuals who attached themselves to causes in response to tragedy—for example, Mrs. Stevens, who founded CHUCK (Committee to Halt Useless College Killings) after her son Chuck died during a college hazing incident.

Reports of the aftermath of September 11 noted that children and adults fared better when they felt connected to others, including their community. When one child in an urban area was asked what helped him to feel less frightened about terrorist acts, he responded that everyone on his block was flying an American flag. For this child, as well as for other children and adults, a connection with a community and a symbol of that community (the flag) served as a reservoir of assurance and strength. Is it any wonder that within a day or two of September 11, stores carrying American flags had exhausted their supply? It is not surprising that when we feel most vulnerable we seek comfort and security through our contact with people, beliefs, faith, and causes.

We would be remiss not to add that a connection with pets has proven to be an important experience for many people in strengthening a resilient mindset. For instance, some therapists have used pets to address emotional issues in their patients. One ten-year-old patient told us that his dog "licks me even when I've done something bad." A nine-year-old girl observed, "My cat loves me even if I don't get good grades or finish all of my homework." Pets may provide a sense of companionship for individuals of all ages, from children to senior citizens. Not only do people report unconditional acceptance from pets, but there is also the joy that occurs when taking care of a pet and watching it grow and develop. In addition, researchers have noted that petting a cat or dog has a calming effect, lowering blood pressure. Based on the amount of money spent on the care of pets in the United States, it is obvious that they play an important role in the lives of many people and families, a role of connectedness. One word of warning: It is a healthy role as long as one's time and energy caring for a pet does not preclude developing meaningful relationships with people.

Mr. Sargent's Quest for Connectedness   We briefly described Ross Sargent in Chapters 1 and 6 as an example of an individual not living a life in accord with his values. We would like to discuss our work with him in terms of the concept of connectedness. He came to see us because of increased anxiety, a lessening of sexual interest, and "a constant feeling of tiredness."

When asked to create a list of what was most important to him, his answers covered a spectrum of connections in his life. He wrote, "My role as a husband, my role as a father to my three children, my health, my church, and success at work." While success at work was listed fifth, in reality it consumed almost all of his time and attention. Sadly, the other priorities came in a distant second. He had little time for his children, came home exhausted each night with little energy for his wife, ate a poor diet, and did minimal exercise, as reflected in a twenty-five-pound weight gain in eighteen months. His attendance at church was infrequent, although he reported feeling comfortable when he was there.

If one possessed a scale to measure connectedness, most of Mr. Sargent's scale would be filled by his work activities. This was unfortunate for two reasons. First, the four priorities he listed as most important in his life would be so small in terms of his actual behavior that they would not register on the scale. Second, his work responsibilities, which would fill the scale, were marked by dissatisfaction and unhappiness. Thus, even at work, where he invested most of his time, his level of stress precluded positive connections to his colleagues or to his job activities.

Mr. Sargent was aware of the discrepancy between his ideal connections and the life he was actually leading. However, similar to Mr. Holland, he felt trapped in a negative script. We discussed with him steps he could take to change his script and to form connections in concert with his priorities. We emphasized that it is difficult to modify one's lifestyle all at once but that he could begin with small steps that would lead to a more comprehensive change.

We reviewed the first four priorities that Mr. Sargent had listed and assisted him in developing short- and long-term goals for each. He felt that he could cut back on some of his work responsibilities, which would allow him to leave a little later for work one morning a week in order to have breakfast with his children and come home early enough on two days to have dinner with them. He said, "I wish I could do this each day of the week." We answered, "We know you do, but it's more important to start with what you feel you can manage and move from there."

Mr. Sargent mentioned how much he loved his wife, but added, "You would never know it from the amount or quality of time I spend with her." He lamented that his unhappiness and exhaustion had reduced his sexual desire and added that "it feels as if our romance has ended. At the beginning of our marriage, it was easier to be romantic, especially because I could just focus my attention on my wife. It's more difficult with kids, but I think I've been neglectful with my wife."

In our discussions with Mr. Sargent, we discovered that he and his wife rarely had time by themselves. He recalled how in the past they had gone out on Saturday nights but they seldom did so anymore. We wondered why.

"I don't know. I guess you get into a certain pattern, you know, what you call a *negative script.*"

"What steps can you take to change it?"

"I think we could definitely plan on going out every Saturday night. Also, we have a lot of relatives who live close by. I think that once in a while one of them could baby-sit so that we can get into town for a getaway evening or weekend."

In terms of his health, Mr. Sargent mentioned that there was a health club next door to his company. He said that some of his colleagues used the club at the beginning or end of the day or at lunch. Because he did not want to take more time from his family, he felt he could get over to the club during lunchtime at least three times a week for thirty minutes of exercise and still have time to eat. He said, "In the past I've told myself that lunch is a good time to catch up on work, but I find I'm not very productive because I've been sitting all morning, and then I'm more exhausted in the afternoon. Yet I keep doing it." Another example of the power of negative scripts!

In terms of his church, Mr. Sargent wondered, "I don't know why I don't attend more often. When I'm at church I feel a sense of serenity and peace. I think for my mental health and spiritual health, it should be built into my schedule."

We asked, "Are all of these changes reasonable? Can you do them?"

Mr. Sargent answered, "They might not be easy at first, but I can't keep going the way I'm going."

More so than other people with whom we have worked, Mr. Sargent desired to address several of his priorities and connections at the same time.

Some individuals prefer to focus on one at a time (such as time with one's children or spouse). However, he believed that these "priorities overlapped with each other." In essence, he wanted to rebalance the scale, a scale that had been weighed down by work commitments that offered little meaningful connectedness. He wanted the scale to reflect enhanced connections with his wife, children, and church, and respect for his own body.

Although, as Mr. Sargent discovered, these changes were easier to list in our office than to accomplish in real life, he was very committed to his goals. As he struggled to author a new script with more meaningful connections, he remarked, "These changes may be difficult, but I would never want to return to what brought me to see you in the first place."

Before we leave this guideline, reflect on the different connections in your life and ask, *Are changes required so that my connections add to a satisfying, resilient life?*

Guideline Three: Be Proactive in Developing Connections and Learn to Take Risks

We have spoken with many people who desire to develop connections with others but take little action to do so. They wait for others to call and invite them to get together. Many may wait their entire lives, someday looking back and wondering why they feel so isolated, why they have so few friends, why they never pursued more intimate relationships.

A basic message of our book is that if one is to possess a resilient mindset and lead a resilient life, one must take personal control of his or her life. While there may be times when good luck appears to shine down on us, the reality is that we often make our own luck and create our own fortunate situations. Mr. Bauer might never have reconnected with his passion for teaching or with his students if he had not taken the initiative to change. Ms. Walton and Mr. Sargent might still be entangled in their negative scripts if they had not sought help in order to take actions that were in accord with their dreams and goals.

Why is it that many people regret feeling lonely and isolated but are hesitant to take the steps necessary to change their behavior and improve their connections? The reasons vary. For some, such as Ms. Walton, each step toward closeness invites possible loss or rejection. The more intimate we are, the more we leave ourselves open to being hurt. However, as we often emphasize, we must consider the alternative of not taking a risk. For others, such as Mr. Holland and Mr. Sargent, closeness requires leaving one's comfort zone even though the comfort zone is not very satisfying. Unfortunately, some people would rather remain in a familiar situation associated with stress, isolation, and unhappiness than venture forth into unknown territory they fear may be even more dangerous. We must all learn to appreciate the benefits of change even as we recognize the possible dangers.

We are not advocating that those unable to swim jump into the deep end of the pool where they are likely to drown. Nor are we advocating that they avoid the pool. We are suggesting that they enter the shallow end and, as they learn to swim, cross over to the deep end. Changes in lifestyle typically are not without risks, but these risks can be minimized if, as we outlined in Chapter 2, you carefully articulate reasonable and achievable short- and long-term goals and plans of action.

"I'd Rather Be Alone than Look Stupid" Lorraine Randolph, a twenty-nine-year-old computer programmer, came to see us due to feelings of isolation and loneliness. She told us that she had one close friend from childhood who had moved away almost two years earlier because of a job change. Although Ms. Randolph appeared articulate, she said, "I hate to get together with people from work or people I don't know very well because I never know what to say."

"What do you mean?"

"Everyone else seems more knowledgeable about world events, about sports, about everything. The other day one of the other women at work invited me to a party someone was having in her apartment building. I know she was trying to be nice. I decided I should go. Within a few minutes I wished that I hadn't. I didn't say anything. I felt I had an IQ of zero. I'd love to be with people, but I feel awkward and stupid when I am."

As we gathered more information, we determined that the issue of feeling inadequate and stupid was one that had haunted Ms. Randolph since childhood but had become increasingly intense in recent years. She described both of her parents as "perfectionists who never really accepted any of my achievements." She dismissed relatively good grades in high school and college with such comments as "The work was easy" or "I didn't have to speak up in class to get a decent grade."

In describing her current life, Ms. Randolph offered a powerful statement: "I hate being alone, but I guess I'd rather be alone than look stupid. Why embarrass yourself?" Although mental health professionals might diagnose this problem as a social phobia, we chose to focus on Ms. Randolph's mindset and the process of her struggles, rather than the descriptive label. Ms. Randolph was so entrapped in a self-defeating script that even when we asked her to think about times when she was with other people and did not feel "stupid," she had difficulty answering. All she could offer were examples when she was training new staff at work; however, as was typical of her style, she downplayed her accomplishments by saying, "It's straightforward stuff I go over when I train new staff. I really don't have to think about what to say."

Because of her anxieties, Ms. Randolph had abandoned a proactive approach for initiating connections with others, paralyzed to do anything. For her, the risks involved in developing relationships overshadowed any possible gains because she feared placing herself in situations in which she might be embarrassed. Sadly, she retreated not only from relationships but also from other forms of connections. She was indeed lonely, isolated, and sad.

In our interventions with Ms. Randolph, we recognized that simply encouraging her to meet other people would accomplish little. We knew she wanted to meet others but that she was fearful of the results. We mapped out a plan that symbolically began with her entrance into the shallow end of the pool. The next step was for her to become accustomed to the water and learn to swim. Once that was accomplished she would be ready to venture into the deep end. Our plan may seem simple and common sense, but as we have written several times in this book, the simple and commonsense approach may not be very apparent to people when they are entangled in a web spun by negative assumptions and beliefs from the past.

As part of the plan, Ms. Randolph initially selected the person with whom she felt most comfortable at work to discuss work-related and then non-work-related topics. We discovered that Ms. Randolph rarely read a newspaper and never read a weekly news magazine; it was little wonder that she felt "ignorant of world events." We encouraged her to begin to read a daily newspaper and a weekly magazine.

We knew that at some point Ms. Randolph would have to swim to the deep end of the pool if she were to progress. She would have to learn to take risks. She did. Rather than wait to be invited to someone's get-together, she demonstrated courage by hosting a small party in her apartment involving a few people from work and a few neighbors whom she knew as acquaintances but with whom she wanted to become friendlier. A few days before the party she jokingly said, "Maybe you could attend in case everyone becomes silent." She smiled and reconsidered, "Nah, then it would be like group therapy."

At our next meeting, we were anxious to learn how things had gone. Ms. Randolph said, "I was nervous, but I think it went OK. People seemed to enjoy each other and I made certain to join in the discussion. At the end of the evening a few people said that we should do this more often. It was nerve-wracking at first, but I'm glad I did it. I know it's only one get-together, but I don't feel as lonely."

We said, "The risk you took seems worth it."

She smiled and responded, "I give you some credit. You kept saying, 'Think of the alternative if you don't take a risk.' Sometimes when you're very frightened and lonely, being alone seems like the only option. It's good to know that there are other options."

As Ms. Randolph discovered, the concept of personal control is not a mere abstraction, but a powerful determinant of a resilient mindset.

Guideline Four: Be Compassionate and Assume the Role of a Charismatic Adult

Earlier in this chapter we reported a question raised by a person who attended one of our workshops: "Don't adults need charismatic adults in order to be resilient?" We answered "yes." We should add that if we are to gather strength from others, we must be open and available to doing so. Especially in times of difficulty, we must learn to accept the comfort and assistance of others. For some people it is more difficult to accept this comfort, especially if their past experiences have led them to distrust others. However, as Mr. Semper, whom we discussed in Chapter 5, discovered, if one is not open to sharing with others and becoming intimate, connections will be ruptured and resiliency compromised.

Earlier in this chapter we noted that our own resilience is nurtured when we serve as charismatic adults to others. Throughout our lives, resilience and connections are strengthened when we contribute to the well-being of others. Children come into this world with a wish or need to be helpful. The act of helping not only fortifies our bond with others, but it serves as a reminder that because we are on this planet, this planet is a better place.

In research we conducted we asked a large number of adults to tell us the most positive and negative memories they held from their school years. We asked specifically about positive incidents that involved something a teacher said or did that enhanced their self-esteem. The following represent the most common theme among the respondents:

- "As a first grade student, I had the responsibility of raising and lowering the coat closet doors because I was one of the taller boys in the class. That made me feel so good because I was so self-conscious about my height."
- "In a one-room school, the teacher had me sit and do spelling with the second graders once I had shown some ability in this subject."
- "My English teacher asked me to tutor a senior who was not going to graduate because she was failing English grammar. I was in tenth grade."
- "In the third grade, I was chosen to help get the milk and straws."
- "In the eleventh grade, my art teacher asked me to paint a mural in the school. I still correspond with her."

As is evident, the most frequently cited positive memory was being provided with an opportunity to contribute to the welfare of others. This need to be helpful is not restricted to children but continues into our adult lives. The ways in which we are helpful will vary from one relationship and one context to the next, but the common denominator is the act of giving. The following are all examples:

- Organizing a charity drive for needy families in the community
- Serving on a committee in your town or city
- Volunteering at a hospice or a nursing home
- Teaching your child to ride a two-wheel bike
- Going on a fund-raising walk for charitable causes

The list is endless. The benefits of engaging in these activities are boundless.

Let's return to several questions we raised earlier, as well as a couple of additional ones. In the context of this guideline for nurturing connections and resilience, consider how you would answer each of the following questions:

- Who are the charismatic adults in your life today?
- What are the things they say or do that make them charismatic adults?
- What people would list you as a charismatic adult in their lives?
- What do you say or do that would prompt them to call you a charismatic adult?
- Who would turn to you for help and support? Why would they do so?
- What charitable activities have you been involved with in the last three months?
- If you are a parent, what charitable activities have you engaged in with your children during the past three months?
- Think of a time that you helped others. What did it involve? How did you feel when you did so?

Compassion and Connections: Essential Features of Resilience It is interesting to observe the number of people who have described the role of compassion in strengthening one's physical and emotional well-being. In an article written years ago, the term "helper's high" was described. The article emphasized that the very act of assisting others triggered a feeling of exhilaration that contained both physiological and psychological roots. In his book *The Art of Living* the Dalai Lama offers a view of compassion that resonates with our own and touches directly on the intimate relationship between compassion and resilience. He writes:

> *There are positive side-effects of enhancing one's compassion. One of them is that the greater the force of your compassion, the greater your resilience in confronting hardships and your ability to transform them into more positive conditions. . . . I also think that the greater the force of your altruistic attitude towards sentient beings, the more courageous you become. The greater your courage, the less you feel prone to discouragement and loss of hope. Therefore compassion is also a source of inner strength. With increased inner strength it is possible to develop firm determination and with determination there is a greater chance of success, no matter what*

obstacles there may be. On the other hand, if you feel hesitation, fear, and a lack of confidence, then often you will develop a pessimistic attitude. I consider that to be the real seed of failure.[7]

The words of the Dalai Lama are poignant and far-reaching. They suggest that a child or adult's self-worth, dignity, hope, optimism, and resilience are nurtured when connecting with others and engaging in acts of caring. When we display compassion, we add value and meaning to our own lives.

In his landmark study of a group of male Harvard graduates who have been followed for more than sixty years, psychiatrist Dr. George Vaillant has explored factors that contribute to emotional health in the elderly. He found that friendships with younger people reinforced enjoyment in old age. These relationships were not those in which the elderly were coddled or patronized by their younger counterparts. Rather, the elderly considered to be the most resilient gave more than they received, sharing life experiences with the younger generation.[8] The act of contributing to the knowledge and welfare of others enhances our sense of connectedness and resilience at any age.

If we are to form meaningful relationships and discover our own sense of worth, we must actively seek opportunities in which we enrich the lives of others. In the process we enrich our own lives. Ralph Waldo Emerson captured this belief when he wrote, "It is one of the most beautiful compensations of life that no man can sincerely try to help another without helping himself."

In offering Emerson's quote we think about Meg, the woman described at the beginning of this chapter. We also think about Marty, a man who attended one of our presentations about raising resilient kids; he came in his role as a grandfather. After our talk Marty walked up to speak with us, accompanied by his daughter and son-in-law. He appeared to be in his mid-sixties. He was very personable. He started the conversation with the statement, "I enjoyed your talk." Then, flashing an infectious smile, he added, "You didn't use big words. I understood what you were saying." We joked, "We really don't know big words."

"That's good," Marty replied, then told us his name and introduced his daughter and son-in-law. "My kids thought it would be good for me to hear you because now that I'm retired I spend a lot of time with my two grandsons. They're wonderful kids. The older one is nine, the younger seven. Let me show you their picture." Marty proudly showed us several photos: the gleam in his eye could have lit the entire room.

We said, "Handsome boys." Marty smiled, "Yeah, they look like me." His daughter and son-in-law laughed and the latter said, "He is a little prejudiced."

Marty was the kind of person you felt you knew from the moment you met him. There was a comfort in being in his presence. He said, "I just wanted to tell you how right you were when you talked about giving to others. My wife died about five years ago. We watched our finances carefully so that we would be able to have enough for our retirement. A month after I retired she died of a heart attack. It was really unexpected. We had been married thirty-seven years. Anyway, I moped around for the first year and didn't do much. I was also getting depressed. I'm glad I had my grandkids and, as much as I love them, I knew I needed to do something to keep me from feeling so down.

"I've always loved kids and I read an article in the local paper about retired people tutoring elementary school kids. I signed up. I tutor a couple of times a week for about ninety minutes each time, and it's been great. I feel so energetic when I'm tutoring young kids."

His daughter interrupted and, with a smile similar to her father's, said, "Dad, are you going to tell about the letter you got?"

"Sure, why not. One of the parents of a kid I was tutoring in math wrote to tell me that for the first time her son seemed excited about school, and he told her what a great guy Mr. Marty is. That felt good!"

Marty's joy was very apparent. We said, "You must really be great with kids."

Marty smiled his infectious smile and said, "I am. So if you ever need help in your practice, just call on me."

Marty's daughter laughed. "Enough, Dad." As Marty and his son-in-law said good-bye and began to walk away, his daughter stayed behind for a moment. She told us, "My dad was really depressed when my mom died. She was his support for thirty-seven years. Working with kids has been so therapeutic for him. And guess what? He is going to be the assistant coach on my older son's Little League team. He can hardly wait. You would think he was coaching a professional team."

Marty's experience provided another example of the way in which the act of contributing fortifies connectedness and resilience. Holocaust survivor and psychiatrist Dr. Viktor Frankl, whom we discussed in Chapter 3, poignantly reinforced this view and the importance of personal control when he wrote:

> *We who lived in concentration camps can remember the men who walked through the huts comforting others, giving away their last piece of bread. They may have been few in number, but they offer sufficient proof that everything can be taken away from a man but one thing: the last of the human freedoms—to choose one's attitude in any given set of circumstances, to choose one's own way.*[9]

Think about the choices you will make in the next few days and weeks and whether they will enrich the lives of others. If they do, you will enrich your own life.

Guideline Five: Remember That Connections Are Constantly Changing

A few years ago, as we were preparing a presentation for first-time parents, we read letters written to the advice column of a national parenting magazine. We were struck by how many of the questions focused on the unexpected impact that the birth of a baby had on the marital relationship. Even months after the birth of the baby, many husbands and wives wrote to share stories of less time for intimacy, decreased sexual drive, and fewer moments of fun.

In our work, parents often describe the time before their first children were born as the wonderful planning days. We jokingly refer to this time as B.C.—not Before Children, but Before Chaos! Parents often develop an idyllic image of the life to follow after the birth of their first child. They envision themselves as calm, patient, nurturing, available caretakers. They often envision their child as angelic in temperament and behavior. They envision their love as growing stronger. How many of us can actually report that our perceptions of parenthood and of our behavior became reality? Despite dreams, hopes, and wishes, no one can foretell the future.

One can explain in part the emergence of postdelivery problems as being attributable to parents getting less sleep, increased attention necessary to meet the needs of the baby, and nursing mothers having less physical energy for making love. However, several letters suggested another issue. One mother wrote that her bond with her infant son was so strong that she felt less interest in her husband. Another woman wrote that all of her husband's attention was directed toward their infant daughter, noting that she felt "replaced."

In our presentation we alluded to these letters, which prompted an interesting discussion among those in attendance. One man asked, "I know you talk about the importance of intimacy and connections, but do you think there is a limit to the amount of energy we have available for our relationships? When a new baby comes along, I think you have less energy for your spouse."

A woman in the group responded, "I think there's some truth to that, but for me and my husband it meant that we had to make more of an effort to spend time together. Actually, in some ways I think the birth of our daughter brought us closer together because the time we had with each other alone was so much more precious and not to be wasted."

As group members shared their experiences, the discussion expanded to other relationships. Some talked about having strong friendships that have continued from their elementary school years to the present, while others described seemingly close relationships in college that no longer existed. Some said the same was true with relatives. Several mentioned first cousins with whom they were very close growing up but from whom they grew apart once they or their cousins moved away as adults. Others maintained strong attachments even though separated by thousands of miles. Their accounts captured our belief that in the course of each of our lives, some relationships will be sustained year after year, while others that once were strong become weak. New relationships and new friendships arise at different points, often replacing some of our former friendships. Most of us can think of friends that we spent hours with in high school or college whom we still remember with fondness, whom we still enjoy seeing at class reunions, but with whom we have little contact at other times.

The same pattern exists for other kinds of connections. Causes and ideals that swayed our lives years before may no longer have an impact on us now, yet other interests and ideals may. One man told us that during his adolescence and early adulthood he rarely set foot in a church, but once his first child was born he felt more motivated to do so. Others have reported an increased sense of spirituality as they enter middle age.

These shifts in connections are to be expected. There are some relationships that by their very nature are long lasting, but if they are to be filled with satisfaction and joy, those in the relationship must be prepared to adjust to expected, ongoing changes. This is especially evident in marital and parent-child relationships. We must examine our priorities in terms of connections and establish which ones are most meaningful at different points in our life. Important friendships in high school may pale in comparison to friendships that we make in our thirties or forties. For parents, involvement with children requires more time and attention when they are young than when they are on their own as young adults. However, even when they are young adults our relationships should remain strong, although with a different quality than when they were youngsters.

We should expect adjustments when our family expands with the arrival of children. Adjustments do not imply a weakening of the connections between a husband and wife. If anything, the goal of any adjustment should be to maintain an intimate mutual relationship while at the same time including a new member in the family. If husbands and wives lament that they have grown apart with the birth of a child, they should honestly examine the quality of their relationship both prior to and after their child was born and determine what they must do to strengthen their marriage.

Couples must be proactive to ensure that a healthy relationship is maintained when any significant change occurs in their lives, not just when a child enters the household. Changes in jobs, a move to a different state, a death of a loved one, or financial reversals require couples to work together, to trust each other, and to offer support. In adopting a proactive approach, couples should consider building in "special times" just for themselves, as Mr. Sargent and his wife did. They must ensure that they have time to discuss their needs, goals, and dreams. They should engage in small gestures that communicate love and caring, and they must never take each other for granted. They should not have to resort to apologetic greeting cards in an attempt to deal with past wrongs.

All of our relationships and connections will undergo change to some extent. Some friendships may wane, often replaced by others. Some relationships in which we allowed ourselves to be used or taken advantage of are best ended. We may lose our passion for certain beliefs and ideals as we adopt new causes. Resilience involves the wisdom and flexibility to modify our goals and expectations and to improve and enhance our ever-changing relationships.

In essence, the problem is not that connections change. They will always change. The problem occurs when our connections are limited or negative, or when we end certain connections without replacing them with new, vibrant ones. When these problem situations exist, isolation and alienation become the dominant forces in our lives. A resilient existence is difficult to achieve in the absence of connectedness.

A Final Thought and Some Sage Words

We raised many questions in this chapter for you to consider, questions that we hope will serve to enhance your connectedness with people and with dreams and ideals. We must constantly examine the ways in which we relate and contribute to others. While we all require the presence of charismatic adults in our lives, our sense of dignity and self-worth is reinforced when we serve in that capacity for others, practicing compassion and caring. We leave this topic with the words of some well-known individuals who poignantly capture the importance of connections and compassion. Charles Dickens wrote, "No man is useless in this world who lightens the burden of it for anyone else." Consider Walt Whitman's words, "When I give, I give myself."

The centrality of connectedness and compassion in our lives is reflected in the number of people who have spoken and written so eloquently of these themes. It is little wonder that these themes have attracted such attention; they are the roots of emotional and physical health and of hope. They must not be neglected if we are to lead a resilient life.

8

Dealing Effectively with Mistakes

The only complete mistake is the mistake from which we learn nothing.

JACOB BRAUDE

Michelle Norwood, forty, was asked by a local organization to give a presentation about a community project in which she was involved. She responded that she was busy and persuaded an associate to speak in her place. In fact, she was not busy, but she was "terrified" of public speaking. When we asked what terrified her, she responded, "What if I make a mistake? What if I forget what I wanted to say? I would feel like a fool." She also acknowledged that although she felt temporary relief by avoiding the speaking engagement, afterward she felt "terrible for being so afraid to do something."

A child struck out twice in a Little League game and immediately screamed at the umpire, "You are blind, you are blind! I wouldn't have struck out if you weren't blind!" Much to the embarrassment of his parents, the child continued his tirade before running off the field.

Ms. Randolph, the twenty-nine-year-old computer programmer whom we met in the last chapter, was so worried that she would be perceived as lacking intelligence that she restricted her interactions with others. She offered the revealing observation, "I'd rather be alone than look stupid."

Gerald Lowell, a thirty-eight-year-old who had recently been promoted to the position of middle school principal, experienced increased anxiety related to his job. He had started his career as a math teacher, eventually moving to assistant principal and then principal. "I dreamed that as a principal I could have an impact on an entire school. But now that I'm a principal I stop to think about every action I take, and sometimes I feel paralyzed to take any action at all. I keep thinking to myself, *What if my decision is the wrong one? What if I make a mistake?* The same thing happens when I'm speaking to a parents group or my staff. I begin to think about each word I'm using. I'm so afraid of making a mistake or looking foolish that I know I'm coming across as insecure and indecisive."

Resilient Mindsets and Attribution Theory

These four vignettes share at least one common theme: individuals burdened by the fear of failure. When this fear dominates our lives, it serves as a significant obstacle to developing a resilient mindset. It is difficult to imagine leading a satisfying lifestyle when one is burdened by constant worries about looking foolish when making a mistake or failing at a task.

Our beliefs or mindset about mistakes plays a major role in determining our actions. In turn, the consequences of our actions influence our mindset so that a dynamic process is constantly operating. This was vividly illustrated with Ms. Randolph. Her belief that she was not very smart prompted her to minimize contact with others. However, this manner of coping, rather than alleviating her anxiety, added to her distress because she felt increasingly isolated and inadequate. By fleeing from interactions with others, she received confirmation that she was not a competent person, a belief that reinforced her negative mindset and led her to withdraw even further. Eventually, with the assistance of therapy, she came to understand and change this self-defeating pattern.

To alter a negative mindset about the meaning of mistakes, it is essential to consider the ways in which resilient people interpret and respond to mistakes compared with those who are not resilient. One helpful framework for articulating the different processes by which individuals perceive mistakes is *attribution theory*. This theory places the spotlight on the causes to which we attribute both our mistakes and successes. In this chapter we will examine attribution theory as it relates to mistakes and failure, and in Chapter 9 we will apply the theory to our successes and accomplishments.

Attributions about our behavior and the behavior of others are shaped by both genetics and life experiences. Genetics influence, in part, how we think about and interpret life. Experience provides the material we use to form ideas about ourselves and others. Though we can't replace our genes, we can learn to interpret our experiences in new ways. For example, individuals with high self-esteem view mistakes as situations from which to learn rather than feel defeated. While they do not delight in making mistakes, they believe that mistakes serve as the foundation for insight and growth. They attribute mistakes to factors that can be changed. They can accurately assess when they need to devise or revise a plan of action to reach their stated goal. In essence, they have learned and accepted that mistakes serve as vital sources of information for future success. Though this learning process may occur differently for each individual, it can be accomplished for all of us.

The late Willie Stargell, a Hall of Fame baseball player for the Pittsburgh Pirates, expressed this positive attitude about mistakes when asked after his retirement what he thought baseball had taught him. His answer resonates with our perspective of a resilient mindset:

> *Baseball taught me what I need to survive in the world. The game has given me the patience to learn and succeed. As much as I was known for my homers, I also was known for my strikeouts. The strikeout is the ultimate failure. I struck out 1,936 times. But I'm proud of my strikeouts, for I feel that to succeed, one must first fail; the more you fail, the more you learn about succeeding. The person who has never tried and failed will never succeed. Each time I walked away from the plate after a strikeout, I learned something, whether it was about my swing, the weather conditions, I learned something. My success is the product of the knowledge extracted from my failures.*[1]

The reactions of some individuals when they encounter mistakes and setbacks stand in stark contrast to Stargell's perspective. They typically attribute failure or the possibility of failure to conditions that they are powerless to change, that are beyond their control. They do not consider options for improvement, believing none exist.

This negative belief is often accompanied by other counterproductive beliefs, leaving little, if any, room for a more benign view of mistakes. One of the more prominent pitfalls of this negative mindset is to generalize the reasons for mistakes and failure far beyond the situation in question. For instance, having an unproductive day at work is interpreted by some as proof of a lack of competence in other life areas. In addition, some are prone to interpret each mistake as a testimony to inadequacy rather than as simply an event to be dealt with. This pattern of thinking erodes confidence, leading to pessimism about possible success in the future. Hope and optimism are in limited supply.

A vicious cycle is set in motion. Feeling hopeless and wishing to avoid the perceived threat of further humiliation fueled by mistakes, some are apt to resort to a variety of ineffective or self-defeating ways of coping. They may avoid engaging in particular activities, as did Mrs. Norwood and Ms. Randolph. Or, feeling pained, they may offer excuses for their shortcomings, often blaming others, as we witnessed with Mr. Butler. Still others may downplay the importance of the situation when, in fact, it is of greater significance than they wish to acknowledge.

Unfortunately, the very attempts to avoid those fearful situations backfire, forcing some down a path of pessimism, self-doubt, and a retreat from challenges. They become increasingly threatened by the possibility of failure. They are vulnerable to slipping into a posture of "learned helplessness," reflected in a mindset that believes "whatever I do will not lead to positive change, so why even try?" Instead of benefiting from the attitude Willie Stargell described as "my success is the product of the knowledge extracted from my failures," they retreat, only to feel more dissatisfied and inadequate. As one man poignantly told us, "I've spent my entire life avoiding the possibility of failure. I feel so unhappy and like such a coward."

Questions to Consider

Similar to the other characteristics of a resilient mindset we have detailed, there are questions to consider that will provide you with a better-defined picture of the ways you understand and respond to mistakes. The better you understand your approach to setbacks, the better equipped you will be to modify counterproductive patterns of thinking and behaving. Answer the following questions on pages 289–290 in Appendix A. Reflect on your answers before reading further.

- List three situations in the past year or two in which you made a mistake or failed at a task.
- Before you attempted each of the tasks, how confident were you of succeeding? Did your confidence level differ from one task to the next? (Your answers to these two questions allow you to examine the

power of your mindset to influence confidence and performance from one situation to the next.)

- When you experienced a failure, can you recall how you explained this situation to yourself? (Your response to this question directly assesses your attributions for mistakes.)
- As you examine the three situations, did you have the same explanations for why you failed in each? (Understanding your expectations provides information about the consistency of your attributions and whether particular situations elicit more constructive explanations than other situations.)
- How did you react to each situation? (Your answer directly addresses the ways you cope with mistakes.)
- With hindsight, would you respond differently to any of the situations now? If so, how would you respond differently? (Your responses to these questions encourage you to consider more productive coping techniques in the aftermath of mistakes.)
- Of the three situations in which you made a mistake or failed, in which situation did you react in a way that pleased you the most? Why did it please you? (Answering these two questions will help compare positive "exceptions" with negative reactions to mistakes.)
- What is the worst thing that has happened to you when you made a mistake or failed in a situation? (Because the fear of mistakes often invites magnification, your response to this question can help you gain a more realistic picture of the consequences of making mistakes.)
- What memories do you have about how your parents or other important adults in your life handled mistakes? (Your answer to this question provides information about the people who served as your models and addresses their influence on your present behavior.)

With your answers in mind, let's examine how these questions assisted Mrs. Norwood, whom we mentioned at the beginning of this chapter.

"What If I Make a Mistake?"

Mrs. Norwood came to see us because of her fear of taking risks and making mistakes. Her refusal to speak at a meeting of a local organization about a project with which she was involved was "the final straw." She said, "I encourage my two kids to try things, but I don't follow my own advice. I back away from so many things. I keep telling myself not to run away from things, but I do. Then I feel worse afterward."

As we gathered information from Mrs. Norwood, we learned that her fear of making mistakes was apparent in her childhood. Although she was a good student, she recalled that even as early as second grade she constantly approached her teacher's desk to clarify a question or an assignment.

"My second grade teacher said to me that I didn't have to come up all the time. I think she was getting annoyed with me, but I was afraid to make a mistake. I've been that way most of my life. It wasn't just in school. I avoided sports. I remember playing soccer when I was in the fourth grade, and in one game a girl on the other team went around me and scored a goal. We lost by one goal and all I could think of was that everyone on my team was blaming me, even though no one said anything."

"Do you have any ideas about why you were so afraid of making mistakes?"

"I've thought about that a lot. I have a younger sister, and she didn't seem worried about making mistakes. If anything, she jumped into a lot of things. I've read that babies are different at birth. My mother told me that even when I was an infant I seemed nervous, that I startled at the littlest thing. I guess I'm just a nervous person."

We agreed that we are all different from birth, but we asked what else might have contributed to her fear of making mistakes.

"I don't want to sit here and blame my parents, because they were loving. But they said things that caused me to worry more, even though I know that was not their intention. They always seemed to focus on what I did wrong rather than what I did right. They would say things like, 'If you weren't so scared, you'd do better on tests and get better grades.' I knew that. It was as if they thought I could just will myself not to be nervous. If I could have done that, I would have. Also, it wasn't like my grades were bad. I was basically a B student, but they felt my average could have been higher if I wasn't so scared about things."

"Even though they may have been loving parents, what effect did their comments about your being scared have on you?"

"Because they seemed to concentrate on my worries and what I had problems with, I think I worried more. I also felt I disappointed them."

As we listened to Mrs. Norwood's account of her childhood it appeared that her parents' love was often conditional.

We decided to shift the focus by asking, "Can you think of a situation in which you weren't worried about making a mistake?"

"That's an interesting question." Mrs. Norwood thought for a short while and said, "I think there must have been, but nothing comes to mind right now. I feel like I'm always worried."

"You said earlier, 'What if I make a mistake?' What do you think would happen if you did make a mistake? What if you gave that talk to the local organization? What is the worst thing that could happen?"

"I might forget what I was going to say. Or, even if I wrote out and read my talk, I might misread words or lose my place."

"What would happen if those things did happen?"

"I would be mortified."

"Mortified?"

"It would be so embarrassing."

"We know that it could be embarrassing. What do you think the people in the audience would think?"

"They would probably be thinking I was scared or I wasn't well prepared. It would be very embarrassing. Wouldn't anyone be embarrassed if they were giving a talk and forgot what they were going to say or weren't very coherent?"

"Most likely they would. But, as you mentioned, you felt worse afterward because you didn't give the talk, especially because you tell your kids to try things and not be afraid."

"I know that, but I don't know what to do to feel less scared."

"That's something we want to help with. We do have another question. You gave us an example of when you were playing soccer and felt that the other team's winning goal was caused by the way you played. Can you think of another time you made a mistake and felt embarrassed?" We asked this to assess what "evidence" Mrs. Norwood was using to arrive at her negative self-evaluation.

"There are plenty."

"Tell us about one."

Mrs. Norwood's answer was intriguing. She paused and said, "I'm sure there are many, but none come immediately to mind. Maybe that's because I don't allow myself to be in a situation where I can be embarrassed."

Mrs. Norwood's response vividly captured the inordinate amount of time and energy she expended in her attempt not to look foolish.

After a few moments she said, "I remember that when my kids were in elementary school, I attended a committee meeting about possible school closings. My kids had already changed schools once because their first school was shut down, and now it appeared that their second school was also going to close. As I began to speak, I became very anxious and called the school that had already closed by the wrong name."

"What happened?"

"Someone corrected me and then I forgot what I wanted to say. I ended up saying something that I thought was foolish, but my husband said it was fine. All I could think about was that I had made another blooper. After it happened, I thought that in the future I should leave comments to people who don't freeze up."

In reading this account of Mrs. Norwood's experience, one might wonder why she was so upset when she made a seemingly small mistake. Most likely, we can all think about instances in our life that were more embarrassing than the one she recounted. However, when one attributes mistakes to personal qualities that cannot be changed and interprets these qualities as flaws of personality, mistakes are magnified and generalized.

We told Mrs. Norwood that we would try to help her to feel less terrified of making mistakes. We also asked her to reflect on the questions we listed earlier in this chapter before our next session. Mrs. Norwood jokingly said, "I haven't had homework assignments in a long time. It might do me some good."

During the succeeding weeks Mrs. Norwood reported that she found the "homework assignments" helpful. They prompted her to articulate several key beliefs that contributed to her fear of mistakes, and in the process these negative beliefs became less formidable and more accessible to modification.

"I thought a lot about 'What's the worst thing that can happen?' It got me to think about times I've seen other people make mistakes. One time someone was introducing a speaker and he temporarily forgot the speaker's name. I felt really bad for the person who forgot the name, but I realized that I didn't assume he was dumb or anything like that because he forgot a name. As a matter of fact, he recovered nicely and actually joked about it. He referred to a television commercial about the importance of getting a good night's sleep. I wish I could do that."

Because Mrs. Norwood seemed in a less tense mood, we asked with some humor, "After you forgot the correct name of the school at the PTO meeting, did they advise you not to attend future meetings?"

She laughed and jokingly said, "Yes they did, but I didn't listen to them."

Our efforts with Mrs. Norwood focused not only on challenging her self-defeating beliefs but also on defining small steps she might take to face, rather than flee from, situations that threatened her. She became increasingly aware of how quickly she magnified the possible negative consequences of mistakes. Although her fear of looking foolish encompassed many areas of her life, it was especially evident when exposed to others, such as during public speaking, a fear shared by many people. One of the most important steps she took was to enroll in a public speaking course. The course not only emphasized techniques for organizing and making a presentation but also taught relaxation strategies that could be used to manage anxiety.

As we have discovered with many other people we have worked with, success breeds success. As Mrs. Norwood altered her negative assumptions and demonstrated the courage to change her self-defeating scripts, each accomplishment provided reinforcement to confront the next challenge. She recognized that some of the strategies she initiated might not be successful but that when they were not she could assess what she might do differently next time.

Steps to Manage Mistakes and Setbacks

Although the process of learning to accept mistakes as information for future success presents many hurdles, there are steps that can be taken to facilitate this journey. Given the link between negative scripts and negative attributions about mistakes, it is not surprising to find that the steps we outlined in Chapter 2 overlap with those for developing a constructive attitude toward mistakes.

Step One: Examine Your Assumptions About Mistakes

The assumptions we hold about why we make mistakes exert a significant influence on our lives. We typically do not identify, reflect on, or challenge these assumptions, so they remain powerful but unrecognized forces directing our actions. When we have asked people in our clinical practice what they attributed their mistakes or failures to, many seem surprised by the question, noting that they had not previously considered these causes.

At one of our all-day workshops we reviewed attribution theory. During the refreshment break a man approached us and said, "I had never heard of attribution theory before today. I have never really thought about the fact that we have assumptions about why we succeed or fail. After you reviewed attribution theory I thought about something that occurred a couple of weeks ago. It's just a small incident, but it confirms what you said."

"What happened?"

"You mentioned islands of competence. Mine is not in the area of being handy around the house. I needed to replace the front doorknob, which had a built-in lock. The guy at the hardware store said it was easy to do. I remember thinking, 'Yeah, maybe for you, not for me.' As I started the job I was expecting failure, which didn't help the situation. Sure enough, when I finished putting in the new doorknob, the lock didn't work. Without realizing it, my first thought was, 'You really are klutzy. You should stick to things you know. Don't try this again.' I called the hardware store and got the name of a locksmith who was able to come over later that afternoon."

This man paused and smiled. "When the locksmith came over and looked at the lock in the new doorknob, he said, 'No wonder it didn't work, it's defective.' I know that's his area of expertise, but I had immediately assumed I did something wrong. As a matter of fact, I told my wife not to ask me to do any more handyman tasks around the house. As I said, it was just a small situation and doesn't have a major impact on my life. But it got me to think about how assumptions we have about mistakes can play a really large role in what we do or don't do."

Changing a doorknob is not an essential feature in this man's existence, but, most likely, he will apply his new knowledge about attribution theory to other areas of his life of greater importance than changing a doorknob.

What are your assumptions about the mistakes you make? To help you with this assessment we listed questions earlier in this chapter. Revisit your answers. The following are simplified versions of these questions for you to consider.

- Think of a couple of times you made a mistake or failed.
- What did you tell yourself when this occurred?
- What was your reaction?

- Did you ask yourself, *Is there anything I can learn from this mistake?*
- Are there times you have refused to attempt tasks?
- Why did you refuse to attempt these tasks? Were you afraid that you might fail?
- How did you feel after you refused?
- Of all the times you made a mistake or failed, what is the time you are most proud of in terms of your reaction? Why were you proud?
- Of all the times you made a mistake or failed, what is the time you are least proud of in terms of your reaction? Why weren't you pleased?

Mr. Millis and Mr. Newman: Contrasting Perspectives We met Mr. Millis and Mr. Newman at the beginning of Chapter 3. They had similar positions in research and development in the same high-tech firm, but their attitudes toward the challenges of their work were in marked contrast to each other. Although research and development activities involve anticipating obstacles, expecting unsuccessful outcomes, and learning from these outcomes, these two men reacted very differently when such outcomes arose.

In our consultation, Mr. Newman reported constant headaches and difficulty sleeping. When a project was not progressing satisfactorily he became impatient with and demanding of his staff, often making critical remarks. When changes in the project were suggested by his supervisor, Mr. Newman became angry, feeling unwarranted pressure.

Mr. Millis shared responsibilities similar to those of Mr. Newman, but his attitude was noticeably different. In discussing the demands of his job, he said, "It's the nature of our work. I expect it and am prepared for it. I would be surprised if a week went by without some unexpected modifications in projects."

Not surprisingly, in our interviews with these two men we discovered strikingly different attributions about mistakes and setbacks, although neither had previously considered the influence of attributions. In many ways the issue was more important for Mr. Newman because his assumptions about mistakes were not in concert with a resilient mindset and lifestyle, while those of Mr. Millis were. In addition, although Mr. Millis had not previously reflected on his attributions for mistakes, it was easier for him to do so than it was for Mr. Newman because the latter was quick to blame others for his difficulties.

Mr. Millis expected that some projects would not yield satisfying results. When that occurred, he did not attribute the failure of the project to shortcomings within himself or others. He did not make excuses that distanced him from a satisfactory outcome. Instead, he believed that successful research and development included projects that were unsuccessful but provided important data that could be used to maximize the probability of future success.

Mr. Newman was burdened by the weight of projects that appeared unsuccessful. Because we interviewed him as part of a consultation role for his company, it was not possible to obtain in-depth information. However, even in our limited encounter, it appeared that he attributed mistakes to personal shortcomings, to weaknesses that were not easily corrected. To protect his fragile self-image, which was dominated by a sense of pessimism, he resorted to blaming his staff and superiors. In this way, he did not have to face his own perceived shortcomings.

Mr. Newman paid a heavy price for this brand of coping, which was similar to the toll experienced by Mr. Butler when we first met him. Mr. Butler cast responsibility for company problems on his managers, failing to examine what he could do differently. When people protect themselves in this fashion, they surrender personal control, an essential component of a resilient mindset. It was little wonder that Mr. Newman experienced both mental and physical turmoil. Not only did each setback drain his limited self-esteem, but his desperate attempts to deal with his discomfort added to his sense of powerlessness and helplessness.

Mr. Newman conveyed the intense stress that was pervading his life. We told him that it might be helpful if he met with a counselor. In making this recommendation we recognized that he attributed his stress to the behavior of others and it might not be easy for him to hear our suggestion that he seek counseling. Thus, we were careful to communicate this recommendation in a way that would minimize his feeling we were criticizing or blaming him. We emphasized that counseling might help him to learn more effective ways to interact with others so that they might be more receptive to what he had to say.

Mr. Newman said he would consider taking such a step. Since our consultation to his company was time-limited, we are not certain whether he did. If we had been Mr. Newman's therapists, we would have helped him become less defensive and more honest in his understanding of and reaction to setbacks. Only in this way could he achieve a feeling of personal control that would be filled with empowerment and hope rather than condemnation and pessimism.

Step Two: Challenge Self-Defeating Attributions

Attributions are assumptions within a mindset. When these assumptions serve as roadblocks to leading a resilient lifestyle they must be defined, understood, and challenged. If we are to be resilient we must strive to ensure that we avoid playing the role of a prosecuting attorney when we offer self-assessments about our mistakes. Instead, we must assume the stance of a defense attorney. In order to lead a more satisfying life, both Ms. Randolph and Mrs. Norwood had to challenge the belief that they were not very smart and that mistakes were a confirmation of limited intelligence.

The following are a sample of the self-defeating assumptions we have heard in our clinical practice. Are some of these familiar?

- I am dumb.
- I will never learn.
- There is nothing I do successfully.
- No one likes to be with me.
- I'm not good at anything.
- I will always be a failure.
- If I try something, I am likely to make a fool of myself.
- My mother said I'd never amount to anything—she was right.

In one of our workshops we offered examples of self-defeating attributions. A participant posed an interesting question: "But what if these self-defeating assumptions are true? What if you really aren't smart or talented? Wouldn't you be deceiving yourself if you tell yourself you are smart when you're not or that you can do something that you can't?"

We answered that it would be deceptive if we evaluated ourselves as much more talented than we actually were. Some people engage in such deception as a way of masking underlying feelings of insecurity. However, more often than not we have encountered individuals who magnify and generalize their vulnerabilities and weaknesses, leaving the impression that their lives are a history filled with mistakes and failures. They focus on their mistakes in the same way that adolescents might focus on one pimple on their face, ignoring many positive features. When this occurs their positive features recede into the background.

Consider the questions we have raised in this chapter as you challenge negative assumptions about mistakes. Examine your answers closely, especially the explanations you devise when you fail at a task. Also, notice whether you fall into the trap of making all-or-none statements (such as "I will never learn"), or whether you generalize a mistake in one area of your life to all areas (such as "I can't do anything right"), or whether you attribute mistakes to a factor that can't be changed (such as "I am really dumb"). In addition, as we will emphasize in the next chapter, begin to focus on areas in which you have been successful.

"If Only I Could Practice What I Preach"   Len Carter, a twenty-eight-year-old mental health counselor, stated during his first session that he was "filled with insecurities." The precipitating event that brought him in was the recent suicide of one of his clients. The director of the clinic in which Mr. Carter worked reviewed his interventions with this particular client and felt that Mr. Carter had practiced good clinical judgment and that no one could have anticipated the suicide. However, Mr. Carter became increasingly haunted by the question of whether he possessed the skills to be a good clinician.

Mr. Carter was an articulate, soft-spoken man. He discussed the events that prompted his call and observed, "I'm doubting everything I say to my clients. Not only do I wonder whether I'm doing my clients any good, but I worry that I actually might be doing them harm. I encourage my patients to deal with adversity, but I have difficulty doing it myself. If only I could practice what I preach."

Although all clinicians are likely to harbor doubts about their effectiveness, especially at the beginning of their careers and following the suicide of one of their clients, Mr. Carter's insecurities loomed larger than most. As he recounted some of his life experiences with us, we began to understand the roots of his self-doubt.

"I was in therapy while in graduate school and thought I had resolved certain issues but they have a way of rearing their ugly heads."

"What issues?"

"I've been struggling with self-doubt all of my life. When I started therapy in graduate school, I wondered whether I had what it took to be a good therapist. But as I discussed this with my own therapist, my doubts about being a good therapist followed a long line of other doubts."

"What kinds of doubts?"

"If I didn't understand something in school, I immediately assumed I didn't have the smarts to succeed. If I had a bad game in sports, I immediately assumed that I had lost whatever skills I might have had or that maybe I didn't have good skills to begin with. I remember that when I started high school I went for tryouts for the freshman basketball team. I had always been pretty good at basketball. But when the tryouts began I felt the other kids were much better than I was.

"Actually, one incident really convinced me I wasn't that good. I was defending a very good player and he scored four quick baskets against me. On the last basket, I turned my ankle a little. The injury wasn't really bad. I felt better by the next morning, but I told the coach it was really sore. I used it as an excuse not to try out because I was convinced that I lacked the ability to make the team and didn't want to embarrass myself. It turned out that the kid I was defending was the best player on the court and probably anyone would have had trouble defending him. But my self-doubts took over. Afterward, I was angry at myself for quitting. What made it worse was that I knew I was better than a couple of the kids who made the team. But at least they tried out. The moment I faced a difficult situation, I quit."

Mr. Carter paused. With a sense of sadness and resignation, he said, "Now I feel like quitting my profession."

We said, "Dealing with a client's suicide is very difficult and could lead any therapist to question what he had done or not done. You told us that the director of your clinic felt that there was no way of predicting that your client would attempt suicide. What do you think about what he said?"

"Rationally, I tell myself he's probably right. But there's this other part that feels there was much more I could have done."

"We know you're really questioning yourself, but why quit as a therapist?"

"I guess it's just my usual way of handling things. As you can see from what I've told you, it's a well-entrenched pattern."

The power of negative scripts was very evident.

"You mentioned that when you were in therapy in graduate school, you thought you had resolved these issues of self-doubt."

"I thought I had, but everything was thrown off by the suicide."

"When you were in therapy, what sense did you make about why you had so much self-doubt?"

"The short version is that I grew up in a home with parents who could have been called 'Mr. and Mrs. Perfection.' Nothing was good enough. I could never please them. I remember getting in trouble in elementary school for pushing over a plant with a couple of my friends. It was a stupid prank. I know it was wrong. We had to clean up the mess and pay for a new plant, which we deserved. But if you listened to my parents you would have thought I was a born criminal destined for a life of crime.

"I remember another time in high school struggling with a math course. I couldn't believe what my father said. Instead of being understanding, instead of our figuring out what might help, he said, 'Maybe you don't have the brains to do math.' I got really angry and he said he was only kidding, but the damage had already been done. Anyway, my father died when I was in college and I don't have too much contact with my mother. We live three thousand miles away from each other, but I think even if she lived nearby I wouldn't have much contact."

We spoke a little more about his parents and then said, "We know having a patient commit suicide is very difficult, but from what you've told us, when you experience setbacks or mistakes you see yourself as inadequate and one of your first responses is to quit."

"That's exactly how I feel."

"Sometimes it can be useful if we can think of a time when we made a mistake or failed, but instead of being critical of ourselves we stuck with the situation. Does any situation like that come to mind?" We wanted to see whether Mr. Carter could recall any exceptions to his usual self-critical response.

"Actually, I remember feeling more comfortable and less defensive with one of my therapy supervisors in graduate school. With some supervisors, I felt as if they were thinking, 'Why is someone so incompetent becoming a therapist?' but with Dr. Penn, I never felt that way."

"What do you think was the difference?"

"Something Dr. Penn said. It's interesting how a comment can stay with you. The first time I met her, even before I discussed any clinical material with her, she mentioned that when she was in training she often felt insecure and at times she wondered whether she was helping her patients. She also said that sometimes she thought that feedback she received from her supervisors was very critical, although it probably wasn't."

"Why were Dr. Penn's comments so helpful?"

"It was as if she were telling me in advance that we all make mistakes, that we all feel insecure, that it's part of becoming a professional. As I'm telling you this, I realize that she was creating a comfortable, nonthreatening atmosphere in supervision. Also, she spoke in a very genuine, caring way. When I presented cases to her, it was one of the only times I can remember not feeling as if I was inadequate."

Mr. Carter stopped.

"You seem to be thinking about something."

"I am. How different Dr. Penn's approach was from how my parents spoke with me."

"We have a question to ask that may be difficult to answer."

Mr. Carter smiled and said, "The way you just worded things sounded just like Dr. Penn. Letting me know in advance that it's OK if something is difficult."

We smiled and proceeded. "If Dr. Penn were the director of your clinic and said that you had done all you could have done with the patient who committed suicide, what would you have thought?" Dr. Penn appeared to be one of the few people in Mr. Carter's life who helped him to be less self-critical and less upset by setbacks; thus, if we could help him apply what he had learned from her to other situations, it might be easier for him to deal with difficult events in his life.

"What an interesting question. I like the director of our clinic, but I know that when he said that he could not find any indication that my patient would commit suicide and that he felt I had used good clinical judgment, I really wondered whether he meant it. I just felt I had really failed. Getting back to your question, if Dr. Penn had said the same thing, I think I would have been more likely to believe her, just given my comfort level with her."

"Do you think you've been very tough on yourself?"

"Yes."

"We've got to figure out a way to place a miniature Dr. Penn by your ear so that each time you make a mistake or face a crisis she can offer encouragement. She could tell you that just because something doesn't work out doesn't mean you're a failure. We bet she wouldn't be thrilled if you told her you were thinking about leaving your career."

"I know she would be upset if I told her that. She actually told me during our last supervision session when she was summarizing my work that she felt I was a talented therapist."

"How did you feel when she said that?"

"Very good. I just felt she wouldn't say something like that if she didn't mean it."

"So we have to figure out how you can stop criticizing yourself and seeing yourself as a failure when things don't work out. In a way, as we mentioned before, you need to listen to Dr. Penn's voice."

"It's a fascinating idea."

Mr. Carter's mindset was dominated by negative thoughts that served as obstacles to leading a resilient life. It was as if an automatic recording was set in motion the moment he experienced any mistakes or setbacks: "I am a failure; I can't do anything right; I am incompetent and shouldn't continue attempting something that will lead to further failure; each mistake proves how inadequate I am."

While these may appear to be overly harsh words, they represent the words that Mr. Carter had brought with him from his childhood. They had become a reality to him, influencing all aspects of his life. Of all his past relationships, it was only Dr. Penn who was able to challenge these self-critical evaluations, but her positive impact was limited to the year she supervised him. In our interventions, which we describe later, we attempted to broaden her influence and challenge the negative attributions that dominated Mr. Carter's existence.

Step Three: Learn Something Positive from Every Situation

A vital step in overcoming self-defeating attributions for mistakes is to address the question, *What can I learn from this situation?* If people are entrenched in a negative script, if they perceive themselves as inadequate or lacking intelligence, if they have not previously considered what they can learn from mistakes, they may quickly answer, "There is nothing to learn from mistakes." For these individuals, mistakes represent a confirmation of their negative view of themselves, and the more hardened this view becomes the less likely they are to free themselves from it.

It is not always easy to discover the learning potential in our mistakes, especially when negative self-evaluations dominate our thinking. However, even if one's self-esteem is high, mistakes are not necessarily greeted with the statement, *I'm so glad I made a mistake because it's another opportunity to improve myself.* Many mistakes trigger feelings of disappointment and doubt. However, if mistakes and failure reinforce negative self-evaluations, there is little opportunity to learn from what went wrong. It was only after Mrs. Norwood and Ms. Randolph examined what they could learn from situations that elicited an inordinate fear about making mistakes and looking foolish that they could move forward and develop more realistic, healthy coping strategies.

As we focus on the theme of learning from, rather than feeling condemned by, mistakes and failure, it is helpful to remember Willie Stargell's view of mistakes cited earlier in this chapter as well as the following observation, which appeared in a report issued by the California Task Force to Promote Self-Esteem and Personal and Social Responsibility:

> *Mistakes are a natural part of life. We learn by experimenting; mistakes and failure can be important parts of our learning process. Einstein flunked grade-school mathematics. Edison tried over 9,000 kinds of filaments before he found one that would work in a lightbulb. Walt Disney went bankrupt five times before he built Disneyland. If we accept our setbacks, we can continue to risk, learn, and move on with excitement and satisfaction.*[2]

Back to Mr. Carter and the Voice of Dr. Penn   As Mr. Carter described significant people in his life, it appeared that only Dr. Penn's words of encouragement served to offset the negative self-evaluations that had become a prominent part of Mr. Carter's mindset. He acknowledged that if Dr. Penn had told him that his work with his patient who committed suicide had met appropriate clinical standards and that he had not mismanaged the case, he would have accepted her judgment.

During our lives we encounter situations in which we have stumbled or failed and are able to consider what we might do differently next time. Reflecting on what we can learn from these setbacks involves changing any negative perceptions we possess when the situation arises again. One may wonder how Mr. Carter could change the situation next time since his patient had taken his own life, but the feedback Mr. Carter received was that there was nothing he could have done differently. So what could he change?

We felt that although all of the analyses of the case suggested that he could not have prevented the suicide, the most important thing he could do differently when a setback occurred in the future (and of course we hoped it would not be one as difficult as a patient's suicide) was to change the way he interpreted the event. If he continued to view each setback as an indictment of his skills and intelligence, it would be difficult to move forward. However, if he could learn to challenge his negative self-evaluations, there would be an opportunity for him to adopt a positive self-image.

When we discussed this step of reflecting on what he could learn from his patient's suicide as well as from future difficult situations, Mr. Carter returned to the metaphor or image we had used earlier. He said with a smile, "I could imagine a miniature Dr. Penn by my ear."

"What would you imagine she would say to you?"

"She would offer encouragement and would certainly remind me that my constant put-downs of myself were not helpful."

"What might she recommend instead?"

"Probably things similar to what you've recommended and probably things I recommend to my clients, but it's often tough to follow your own advice. I think she would remind me that I have many talents and that when I make a mistake or when something doesn't work I can focus on what I can learn and not put myself down and constantly doubt myself. I think she would emphasize that failing at something doesn't mean you're a failure as a person. That's a thought I have to learn to keep in mind."

"Do you think that reminding yourself of what Dr. Penn would probably say can be helpful?"

Mr. Carter answered honestly, "I'm not certain, but I don't really want to give up the work I'm doing. I've got to remember what she would probably say as well as what my clinic director told me."

Living with self-doubts and self-recrimination for years makes changing these negative thoughts and scripts seem like a herculean task. However, Mr. Carter also recognized that running from setbacks was not a desirable response. He struggled for many months to attend to what he could learn from setbacks, including changing his typical negative self-perception. He also struggled to answer the questions we posed earlier in this chapter in an attempt to gain a more precise picture of the assumptions or attributions that directed his behavior.

His confidence and self-assurance improved slowly but steadily. When self-doubt arose, he reminded himself of Dr. Penn. His connection to her voice was a vital component of his improvement. Little did Dr. Penn realize how she had served as a charismatic adult in Mr. Carter's life, even in absentia.

Step Four: Decide on a Plan of Action to Attempt New Scripts Based on New Attributions

Once we have become aware of and challenged negative attributions about mistakes and failure and once we have adopted the view that mistakes are experiences to learn from, our next step is to translate this new, more positive mindset into a specific action plan. This step closely parallels our description of the process for changing negative scripts outlined in Chapter 2. It involves a consideration of the following components.

First, ask yourself what are different things you can do either to change your behavior so that mistakes are less likely to occur or to change how you view and respond to mistakes when they do occur. This is closely linked to the previous step of considering what you can learn from a setback or failure. It also highlights that change may be expressed through a new evaluation of the situation, as occurred with Mr. Carter, as well as through new behaviors; these two components are closely linked because a new, more positive evaluation typically leads to new, more constructive behaviors.

We wish to emphasize that by directing attention to what you can do differently, you also assume personal control for your life rather than passively accepting the negative thoughts and scripts that have existed. As we know, this sense of personal control is a major feature of stress hardiness and resilience.

Second, after reviewing several possible options to change how you view and react to mistakes, select one that you believe has the greatest probability for success.

Third, once you have selected a new action plan, anticipate the possible obstacles to success. The more prepared you are for obstacles that may arise, the better equipped you will be to manage these obstacles in a constructive manner in concert with a resilient mindset. As you reflect on possible obstacles, it may be helpful to consider once again your answers to some of the questions we posed earlier, as well as several new questions.

- Think of a few times you made a mistake or failed. What did you tell yourself when this occurred?
- What was your reaction?
- If you make a mistake or fail in the future, what do you want to tell yourself? Is this different from what you told yourself in the past?
- If it is different, how do you think it will affect your behavior?
- What difficulties do you anticipate encountering as you use new words and actions to deal with mistakes?
- How will you manage these difficulties so that you can move forward?
- Of all the times you made a mistake or failed, what is the time you are most proud of in terms of your reaction? Why were you proud?
- Of all the times you made a mistake or failed, what is the time you are least proud of in terms of your reaction? Why weren't you pleased? How would you change?

This series of questions will help you think about how you managed past mistakes and how you might handle them in the future.

Fourth, perform the new script that you have devised that you believe will help you lessen the fear of mistakes. As you engage in this new script, judge its effectiveness.

Fifth, if your new attributions about mistakes or your new behavior are not successful, avoid negative self-evaluation. Instead, return to Step Three and ask what you have learned from this setback, then proceed to Step Four again to consider new options and a new plan of action.

The Journey of Mr. Hopkins You have read stories within this book of individuals who have had the courage to shed the shackles of long-held negative self-perceptions and engage in unfamiliar behaviors that allowed them to experience a more satisfying, resilient lifestyle. Greater self-awareness and self-assurance permitted them to replace ineffective coping techniques (avoiding situations, quitting, blaming others) with coping behaviors that led to a sense of accomplishment.

Mr. Carter, Mrs. Norwood, Ms. Randolph, Ms. Gateman, and Mr. Butler quickly come to mind as individuals who held negative attributions about mistakes and consequently engaged in counterproductive behaviors. In the process of making changes in their lives, they considered the questions we posed in this chapter. They examined their assumptions and fears about making mistakes and looking foolish. Once this was accomplished they slowly assumed new behaviors that were in accord with their goals and wishes, behaviors that were realistic and achievable.

In ending this chapter we would like to describe the remarkable journey of Peter Hopkins, a forty-two-year-old owner of a heating and air conditioning business, and his wife, Patty. Mr. and Mrs. Hopkins consulted us about the school program for their eight-year-old son, who was diagnosed with learning disabilities. During our consultation, Mr. Hopkins shared his childhood and adolescent experiences.

"Growing up, I had some learning problems. I struggled to learn to read. Also, I had some expressive language problems, so I avoided long conversations. One of my uncles said I was shy. Maybe I was, but I figured, why say anything when you're convinced that anything you say sounds foolish? My parents were supportive and even encouraged me to see a psychologist. I went once when I was about twelve years old. I told myself it wouldn't help, and it didn't because I refused to talk. Looking back, I felt that nothing could help, so why go see a shrink? Probably I should have given the psychologist a chance."

"It sounds like you weren't ready for therapy."

"I wasn't. But I continued to struggle in school and in my relations with other kids. I finally graduated from high school and enrolled in a local community college. That's where I met Patty."

When he said this, he reached out and took his wife's hand in an affectionate way. He laughed and said, "I felt an attraction to her immediately, but I was too shy to say anything. I felt that anything I said would sound dumb. Fortunately, she chased me."

Mrs. Hopkins laughed and said, "Well, if I waited for you to make the first move, I'd still be waiting."

Mr. Hopkins said, "As we got to know each other, I talked about my worries about saying things. Patty's a very easy person to talk with. I even told her that I was thinking about dropping out of college because I just sat in class worried that I might be called on. When you think you're not very smart, you find ways of avoiding situations that might reveal how dumb you are. The problem is that it catches up with you."

"That's a very perceptive observation. Just from the little we know you, it seems that you've really changed. You have your own business and you're articulate in expressing your thoughts. What changed?"

Mr. Hopkins smiled again and responded, "Patty basically became my psychologist. She pointed out some things that should have been obvious to me but were not. She said that the more I kept from saying things and the more I limited my conversations with other people, the more I was going to feel like a failure. She had taken a psychology course and read about a technique called something like 'behavior rehearsal.' Some people need tutoring in math or reading. I needed tutoring in feeling more comfortable dealing with mistakes and not immediately seeing myself as stupid."

We turned to Mrs. Hopkins, who was co-owner of the business with her husband, and said, "You could easily have an advanced degree in psychology."

She smiled and said, "I appreciate that. Actually, I have to use psychology all of the time, not only with Peter and our kids but also with our customers."

We wondered, "How did you use behavior rehearsal?"

Mr. Hopkins answered, "Patty and I would rehearse how to answer questions in class and what to say if I didn't know an answer. We also rehearsed different interactions with other people. She made it tough at times. When I wasn't sure how to answer and felt dumb, she would remind me that few, if any, people know the answers all of the time. One of the things I really learned was that my attitude about mistakes was a bigger problem than actually making mistakes. I was so afraid that I would come across as a nitwit that I made excuses to avoid many situations. With Patty's help I began to take small steps to change. Nothing big, but each time I volunteered an answer or went out of my way to talk with another student, I gained more confidence. I also reminded myself that if I didn't know an answer, it didn't mean I was dumb."

We were very impressed not only by the journey Mr. Hopkins had taken but also by the insights of his wife, who was truly his charismatic adult. Mrs. Hopkins intuitively knew about attribution theory (even if she did not know it by name) and was aware of strategies that could be applied to change negative attributions and self-defeating behaviors. Mrs. Hopkins helped her husband recognize that mistakes and setbacks are likely to occur in anyone's life and that a major issue is when one's "attitude about mistakes was a bigger problem than actually making mistakes."

Mr. Hopkins offered a wonderful perspective of his journey. He said, "When I look back at my life when I entered community college, the person I was then seems like an entirely different person than I am now. If I had continued down the road I was on back then, I hate to think about where I would be now."

Concluding Thoughts About Mistakes

As Mr. Hopkins so eloquently described, mistaken attitudes about mistakes are a bigger problem than making mistakes. Resilient people view mistakes as experiences to learn from. If you are to lead a resilient lifestyle, you must recognize that mistakes and failure are a natural occurrence within that lifestyle. Your choice is the manner in which you respond to these events. As you consider the influence of mistakes on your life, you might wish to reflect on the following observation by Jacob Braude: "In order to profit from your mistakes, you have to go out and make some."

We believe this sentiment captures the essence of this chapter and the place of mistakes in a resilient mindset. It is well worth considering.

9

Dealing Well with Success
in Building Islands
of Competence

In Chapter 1 we met Jill Alexander and Marian Baker, two women who held very different assumptions about the reasons for their vocational success. Both were complimented for their accomplishments. Ms. Alexander reacted to praise with the following thoughts: "I really worked hard on this project. I really put in a lot of energy. I feel very good. I think I'm ready for a more challenging project." She also commented, "I planned the project very carefully and had clear goals and plans."

Similar to the different perspectives possessed by Mr. Millis and Mr. Newman about mistakes and setbacks, Ms. Baker's view of success was in marked contrast to Ms. Alexander's. Upon being congratulated by her coworkers, she thought, "I was lucky on this project. I'm surprised it worked. I bet all of my faults will be exposed sooner or later." While Ms. Alexander easily accepted credit and ownership for her success, Ms. Baker did not or could not.

Drew Arsdale consulted with us because of "increased anxiety and insecurity." A forty-one-year-old account executive, he said, "I have a well-paying job, a lovely wife, and three great children. I know that other people see me as successful and competent, but I certainly don't feel that way. I don't know if I've truly ever felt capable, even though it may seem that I am. I always have doubts. I always think any success I have will be lost."

Mr. Arsdale described intensified anxiety after the loss of a major account several months earlier. "The client was dissatisfied with my work. I think he expected too much. But when he left to go with another agency, I began to worry that my other accounts would also leave. I began to feel that whatever successes I had in the past were like a house of cards that could be swept away at a moment's notice. I actually started to feel that I didn't deserve to have many of those accounts in the first place."

Resilient Mindsets, the Experience of Success, and Attribution Theory

In Chapter 8 we used attribution theory to explain the different assumptions or mindsets that people possess about mistakes and failure and how these assumptions are linked to the presence or absence of a resilient mindset. Attribution theory also applies in helping us understand the ways people interpret and respond to success.

Attribution theory research finds that people with high self-esteem and confidence, such as Ms. Alexander, tend to perceive their accomplishments based in great part on their resources and efforts. While they freely acknowledge the assistance of others, they also recognize their contributions to success. This recognition is a vital feature of a resilient mindset. When we accept realistic ownership for our achievements, we are more confident of future success. We are also better prepared to deal with the inevitable mistakes and setbacks that arise in life because we believe that we have the competencies to deal with these obstacles and move forward. In these circumstances we are filled with self-assurance rather than self-doubt.

The portrait is much different for individuals such as Ms. Baker and Mr. Arsdale. They attribute success to luck or chance and thus lack the confidence to believe that they will be successful in the future. When we believe that luck or chance are the main contributors to our achievements, we are less assured of continued accomplishment because luck is an uncertain commodity. Though a modicum of chance may operate in any situation, ongoing success is based on the belief that we have control over our destiny. What is perceived as luck often represents the ability to take advantage of fortuitous situations.

Individuals lacking a feeling of personal responsibility for their accomplishments are especially vulnerable to the negative impact of mistakes. Believing that their accomplishments are not based on their abilities, they are quick to interpret mistakes as a reflection of their basic flaws or inadequacies. In Chapter 8 we detailed the negative consequences of holding these kinds of attributions about mistakes.

A Lack of Satisfaction

Another dimension that distinguishes individuals in their attributions for success is the level of satisfaction they experience when attaining their goals. Those possessing a positive mindset, such as Ms. Alexander, experience contentment and joy when they achieve their goals. A sense of personal satisfaction pervades their lives. As one man told us, "When I accomplish something, I don't immediately move on to my next goal. I enjoy the moment. You could say that I stop and smell the roses."

Unfortunately, the Ms. Bakers and Mr. Arsdales of the world are less likely to experience this kind of satisfaction. They are burdened by thoughts that they are not truly responsible for their achievements and thus do not deserve any accolades, either from others or from themselves. It is difficult to "enjoy the moment" when you are worried that success is illusory and unlikely to occur again.

A man spoke with us at the conclusion of one of our workshops. He said, "When you were describing attribution theory, I thought you were talking about me."

"In what way?"

"In all ways. First of all, I really get down on myself when something doesn't go right, and I keep thinking that I'm not very bright or talented. But even when I succeed at something, I fit the picture you described. You would think at those times I would, as you say, 'enjoy the moment,' but I don't."

The man paused and added, "I'll give you an example. I liked to play baseball as a kid. I still remember that when I played Little League I was a pretty good pitcher. As I was striking out the last batter in the game, my first thought was, 'I was lucky to get him out. I wonder if I'll be as lucky the next game. I wonder if I can win the next game.' All I could think of was the next game, so I couldn't enjoy myself at the end of the game we had just finished. Do you know that thirty years later I'm still struggling with the same self-doubts and lack of enjoyment?"

We spoke with this man for a few more minutes. Although we are cautious not to recommend a consultation with a mental health professional to each person who speaks with us about a personal problem at the end of one of our workshops, we suggested such a consultation in this instance because of the obvious distress this man was feeling. It was evident that he required assistance to change the self-defeating attributions that burdened him with a great amount of psychological pain, robbing him of the self-satisfaction that derives from realistic achievements.

Acceptance, Not Narcissism

In discussing attributions for success, we wish to make clear that assuming realistic credit for one's accomplishments should not be confused with egotism, narcissism, or just plain bragging. When individuals are comfortable with their achievements, when they possess a resilient mindset and are leading a resilient lifestyle, they do not feel a need to broadcast their successes. People feeling insecure about their achievements and appearance to others often cope with these negative thoughts by letting the world know how wonderful they are or by ignoring or minimizing the accomplishments of others. Their words of self-praise are born of self-doubt, not of satisfaction or contentment.

In this regard, it is interesting to note the work of Jim Collins, director of a management research laboratory in Boulder, Colorado. Collins and his colleagues examined what was required for a good company to become a great company. They developed criteria to define *great* and discovered that those companies that met these criteria shared certain characteristics in common, one of which was the presence of what they called a "level 5 leader."[1]

Collins's description of a level 5 leader resonates with the tenets of attribution theory. He notes that such leaders accept realistic responsibility for poor results without feeling defeated or blaming others. They also demonstrate "personal humility" for the achievements of the company, recognizing the contributions of others and not placing the spotlight on themselves. These leaders hold high standards, possess an image of excellence, and have a firm sense of personal control, but they have no urge to flaunt what they have accomplished because they feel secure in what they have achieved.

In essence, assuming realistic ownership for success and humbly highlighting the good work of others are not mutually exclusive. While level 5 leaders may take some of the focus off themselves by asserting that some luck or a competent employee played a large part in their success, what

Collins calls their "unwavering resolve to do whatever must be done to produce the best long-term results, no matter how difficult" indicates their appreciation of the significant role they play in bringing about positive change. Collins's examination of level 5 leaders and their awareness of not placing themselves in the spotlight but instead recognizing the input of their staff dovetails with the observations of Kouzes and Posner about effective leaders. The latter note:

> *Remember to say thank you! Study after study points out just how fundamental all this really is. For example, one survey examining employee turnover found that the chief reason people give for leaving is that they get "limited praise and recognition." When asked what skills their managers might develop to be more effective, employees placed at the top of the list "the ability to recognize and acknowledge the contributions of others."*[2]

The attributions of resilient people toward mistakes and successes are realistic, characterized by a belief that problems can be solved, that the solutions must first be found within oneself, and that when success arrives it need not be accompanied by self-glorification.

The Fear of Success

In one of our workshops we discussed fears of failure and success. Several participants responded that they could understand fear of failure because that could prompt feelings of humiliation or incompetence. But they had difficulty comprehending the fear of success and wondered how such a fear might be related to attribution theory.

We have worked with individuals who not only have difficulty accepting their accomplishments but actually fear success. A major force behind the fear of success is the belief that one doesn't deserve success and will not easily duplicate it. Burdened by low self-esteem, such individuals believe that their success is deceptive and not of their own making. Thus, the more they succeed, the more afraid they are of being uncovered as a "fraud." They believe that with each success, others will have higher expectations for them. More demanding expectations are fraught with danger when you believe that your accomplishments are based on factors outside your control and beyond your ability.

We witnessed this dynamic with Carla Palmer, a thirty-year-old clothes buyer for a department store chain. After being offered a promotion, she became anxious and contemplated turning down the position. She discussed her feelings with her husband, Joel, attributing her anxiety to the increased hours that would probably accompany her new responsibilities. Mr. Palmer thought this was a wonderful opportunity for his wife, even if additional hours were involved. He knew that this promotion was something his wife had desired. He said that while it was her decision, he supported accepting the job, saying that once she was in the position they could evaluate how demanding her new responsibilities and time commitments would be. He asked his wife, "How will you feel if you don't accept the promotion?" She answered, "I'm not sure."

Mrs. Palmer requested a few weeks to consider the offer. Her request was granted. Her boss told her that he thought she was ready for the promotion and reassured her that her hours of work would not increase very much.

During the next few days, as she was reflecting on the promotion, her anxiety "skyrocketed." She told her husband, "I don't know why I'm feeling so anxious. You would think I'd be happy, but I'm not."

He was concerned about the intensity of her anxiety as well as her confusion about whether to accept the position. He suggested that she speak to a therapist before making a final decision. She came to see us.

During our first session we asked Mrs. Palmer whether she had previously experienced this kind of anxiety or indecision.

She responded, "No. I don't remember ever feeling this anxious. If anything, I see myself as a pretty confident person. I'm not certain why this promotion is causing me such distress."

"How would your life be different if you accepted the new position?" We asked this in an attempt to encourage Mrs. Palmer to articulate what might be triggering her anxiety.

"I think the added responsibilities would involve many more hours of work. I know that my boss said my hours would not increase that much, but I think they would. If that happened it would interfere with the time Joel and I spend together. Also, Joel and I have talked about beginning a family. If I take this job it might mean waiting longer to have children."

"Why's that?"

Mrs. Palmer answered, "Well, I guess it doesn't have to mean putting off having children, but it could."

"What does your husband think about the promotion?"

"He was actually very happy for me. He knows that one of my goals was to reach a top managerial level and feels that as a couple we can handle the promotion and continue to have a good marriage. He feels I should accept it and see what happens. He said that if it doesn't work out, it doesn't work out, that it's not the end of the world. I wish I could be as relaxed about this."

"So from what you say, your main hesitation has to do with the possibility of increased work hours interfering with your relationship with your husband. Yet he doesn't feel that way. Are there any other reservations you have about accepting the promotion?"

"I can't think of any."

"It's something we might want to consider at our next meeting. People can experience anxiety about new situations and not be aware of the many reasons they're anxious. It's helpful to identify these reasons so that we can deal with them."

At the conclusion of our initial session with Mrs. Palmer, we felt that while the possibility that her promotion would demand more hours of work was prompting her anxiety, the intensity of her worries suggested that other factors might also be contributing to her psychological turmoil.

At the beginning of our next session, Mrs. Palmer explained that she could not think of any other reasons why she would be so worried about accepting the promotion. She also said that her anxiety level continued to be very high.

"Maybe my anxiety should tell me that something is not right about my accepting the promotion."

We responded, "It's obvious you're experiencing distress. Maybe it is an indication that you shouldn't take the new position, or maybe distress is a cue that something about your thoughts or in your life warrants change. But if we can figure out why you're feeling so anxious about it, you can make a more informed decision. Also, we want to make certain that you're not giving up an opportunity that you'll regret later on."

Mrs. Palmer nodded. "But I can't think of what else it could be other than the increased hours."

"Can you think of another time in your life when you felt this anxious about making a decision?"

Mrs. Palmer smiled. "When Joel asked me to marry him. Well, not really. It took me all of five seconds to say yes."

We returned her smile and said, "We'll reword the question. Can you think of another time in your life when you felt very anxious about making a decision that involved a promotion and increased responsibilities?"

"I've been working for the same department store chain since I finished college. I've had promotions along the way, but compared with the current one they've been small."

"In terms of responsibilities, what makes this one large?"

"A couple of things. In the past I had only one or two people reporting to me, but in this position I would have an entire staff reporting to me. Also, if I accept the promotion I will have more of the final responsibility for what we buy. Although I held some of this responsibility before, I reported to another person. He would go over my decisions and really have the final say. It's his job that I've been offered because he's leaving to go to another company. If I take it, for all intents and purposes I will make the final decisions."

"Putting aside the possible extra hours that would be involved in the new position, what do you feel about the additional responsibilities of having a large staff report to you and having more of the final decision-making power?"

Mrs. Palmer responded, "Do you know that just talking about this is making me more anxious?"

"In what way?"

"After my boss offered me the promotion, I had an initial feeling of exhilaration, but that was quickly followed by anxiety."

"Without wanting to sound like a broken record, what do you think this anxiety might be about?"

"I'm not certain."

"We have a question to ask that might not be easy to answer, but it might help us to have a better idea of why you're feeling so anxious and indecisive."

"What is it?"

"Do you have any worries about being able to handle the responsibilities that come with the new job?"

"Wouldn't taking on new responsibilities lead anyone to worry more?"

"That could certainly happen, but we're wondering whether taking on the responsibilities that your new job requires has led to anxieties you didn't expect. We know you said that this promotion brings with it many more responsibilities than your previous promotions, so it might also be leading to fears you hadn't anticipated."

"I can see what you're saying. I know that I have some doubts about being able to handle my new responsibilities. I'm going to say something to you that I haven't even discussed with Joel. I think it sounds silly, but it's probably important to mention."

"What's that?"

"When I was offered the job I wondered if I deserved it. I was almost going to say to my boss, 'Are you sure you have the right person? Why me?' But isn't that a natural reaction to being offered such a big promotion with new responsibilities?"

"It can be, but what's most important is to figure out what it meant to you and what you experienced."

"Well, I know I questioned whether I could handle the position, even though my boss didn't seem to have any doubts about it. I remember thinking, 'Leave well enough alone. You've done fine up to now. Why take on something that may be way over your head? You may hit a brick wall. People will expect things from you that you can't deliver.' Oh, oh, I'm getting anxious just saying that."

We waited for a moment. Mrs. Palmer continued. "Here's something else that might seem a little foolish. I've been in my current job for a couple of years. I could tell from my performance reviews that my boss was very pleased, and I sensed that if a higher position in the company became available I would be one of the top candidates. On the one hand I was very excited by that prospect, but on the other hand I was anxious. As I'm telling you this, I remember thinking, 'Slow down. If you do too good a job, they may ask you to move up the ladder and you'll open yourself up to scrutiny.' But why would I think that?"

"We're not sure why you would think that, but at least we have a better sense of what your anxieties are about."

Mrs. Palmer's anxiety and indecisiveness from the perspective of attribution theory contained self-defeating elements that served as obstacles to a resilient lifestyle. Although by her own accounts she had been successful in her work, she harbored doubts about whether her accomplishments were deserved. These doubts prompted her to be cautious about being too successful lest she be asked to assume more demanding responsibilities that she believed would lead to failure. A fear of success was present because she had not established a sense of ownership for her achievements. This situation left her vulnerable to a fear of failure.

Mrs. Palmer had not been aware of this mindset as a source of her anxiety. As she began to understand the assumptions that affected her emotions and behaviors, she was able to take action to change. The questions we posed in the last chapter about mistakes, as well as the questions that we raise later in this chapter about attributions for success, helped Mrs. Palmer to articulate the source of her anxieties and begin to take steps to overcome these obstacles. We will discuss our interventions with Mrs. Palmer later in this chapter.

Identifying Our Islands of Competence

As we examine the mindset of resilient people in terms of their attributions or assumptions about success, it is important to emphasize a metaphor we use in our work: *islands of competence*. Resilient individuals never minimize or deny their problems and can identify their islands of competence, or strengths. These islands serve as sources of satisfaction and pride, especially when we assume personal responsibility for fortifying these islands and when significant people in our lives demonstrate appreciation for our accomplishments. As we witnessed with Mr. Arsdale, Ms. Baker, and Mrs. Palmer, when we perceive our successes as outside our control, it is less likely that we will be able to identify meaningful islands of competence. In this situation, these islands are similar to mirages in a desert, lacking substance and reality.

Questions to Consider

In Chapter 8 we posed a number of questions for you to consider about the ways in which you understand and respond to mistakes. We have new questions for you to consider relevant to your experiences with success. The more we appreciate the meanings we ascribe to our accomplishments, the better equipped we will be to change any self-defeating patterns of thinking and behaving that might be present in our lives. Respond to the following questions, using the space provided on pages 291–293 in Appendix A. Reflect on your answers before reading further.

- List three islands of competence that you possess.
- How important are these islands to you in terms of your everyday life? (Your response to this question helps you to determine whether what you believe to be your strengths are in fact important areas in your life.)

- Think of three significant people in your life. What would each say about the importance of the islands of competence you have listed? (Your answer to this question assesses whether you believe significant others in your life view your strengths as relevant.)
- List three situations in the past year or two in which you were successful at a task.
- Before you attempted each of the tasks, how confident were you of succeeding? Did your confidence level differ from one task to the next? (Your answer to these two questions allows you to examine the influence of your mindset in determining confidence and performance from one situation to the next.)
- When you experienced success, can you recall how you explained the situation to yourself? (Your response to this question directly assesses your attributions for success.)
- As you reflect on these three situations, did you entertain the same reasons why you succeeded at each? (Understanding your expectations not only provides information about the consistency of your attributions, but also whether particular situations elicit more constructive explanations for success than other situations.)
- How did you react to each situation? (Your answer directly addresses the ways in which you manage your achievements.)
- What memories do you have about how your parents or other important adults in your life handled success? (Your answer to this question provides information about the people who served as your models and examines their influence on your present behavior.)

With your answers in mind, let's examine how these questions aided Mr. Arsdale, the account executive we met earlier in this chapter, to overcome self-doubt and feel comfortable about his achievements.

"A House of Cards"

Mr. Arsdale is similar to numerous people who appear successful to others but experience little satisfaction from their achievements. As he put it, "I know that other people see me as successful and competent, but I certainly don't feel that way. I don't know whether I've ever truly felt capable, even though it may seem that I am."

Before describing our interventions with Mr. Arsdale, we want to address a question we are often asked about individuals like him: "If people have so many self-doubts, how can they continue to be successful in what they do? Wouldn't they eventually give up?" Some do give up and retreat from challenges. However, many others continue to work hard because of internal or external pressures but, sadly, receive little satisfaction even when they succeed. A sense of joy is illusory or transitory at best. Thus, although they may harbor self-doubts, these doubts do not prevent them from engaging in the task at hand; however, when so engaged, they lack the zest or excitement present when one feels a sense of ownership for one's accomplishments.

Mr. Arsdale was in obvious distress when we met him. While the precipitating event was the loss of a major business account, in reality this event was the proverbial straw that broke the camel's back. It triggered a cascade of self-doubt that had been building for years, ready to erupt at any moment. Past successes could not withstand this eruption. Mr. Arsdale sadly noted, "I began to feel that whatever successes I had in the past were like a house of cards that could be swept away at a moment's notice."

Mr. Arsdale painted a portrait of lifelong insecurities. He remembered feeling burdened by low self-esteem from an early age. With some emotion he observed, "I couldn't allow myself to fail. I'm not sure why I put so much pressure on myself, but I did. In comparison with many of my friends, my parents were pretty encouraging, but I had high expectations for myself. My parents even told me that they wished I wasn't so hard on myself. The sad thing is that even when I met these expectations, I wondered whether I could continue to achieve. When things didn't go well, I really wondered how I had succeeded in the past, especially with some of my accounts."

Mr. Arsdale's description of his thoughts and responses captured the basic premises of attribution theory.

We asked, "Can you think of a time you succeeded and felt a sense of accomplishment?"

"If things are going OK for a while, I begin to feel maybe I do have ability, maybe I'm not just lucky. But as soon as there's a setback, like losing an account, all of the self-doubts come back and they stay around for a while. Then it's harder for me to feel any satisfaction when something good happens because I'm already thinking about what might go wrong. Have you ever seen that cartoon with a black cloud always hanging over someone's head? That's what I feel like."

"What do you think when something you do doesn't work out?"

"I feel really lousy, especially if it's something important, which these days has to do with work. But, you know, I can also dwell on a loss in things not related to work, such as a tennis match or a pickup basketball game."

Similar to what we witnessed with Mrs. Palmer, Mr. Arsdale held negative assumptions about failure and success that served to reinforce each other. Each setback prompted him to question his competencies, lessening his feeling of accomplishment even when the outcome was positive. Although Mr. Arsdale possessed some insight into the ways he interpreted mistakes and successes, we thought it would facilitate our interventions to review attribution theory with him. We have discovered that describing this theory in a practical, concrete fashion can be very beneficial. Knowledge of this theory can reinforce a sense of personal control by providing an understanding of one's behavior and feelings. When we are aware of our mindset, we are in a better position to change those features that cause distress.

Mr. Arsdale was fascinated by attribution theory. He jokingly said, "I guess if they have a whole theory about the way I'm thinking, I'm not the only person in the world who thinks this way."

We agreed. We also asked him to consider a number of the questions we posed in Chapter 8 and this chapter. As he reflected on the questions, it became even more obvious to him how quickly he viewed any setback as a testimony to his incompetence and how quickly he dismissed any success as lucky or undeserved.

Mr. Arsdale struggled with the question that asked him to list three of his islands of competence. "I was all set to write 'I am a good husband and father,' but then I wondered whether being a good husband and father is an island of competence."

"Why wouldn't it be?"

"Even though I immediately listed it, I wondered whether islands of competence had more to do with certain achievements, like being good in sports or being a good electrician or being a good salesman."

"Anything can qualify. There's no right or wrong answer. It's what you believe is important. That's why we have a question, 'How important are these islands to you in terms of your everyday life?' Most people would consider being a good husband and father important."

"I know that I work hard on those areas, and I think my wife and kids would agree."

We reinforced the importance of connections as something that gives meaning to our lives. We asked Mr. Arsdale the other two islands he had listed.

"To be honest, I could only think of one other. I've always been pretty good with my hands. As a kid I loved to build things out of wood. Today, I love to build furniture. I just finished a toy chest for my daughter. She loved it and I loved making it." As Mr. Arsdale said this, his entire face beamed.

"If we go back to attribution theory, when you finished the toy chest, what were you thinking and feeling?"

"I was feeling great. I was really proud. In terms of attribution theory, I would say I felt that the toy chest turned out so good because of the time and effort I put in. Also, without sounding immodest, I think I'm pretty good using my hands to build things."

"We bet you are."

"Would you like to see a photo of the toy chest?"

"You carry one?"

"Yes, mainly because of how happy my daughter looks standing next to it."

"We'd love to see it."

Mr. Arsdale took out the photo from his wallet. Although it was a small photo, the look on his daughter's face was clearly one of pure delight, and the toy chest was beautiful.

"You have an adorable daughter and the toy chest you made is very impressive."

Mr. Arsdale was genuinely appreciative of our assessment and simply answered, "Thank you."

"We have an important question to ask you."

"Go right ahead."

"It's obvious that you see yourself as pretty skilled in building things, and from what we've seen you *should* see yourself that way. Here's the question. While building something, have you ever made a mistake or has something not gone as planned?" We asked this question to evaluate whether Mr. Arsdale's attributions for mistakes were less critical and more constructive when engaged in a task in which he felt more self-assured. We were also searching for exceptions to his more negative outlook as a basis for beginning to modify this outlook.

Mr. Arsdale smiled. "I can see where you're going."

We smiled and said, "Maybe we shouldn't have reviewed psychological theories with you."

"Actually, it's a good question. When you're building something, it's not unusual for something not to come out right. I remember one of the first things I built after we were married and had moved into our new house was a bookcase. Nothing too fancy. Somehow I mismeasured the space where I was going to put the bookcase and the bookcase wouldn't fit."

"What happened?"

"I felt foolish. I remember thinking, *How could you not take the correct measurements?* Then I decided I had several choices. I knew that I didn't want to start over because I'd put a lot of work into it. I thought about putting it somewhere else in the house where it might fit, but I really wanted it in the family room. So I decided to take it apart and cut it down to size. It was harder work than I expected. Actually, if I knew how hard it was going to be I might have found another room for it. But when it was done, you would never have known it was cut down."

"Do you have a photo of it?"

Mr. Arsdale smiled and said, "Actually, I do, but not with me."

Becoming more serious, we said, "So there are times when you feel what you have accomplished is a result of your skills and not just luck."

"As we're talking, I guess I would say yes."

"And there are times when things don't go right, you don't automatically question all of your abilities or wonder whether you can correct the situation?"

"Yes, again."

"So one of the things we have to do is apply this more positive attitude to situations such as work."

Mr. Arsdale readily agreed, but added, "But what if you're not as competent at work as you are at building things?"

"That's a good question. If we had a scale to measure competence, it might turn out that you're higher on the scale for building things than when you're involved with work activities. But that doesn't mean you have to be overly critical of your abilities at work when things don't go as well as you would like. Imagine if you put yourself down while building things. You might never have finished the bookcase or the toy chest."

During the next few sessions, our interventions with Mr. Arsdale continued to focus on understanding and challenging counterproductive assumptions. We discussed the importance of examining the possible reasons for losing an account so that he might change his approach in the future. Most important, we emphasized that he should "catch" himself when he began to question whether his accomplishments were deserved and remember that while luck might play some role in any success, ongoing success is based on one's effort and skills.

As we noted in Chapter 2, changing longstanding negative mindsets and scripts is a process that takes time. It is not unusual for self-defeating thoughts and behaviors to reemerge when we face difficult situations and obstacles. For example, Mr. Arsdale was gaining greater confidence and assuming increased ownership for his achievements when he lost another account. Self-doubts about his competencies and past achievements quickly arose. However, given his increased understanding of the assumptions he held about both failure and success, he was able to challenge his negative thoughts and move forward.

Initially, Mr. Arsdale listed only two islands of competence (being a good husband and father, being good at building things), not the three we requested. Eventually, he added a third, which was related to our interventions with him. He said, "I'm not sure this is really an island of competence, but I think I've become pretty good at changing negative scripts." While Mr. Arsdale may have questioned whether this was an island of competence, we felt it was.

Steps to Develop a Resilient Outlook About Success and to Nurture Islands of Competence

Our interventions with Mr. Arsdale were guided by three major steps to help him achieve a greater appreciation for and acceptance of his strengths. The first two steps parallel those that we described in the previous chapter about managing mistakes. As you consider the three steps, reflect on your answers to the questions we raised earlier in this chapter and what measures you might initiate to nurture a resilient mindset.

Step One: Examine Your Assumptions About Success

As we noted when discussing mistakes, we typically do not stop to think about our attributions for success or failure. Yet these attributions or assumptions are influential in determining how satisfied and successful we are. Earlier in this chapter we described a man at one of our workshops who apparently recognized for the first time the ways in which his assumptions dampened feelings of success. He recalled how, as he was striking out the last batter in a Little League contest, he could not enjoy the moment but instead was preoccupied with worries about whether he could repeat his performance in his next game.

The impact of one's attributions was highlighted at a parenting seminar we conducted. A woman in attendance declared that our description of attribution theory "really hit home." She had recently returned to college after dropping out eighteen years earlier. She was forthright in stating that she had left because she thought she was not capable of doing the work. Then, as her children grew up, she felt an urge to return to college part-time.

She revealed, "I was scared, but I said that I would begin by taking one course and see what happens. I took my first test last week and got it back today. I couldn't believe it, but I earned an A–."

We asked, "How did you feel about this grade?"

"The first thing I did was to check to see whether this was *my* test. Then I looked to see whether the professor had added my score correctly. Then I actually said to myself that the professor must have felt sorry for me and given me a better grade. Finally, I said that if this was my test, I was lucky to earn an A–; I probably won't be able to do it again."

"How has the information we've been discussing about attribution theory changed your mindset?"

She said with a smile, "I guess the people who wrote about attribution theory knew all about me. Now I have to work on accepting my successes."

Mr. Arsdale and Mrs. Palmer could not move forward until they were able to examine their perceptions of their successes, perceptions that were riddled with self-doubt and anxiety. Both discovered the degree to which they questioned their competencies, even when successful, wondering whether these past successes were deserved.

What are your assumptions about your accomplishments? To what factors do you attribute your achievements? To help you with this self-assessment, revisit your answers to the questions we listed earlier in this chapter. The following are several simplified versions of these questions:

- Think of a couple of times you succeeded in the past few years.
- What did you tell yourself when this occurred?

- Why do you think you succeeded?
- What was your reaction to your success?
- In what way, if any, did it change your behavior in the future?

"We Lived Comfortably, but We Weren't Comfortable" As we mentioned, Ms. Baker was quick to downplay her accomplishments. Her immediate thoughts when congratulated by coworkers for a successful project were, "I was lucky on this project. I'm surprised it worked. I bet all of my faults will be exposed sooner or later." Although these thoughts were explicit, we were to discover that Ms. Baker did not appreciate their full meaning and the extent to which they influenced her happiness and well-being.

In our first few sessions, Ms. Baker discussed her feelings of unhappiness and observed that "depression runs in my family." When we asked her to elaborate, she said that her mother and father were "gloomy, pessimistic people," as was her brother.

"You could write a book about my family. My parents always seemed to see the glass as half-empty. I promised myself that I would not be the same way. I know that my parents did the best they could and I know they loved me, but my house was not filled with happiness. It's sad, because both of my parents are accomplished people. My mother is a lawyer and my father a businessman. We lived very comfortably, but we weren't comfortable. What I mean is that my parents didn't seem to take comfort in what they had."

"You mentioned that you promised yourself that you would not be the same way. How has that worked out?"

"That's one of the things that brought me in here. I feel I've caught the sadness." Ms. Baker explained that she didn't feel very happy. "I'm thirty-three years old, single, and lonely. I don't feel I've done very much with my life, but when I look at my parents I realize that they don't feel they've done very much with their lives, even though they've been successful."

During the next few sessions we discussed the poignant comment, "I feel I've caught the sadness." As you read Ms. Baker's comments, focus on her interpretation of her success.

"You mentioned that you feel when you achieve something, it's lucky, and that someday your faults will be exposed."

"Yes, that's how I feel. Sounds pretty sick, huh?"

"Have you ever been successful at something that led you to feel satisfied, that you had really achieved something?"

Ms. Baker didn't hesitate. "I don't think so. I told you that I feel I caught the sadness in my family."

"You answered our question very quickly. Just take a moment or two to think about it. Maybe there's never been a time that you accomplished something and felt satisfied, but maybe there's been at least one time."

Ms. Baker thought for a few seconds and responded, "I know that I've been successful at work, but I don't feel successful."

"Why not?"

"I downplay my achievements. Why toot one's own horn?"

"One can feel satisfied without tooting one's horn."

Ms. Baker responded, "I guess you're right."

"But the way you're saying it, you're not certain."

"I'm not."

We observed, "Not only don't you toot your own horn to others, but you seem to feel there's no reason to toot it even to yourself."

"You're right."

"What makes that difficult?" We asked this to help Ms. Baker articulate the struggles she faced in accepting ownership for her success.

"I'm really not sure. I've read some psychology books, so I can say part of it is that my parents weren't models to help me with this. I'm not blaming them, just trying to be realistic."

"Do you know why we're asking you questions about how you experience success?"

"I guess to help me feel better when I am successful."

"Yes, especially because you tend to minimize your contributions. When people do that, sadness will continue."

This dialogue served as the initial foundation for modifying Ms. Baker's assumptions about success. The more able we are to identify these assumptions, the greater the probability of changing them. Ms. Baker was trapped in a family web of unhappiness. Similar to Mr. Arsdale, Ms. Baker and her parents appeared successful to outside observers. However, outward appearance hid an inner sadness and lack of satisfaction that permeated their existence. An appreciation of the influence of mindsets and an identification of the self-defeating beliefs of her own mindset were critical components in Ms. Baker's journey toward a resilient lifestyle.

Step Two: Challenge Self-Defeating Attributions

Once we are aware of the assumptions or attributions that guide our behavior, we must question and challenge those that serve as obstacles to resilience. The following represent a sample of self-defeating assumptions about success that we have heard.

- I was lucky.
- If people knew the real me, they wouldn't congratulate me for what I have done.
- I really don't deserve what I have earned.
- Hard work has very little to do with success. You have to be in the right place at the right time.

We are not denying that there may be some truth to these statements, especially the last; however, to attribute success exclusively to luck or being in the right place at the right time is to deny a sense of personal responsibility. Once this kind of denial dominates our thinking, it is difficult to develop a resilient lifestyle because a major feature of that lifestyle is missing: namely, a feeling of personal control.

Mrs. Palmer's Promotion A seemingly sought-after promotion triggered anxiety in Mrs. Palmer that she did not expect. In our sessions it became apparent that her assumptions for both success and failure served as roadblocks to a feeling of satisfaction and accomplishment. She was burdened by doubts about her capabilities, doubts that were magnified when confronted with the reality of a more demanding, more responsible position.

Our discussions helped Mrs. Palmer identify and clarify these assumptions. She recalled that although she had "relished" the possibility of being promoted to a top position, anxious thoughts crept in, such as, "Slow down. If you do too good a job, they may ask you to move up the ladder and you'll open yourself up to scrutiny." She wondered why she would have such thoughts, especially because her life was characterized by ongoing success and she had a very supportive husband and boss. She also described her parents in positive terms, noting that they were always "encouraging" and "provided me with what I would call unconditional love."

What were the factors that served as a catalyst for Mrs. Palmer's anxiety and fear of both success and failure? There is no easy answer. As we have noted in this book and in *Raising Resilient Children*, the mindset we develop is based on a dynamic, complex interaction between inborn temperament and life experiences. A simple one-to-one relationship between particular childhood experiences or childhood temperament and our adult personality does not exist, especially because an adult personality is not set in stone when a person reaches the age of eighteen or twenty-one. Many experiences await us as adults that will continue to shape our mindset, a situation we vividly witnessed in the last chapter with Mr. Hopkins, who never abandoned his quest to learn to read.

People can grow up in seemingly supportive homes, as Mr. Arsdale and Mrs. Palmer reportedly had, and yet, perhaps because of their temperamental characteristics, be confronted by inordinate self-doubt and self-defeating assumptions. Others can be exposed to parents who were not encouraging and who practiced conditional love, but still enter their adult lives without being hampered by negative self-thoughts.

The insecurity displayed by individuals who grew up in homes with critical, unsupportive parents is easily understandable. However, as we mentioned, others may experience such negative environments without developing self-doubt and self-defeating attributions.

In our work with Mrs. Palmer, we could not pinpoint the roots of her anxieties. Although articulating the causes for our feelings and behavior can permit us to gain a better understanding of why we feel and behave the way we do, which helps us to confront our problems with greater clarity, we do not believe that it is always necessary to possess this understanding to move forward. It is helpful, but not a necessary condition for change. This belief is advanced by Bill O'Hanlon in his book *Do One Thing Different*. As a matter of fact, similar to O'Hanlon, we believe that some therapists may fall into the trap of spending too much time to "uncover" the past and in the process fail to focus adequately on what patients can do in the present and future to change negative mindsets.

We accepted that Mrs. Palmer's experiences with the main figures in her life had been and continued to be supportive. Yet she was currently beset by fears of success that were based, in part, on her feeling that in her new job her skills would be stretched to the limit and her deficits would be exposed for all to see. In answering the questions we raised in therapy, as well as those listed earlier in this chapter and Chapter 8, she became increasingly aware of her attributions, even if she could not understand the basis for their existence. We encouraged her to challenge these self-defeating attributions. In many ways it was easier to accomplish this step with Mrs. Palmer than with other individuals, given her benign upbringing and the many successes in her life.

We asked, "You mentioned that before you received the promotion, you began to think that if you did too good a job, they might offer you the promotion and that the increased responsibilities would open you up to greater scrutiny. But wasn't your work in the company already being scrutinized for them to consider you for promotion?"

"Yes, but the promotion brought more responsibilities, which would have a greater impact on the company. Also, there would be more scrutiny from top management as well as from the many more people who would report to me."

"But in the past, scrutiny of your work led to high praise, not to criticism. Why would you expect it to be different now?"

"As I mentioned, I think having more responsibility for the bottom line—you know, profits—and being more responsible for the performance of more staff."

"But you seem to believe that you're not prepared for these increased responsibilities. Yet, as you described, it's not as if you were being promoted after six months on the job. You've had years of experience in your company preparing you for this." We mentioned this not as an attempt to convince Mrs. Palmer that she could succeed at her new position, but rather to have her begin to question the doubts that were spinning out of control and prompting her anxiety.

"I hear what you're saying, but it's easier said than done."

"We agree. Maybe we can help a little more with this train of thought. What do you see as your islands of competence, especially in terms of your work?"

"I've been thinking of my islands of competence since you first gave me that list of questions. In terms of work, I would say that my strengths are that I consider different alternatives in making decisions about the products we buy and do not act impulsively; that I listen carefully to the input of others; that I don't need to occupy center stage but can share our successes with others; and that I've been told I'm a real 'people person.' I think those would be the main strengths."

We smiled and asked, "What islands of competence do you think you need to be successful in your new position?"

Mrs. Palmer returned the smile and said, "Ah, you psychologists have an interesting way of making a point. I think some of the main skills I listed as my strengths are the skills necessary for success in the position I was offered, but I still wonder whether I can handle it."

We decided to shift focus more directly to her fear of failing and being exposed. We asked, "In your previous positions, did you ever make mistakes?"

"Yes. Some products that I was involved in buying did not sell very well. Also, in my first supervisory position, I think I came across as not decisive enough. I waited too long to make a decision and it increased the anxiety of the two people who reported to me."

"What happened?"

"My immediate supervisor, who was always supportive, gave me feedback about considering options but not delaying making a decision. This particular supervisor really helped me to see how you could balance thoughtfulness with decisiveness."

"So, even with this feedback about your performance, they kept you on the job?"

Mrs. Palmer smiled again. "Yes."

"What about when you bought merchandise that did not sell well?"

"Actually, in that position, my immediate boss made the final decision, not me."

"But did you have some input?"

"Yes."

"What happened?"

"None of us felt great about it, but sometimes you can misjudge a product, even with careful research."

"So some miscalculations about what you buy and sell are part of the territory."

"Yes. It's OK as long as the miscalculations don't take over the entire territory."

"Did they ever for you?"

"No."

"As we're trying to put together all that you've said, your strengths, or islands of competence, seem to be an excellent match with the responsibilities of your new job. Also, some mistakes about the anticipated sale of certain merchandise are to be expected as long as they are kept to a minimum. You've handled feedback in the past very well. All of your previous work with the company has prepared you for the new position. We think it's important to keep these factors in mind as you make your decision about the promotion."

In the next session, Mrs. Palmer noted that her anxiety had decreased. "The moment I begin to get anxious, I think of the questions you asked about how I've dealt with success and failure in the past. I've found that by doing this, my anxiety does not get out of control. I use it as a cue to think differently. I'm actually asking questions like, *What's the worst thing that can happen?* or *Why do I feel I've been successful in the past?* It's helped me to think about these issues."

Mrs. Palmer accepted the promotion. Although we could not predict with certainty that she would be successful in her new position, just as she and her staff could not always predict which merchandise would be profitable, we felt that there was a strong likelihood that she would do well with her new responsibilities. She was well trained, had solid experience, and had skills well matched to those required for the job. In fact, she not only performed well in a senior management position but also reported that this new position brought her much satisfaction. To get to this point, it was necessary for her to understand and challenge assumptions that served as roadblocks to success.

Step Three: List Your Interests and Islands of Competence and Pursue Them

This step is closely related to our discussion in Chapter 6 about accepting oneself and living a more authentic life. You might wish to review that chapter as you identify your islands of competence and consider the degree to which you expend time and energy with these islands. In Chapter 6, we asked you to consider the following questions:

- List two or three activities that you enjoy doing.
- How frequently do you engage in these activities?
- List several areas that you believe represent your strengths.
- How important are these strengths in terms of your daily routine? (We noted that if people perceive their strengths as unrelated to their daily existence, they are unlikely to feel competent and

successful. We might add that if significant others in our lives do not perceive our strengths as very important, it may dampen our enthusiasm for these strengths.)

- List three or four short-term or long-term expectations or goals you have for yourself.
- How do these goals relate to what you perceive to be your strengths and weaknesses?
- Next to each goal, list what steps you have taken to achieve that goal.

Earlier in this chapter we asked you to reflect on the following questions, which overlap with those listed in Chapter 6:

- List three islands of competence that you possess.
- How important are these islands in terms of your everyday life?
- Think of three significant people in your life. What would each say about the importance of the islands of competence you have listed?

It was easier for Mrs. Palmer to accept the promotion that had been offered when she recognized that her strengths dovetailed with the requirements of her new position. A prominent part of our intervention with Mr. Arsdale was to focus on his perceived islands of competence. We were able to use one of these islands, his love of building things, as an avenue to discuss and overcome his negative reactions to setbacks at work and in other arenas of his life.

If we are to feel a sense of pride and ownership for our successes, we must engage in those activities that represent our interests and islands of competence. This statement should not be interpreted to imply that we are recommending people avoid all other activities. Not only would this be impossible to do, but it would lead to a narrow lifestyle characterized by a constant retreat from challenges. If we are to be resilient we must occasionally confront areas that do not represent our strengths. We may find that with practice and perseverance, areas of vulnerability may be transformed into islands of competence, as Mr. Hopkins and Mrs. Norwood discovered.

In reality, it is easier to confront and manage our vulnerabilities when we also spend time involved in activities that represent our interests and strengths. Involvement in these activities not only nurtures a feeling of emotional and physical well-being, but it also reinforces a sense of ownership and personal control for success. These are significant components of a resilient mindset. Fortified by experiences of success and a belief in personal control, we are much better equipped to deal with life's hardships and setbacks.

There may be times when what we have designated as our islands of competence are not seen in a positive way by significant others in our lives. We should not ignore what others think, nor should we immediately abandon those areas that bring us a feeling of satisfaction and accomplishment. Instead, we should consider the input of these significant others in making possible adjustments to our lifestyle. To take a simple example, if playing golf is an island of competence but leads to a great deal of time away from one's family, one need not give up golf, but simply lessen the amount of time consumed by this activity. A resilient lifestyle is a balanced lifestyle.

We have discovered in our clinical practice and workshops that many people become so preoccupied with problems and negative thoughts that they neglect their islands of competence. They report that their interests and strengths, such as exercising, playing a sport, reading for pleasure, spending time with their children, painting, or doing charitable work, are pushed to the background when they are beset by problems. However, it is precisely when we are confronted with difficulties that we must be increasingly vigilant to balance our lives and ensure time for activities that bring us pleasure and a sense of accomplishment. If we wear blinders that allow us to focus only on problems, we will restrict those experiences that bring us enjoyment and add to our sense of personal control. In such a scenario, we are likely to become trapped by a lack of authenticity and feelings of dissatisfaction that affect all areas of our life.

Concluding Thoughts About the Experience of Success

In this chapter we detailed the importance of success and accomplishment in leading a resilient life. However, we must not forget that it is our interpretation of success that determines its impact. Consider the many questions we posed as you reflect on your life. If you tend to view your achievements simply as good fortune or if you fail to build on your islands of competence, the experience of success will be compromised.

Different people have different islands of competence. We have learned that whatever these islands are, if they represent our passions and we pursue them with a sense of empowerment and joy, our lives will be infused with meaning and authenticity. With this in mind, we would like to end this chapter with Ralph Waldo Emerson's view of success. As you read his words, consider how you would define success and whether the activities in which you engage are in concert with your definition of success.

> *To laugh often and much;*
> *To win the respect of intelligent people and the affection of children;*
> *To earn the appreciation of honest critics and endure the betrayal of false friends;*
> *To appreciate beauty, to find the best in others;*
> *To leave the world a bit better, whether by a healthy child, a garden patch or a redeemed social condition;*
> *To know even one life has breathed easier because you have lived.*
> *This is to have succeeded.*

For us, Emerson has captured the mindset and lifestyle of resilient people.

10

Developing Self-Discipline and Self-Control

Know prudent, cautious self-control is wisdom's root.

ROBERT BURNS

Self-control is a cornerstone of a resilient lifestyle. It is a skill that develops gradually from childhood and affects all avenues of our lives. Each problem we solve, each decision we make, each interaction we have, each display of emotion involves the presence of self-control to some extent. Unfortunately, many people struggle with this component of a resilient mindset, as is evident in the following examples.

"I Was Just Trying to Emphasize a Point"

Tyler Easton, a forty-year-old insurance salesman, called us at the recommendation of his office supervisor. His supervisor had received several complaints about Mr. Easton's approach with prospective clients, one describing him as "rude" and "heavy-handed." Another was so annoyed with Mr. Easton's behavior that he wrote to the supervisor, "I would never consider buying a policy from Mr. Easton. He wouldn't get off the phone, even when I politely told him that I was already working with an insurance agent I respected. When I said this to Mr. Easton, he actually yelled, 'Just because you've been working with someone for years, doesn't mean he's doing the best job for you!' At that point I hung up. Much to my amazement, he called back and told me that I was hurting my future and my family's future by not listening to him. I hung up again, and thankfully he didn't call back."

When confronted by his supervisor with these complaints, Mr. Easton said, "Being an insurance salesman is a tough business. Most people don't understand what's in their best interest. I was just trying to make the point that they would do well to listen to me. I may have gotten a little loud, but I was just trying to emphasize a point." The supervisor told Mr. Easton that being a good salesman did not entail "losing your temper or being rude" and that he needed help with his temper.

During our first session with Mr. Easton, he said he didn't need to see a therapist. "I'll tell you who should be coming in to see you, the people who lodged the complaints against me. Sometimes people don't know what's good for them and they need people like me to help them. I agreed to see you because my supervisor suggested it. I was concerned that if I didn't make an appointment it could jeopardize my job."

In our interview with Mr. Easton we learned that his first marriage ended in divorce and his second wife was considering divorce. Each marriage had produced one child. Mr. Easton did not often see his older child, a ten-year-old boy, because his first wife had moved to the Midwest.

When we asked him why he thought both of his marriages were problematic, he responded, "My first wife felt I was too impulsive. She accused me of making decisions without consulting her. She said that I lost my temper a lot. I don't agree. I think she's such an indecisive person that she would view anyone acting decisively as being impulsive. What she called losing my temper was just my trying to emphasize a point."

When asked about the shakiness of his current marriage, Mr. Easton said, "The big mistake I made was to marry a second wife who is just like my first wife. She has some of the same complaints. It's almost like my present wife consulted with my first wife. I hear the same things. 'You don't stop and think. You make rash decisions. You lose your temper too often.' It would be nice to meet a woman who understands me."

We will return to Mr. Easton later in this chapter.

"It's Not Really Me"

Arlene and Mason Berkley, both thirty-six years old, came to see us because of "family issues." The main issue was Mrs. Berkley's response to their two sons, ages six and nine. Mrs. Berkley said, "They're good kids, but I lose my temper with them a lot over silly things. If they haven't picked up their toys, I begin to shout and yell. A couple of weeks ago, I actually picked up one of their toys and threw it against the wall. I don't know why I can't control myself better. When I do these things, it's not really me."

We wondered, "Not me?"

"No. I feel I'm really a kind person, so when I do these things, it's out of character."

"What do you think contributes to your being out of character?"

"I don't know."

"Does it happen at times that don't involve your two sons or is it just with them?"

Mrs. Berkley glanced at her husband and then said, "As Mason can tell you, it happens with other people and in other situations."

Mr. Berkley observed, "It's difficult to have any kind of conversation with Arlene. Soon she's yelling and screaming. Almost anything can set her off, especially if she feels you don't agree with her or listen to her. I know that she keeps saying 'It's not really me,' but these aren't isolated incidents. They occur all of the time and I think they're getting worse. Arlene can be very kind and thoughtful, but these outbursts are really her. If they really weren't her, they wouldn't be happening so often."

We will return later to our work with the Berkleys.

Being Loud or Having a Tantrum?

In a consultation we did with a business firm, we were asked to focus on one particular department with a high turnover rate. In exit interviews, several departing staff described the manager of the department as "angry," "easily upset," "unpredictable," "scary," and "a yeller." One person said, "You never know what to expect. One moment he can be charming and calm, and then if something doesn't go right he loses it. He can be abusive."

These comments prompted the consultation. Current staff confirmed what departing staff had observed. This manager's interpretation of the situation was similar to what we had heard from Mr. Easton; he tended not only to dismiss the staff's complaints but actually to blame them for his behavior, with such statements as "If they did what they were supposed to, I wouldn't have to be so loud in motivating them." He used the word "loud," while his staff described the same behaviors as "temper tantrums" and "abusive." His company placed him on probation, and when things did not

improve they dismissed him. When he left, he accused his staff of con-
ducting a "witch hunt."

Self-Discipline, Self-Control, and Resilient Mindsets

Mr. Easton, Mrs. Berkley, and the department manager shared at least one
characteristic in common: they all had difficulty with self-discipline and self-
control, a vital component of a resilient mindset. Research indicates that
from an early age, self-control is a necessary skill for success in all arenas of
life.[1] Daniel Goleman and his colleagues have highlighted *self-management*
as a key feature of emotional intelligence and effective leadership.[2] Within
the rubric of self-management they describe such features as *emotional self-
control* (keeping disruptive emotions and impulses under control), *transparency* (displaying honesty and integrity), and *adaptability* (flexibility in
adapting to changing situations or overcoming obstacles).

Goleman's emphasis on self-control, or self-management, is justified.
When people lack self-control, they typically

- act before they think,
- fail to plan ahead,
- have difficulty regulating the expression of their emotions,
- do not anticipate consequences,
- possess a distorted view of personal control, and
- have an impulsivity that interferes with empathy and satisfying
  relationships with others (because taking the perspective of another
  person requires reflection).

Given these circumstances, it is difficult for people struggling with self-
discipline or self-control to develop and maintain a resilient life.

Psychiatrist Joseph Strayhorn notes, "Self-control problems do not con-
stitute any one psychiatric disorder but are a central component of many of
them. . . . A very large amount of suffering could be relieved if there were
efficacious methods to increase self-control skills, widely applied."[3]

Balance, Not Overcontrol

Before proceeding, we should emphasize that any positive characteristic
taken to an extreme can lead to negative outcomes. Thus far, we have

focused on a lack of self-control as detrimental to one's physical and emotional health; the other extreme, excessive self-control, is also harmful. If people have difficulty arriving at a decision; if they constantly ruminate and second-guess themselves; if they fear spontaneity, always finding refuge in the same predictable routine even if that routine is not very satisfying, then they are also restricting their happiness and their possible accomplishments. As Strayhorn emphasizes, "Obviously not every decision to delay or forgo gratification is a good one. Miserliness, puritanical sexual joylessness, workaholism, overexercise, and anorexia nervosa may be conditions representing overavoidance of certain types of pleasure."[4]

Throughout this book we have highlighted the importance of leading a *balanced* life. When applied to the concept of self-control, balance implies that people are using problem-solving skills and setting realistic limits on their behavior without placing themselves in an emotional straitjacket.

Questions to Consider

In helping you to assess how you fare in the dimension of self-discipline and self-control, we have listed a number of questions for you to reflect on. Some of the questions, especially those dealing with establishing short-term and long-term goals, touch on the steps we outlined in Chapter 2 for changing negative scripts. This is not surprising because the various components of a resilient mindset are not isolated, but rather interact with each other. Before reading beyond this section, consider and respond to the following questions that appear on pages 293–295 in Appendix A.

- List a couple of important decisions you have made in the past year.
- When you made these decisions, did you define both short-term and long-term goals? (Your answer to this question helps you to determine whether your decisions and actions are guided by clearly articulated objectives.)
- If these decisions involved interactions with other people, did you consider how they would respond to your words and actions? Did the way you communicated and acted increase the likelihood of these other people understanding and responding constructively to your point of view? (These questions are similar to those pertaining to empathy that we raised in Chapter 4. They provide a glimpse into how reflective and empathic you are.)

- Did you think about several possible alternatives when making these decisions? (Your response to this question offers information about whether you consider more than one solution.)
- Looking back at the decisions you made, would you change them in any way? (Your answer helps you to assess whether you use past decisions to guide your future behavior. If so, it indicates the extent to which you are learning from past experiences and displaying self-control.)
- In the past year or two, have there been any occasions when you feel you have acted without considering the consequences? If so, why do you think this occurred? (Your response to these two questions helps to define whether you have difficulty at times with self-control and under what circumstances these difficulties emerge. It helps you to assess the degree to which you are consistent across a wide spectrum of situations.)
- Think about two situations you encountered that elicited strong emotions in you: one in which you believe you expressed these emotions in an appropriate and effective way, and one in which you did not. What was the difference between the two situations? (Answering this question helps you to define conditions that either contribute to or lessen your self-control.)
- Do you feel that you have difficulty making decisions? Are you hesitant to make decisions or take certain action? If so, why might you be hesitant? (These questions focus on whether you may demonstrate too much control, often fearful of leaving your comfort zone or making mistakes.)

Returning to Mr. Easton

As you reflect on your answers to these questions, let's examine the journey that Mr. Easton embarked on as he attempted to respond to these questions. During our first meeting with Mr. Easton it was evident that he lacked several characteristics of a resilient mindset. A sense of personal control and responsibility was noticeably absent as he cast blame on clients, prospective clients, his ex-wife, and his current wife. He also felt that he was forced to see a therapist, emphasizing that it was not his choice. Not surprisingly, empathy was limited because he failed to consider the perspective of others, constantly attempting to justify his perceptions and actions. He had difficulty accepting setbacks. Finally, his impulsivity and anger bore testimony to a dearth of self-control.

Individuals such as Mr. Easton present several obvious challenges to therapists. Because they are prone to blame others and not accept responsibility for their actions, they see little purpose in speaking with a therapist. Mr. Easton told us that the "overly sensitive" people in his life should be in therapy, not him; basically, he saw himself as well adjusted and he constantly offered reasons to justify his actions. In addition, when people are impulsive and act before they think, they are less inclined to examine their feelings, actions, and coping styles. This self-examination is an important ingredient of therapy. Instead, they are poised to hear any comments about their behavior as criticism, prompting them to become annoyed and disenchanted with the therapist.

We understood that an initial task with Mr. Easton was to create a climate in which he would feel secure enough to reflect on his life without quickly diverting blame to others. In order to accomplish this task, we validated his perceptions and experiences. To validate did not mean to agree with his perceptions but simply to affirm that we understood his point of view. During the first few sessions, whenever he challenged or dismissed criticisms that had been directed at him, we said that we could understand how he could become annoyed when others did not listen to him or when they appeared to be indecisive.

In this initial phase of therapy, Mr. Easton echoed a familiar theme: "It would be wonderful if you could talk with my wife, ex-wife, and dissatisfied clients so that they could see that I'm just trying to be of help and that it's their indecisiveness that has caused the problems." We dealt with his tendency to place the onus for change on others by conveying the message, "It might be helpful if we could change the attitudes of these other people, but we do not have the influence to do so. Instead, we could look at what you might do differently to influence their perception."

When we made this comment, he responded quickly, "Why should I change when these other people are the ones who have to be more reasonable?"

"That might be, but we have to figure out a way for them to become more reasonable. That means that you may have to change your approach."

Mr. Easton responded, "Are you saying I'm the one at fault?"

"We think it might be more useful not to look at the problem in terms of assigning fault but rather in terms of asking the question, *What is it that*

I can do so that I develop better relationships with people in both my personal and professional life? This doesn't mean blaming yourself, but rather taking responsibility for changing things."

These remarks were intended to reinforce a sense of personal control and to change negative scripts, two features of a resilient mindset. By minimizing issues of fault and blame while highlighting personal control, we hoped to help Mr. Easton feel less accused and more receptive to hearing our message. Once he arrived at the point of not equating making accommodations with "giving in" or "being taken advantage of," he was able to contemplate what steps he could take to change things.

As he became less defensive in our sessions, we were able to introduce themes related to his impulsivity, limited self-control, and lack of empathy. We said, "You've mentioned that your wife, ex-wife, and several clients have described you as impulsive and making rash decisions. We know that you haven't seen it that way, but do you think that sometimes, without intending to, you give the impression that you're that way?"

Mr. Easton said, "I can see why they might get that impression, but I feel that I'm responding that way to make a point. I have to do it because too many people are afraid to make decisions."

We challenged this statement with an empathic tone. "You may feel you have to act this way to make a point, but if people are not getting the point, then your approach isn't working. You have to think about what point you're trying to make and how to make it so that other people will understand and respond positively to what you're saying."

Our statement was guided by several objectives, including encouraging Mr. Easton to define his goals and examine his behavior, and reinforcing empathy by having him consider the perspective of others. These are essential qualities of a resilient mindset. We also asked Mr. Easton to consider the questions we posed earlier in this chapter. Our goal was to create a secure platform from which Mr. Easton could begin to change his defensive, impulsive style and recognize that his style contributed to the many problems he faced in his personal and professional life.

Several months after Mr. Easton entered therapy, we had an especially productive session with him.

He said, "A couple of days ago, something happened with my wife that may seem small, but I was really pleased with what she said to me."

"What happened?"

"We needed a new television. In the past I would have just gone out and bought one right away without consulting her. This time I asked whether she would like to go with me to look for one. She was delighted and even did some research in advance about comparable models and prices. We went to a couple of places and looked at several different models. When we discussed what we had seen, I thought for sure that she would be indecisive and we would be debating for months which one to buy. Much to my surprise, it didn't take long for her to offer an opinion."

Mr. Easton added, "I said to my wife that I was really pleased with how quickly we could, or perhaps it would be more accurate to say how quickly *she* could, make a decision. She thanked me and said, 'It was easier for me to make a decision because you took the time to listen to my opinion and not rush ahead and make a decision before I could say anything.' She even told me that it was much more enjoyable to be with me when I didn't rush into things and I actually listened to her. She said that she felt more respected."

Mr. Easton smiled as he said, "And she even had a compliment for you. She said 'Your therapist is doing a good job.'"

We returned the smile and said, "Sounds like your wife has good judgment."

In a more serious vein, we asked Mr. Easton whether he could explain what had helped him to become less impulsive and more reflective. There are a couple of reasons we asked this question. We believe that when people make changes in their style of thinking and behaving, it strengthens their progress if they are able to articulate what has contributed to these changes. The greater their understanding of those factors that lead to increased self-discipline and a more resilient lifestyle, the more likely it is that these factors can be recruited and reinforced every day.

The second reason that prompts us to ask people for their understanding of changes that have taken place in their lives is based on the tenets of attribution theory. If people attribute positive modifications in their lifestyle to luck or chance, or simply to having a good therapist, then they are minimizing their role. It is important to reinforce the belief that they are active participants in changes that transpire in their lives. Certainly it is reasonable for individuals to acknowledge the help of a therapist or others, but if they believe that their success is based solely on the input of their therapist and not on their own resources and efforts, then that therapist has unintentionally failed to promote a more resilient mindset, one permeated with a sense of personal control and personal responsibility. We have frequently reminded our patients of their contribution to a healthier life.

When we asked Mr. Easton whether he could define the changes he had made to display more self-control, he thought for several moments and then offered an impressive observation.

"I think it's several things. Although I didn't want to admit it, I wasn't happy with what I was doing. But it was easier to blame others than to face my own shortcomings. The questions you asked forced me to think about how I made decisions and whether I was as impulsive as my wife and ex-wife had said. I also thought a lot about empathy. I thought about the prospective client who hung up on me when I shouted at him. I put myself in that person's shoes and wondered how I would feel if someone acted the same way toward me."

Mr. Easton hesitated and observed, "I must admit that when I first thought about how I might feel if someone yelled at me, I fell into an old pattern of thinking. I told myself that no one would act that way toward me because I would have listened to what an insurance salesman had to say in the first place. Then I realized that this was just another excuse. In fact, I would also have hung up the phone if someone treated me the way I treated that client. Also, I would have been very angry if I hung up on a person because they were being rude and then they called me back to tell me I was making a mistake. As I'm telling you this, I can't believe that I actually did it. I also can't believe I once felt that I was justified in doing it."

Mr. Easton added, "It's not easy to look at yourself and admit that you have to change. But as you've asked me several times, 'What are the alternatives?' I knew that if I didn't start to change I would probably be faced with a second divorce and I might lose my job. One of the most important steps I had to take was to honestly examine what I was doing and recognize that I had to be responsible for my life. I had to accept what you've called *personal control*. During much of my life I've lacked self-discipline. Even as a child I struggled with this problem in school, at home, and on the playground. I guess I was just born this way. You know, if you behave a certain way for a long time, after a while you just resign yourself to the fact that this is who you are and there is not much you can do about it.

"Throughout my life I've acted rashly without carefully thinking of the consequences. I don't think I ever developed these abilities. Instead, I guess I deceived myself with the message, 'You know what you're doing is right, so just do it, and if it doesn't work it must be someone else's fault.' For a couple of years my parents even had me take a medication. Maybe it helped my behavior. To be more accurate, it seemed to help that my behavior didn't bother others, but it really didn't change the way I thought or felt. After talking to you, it finally dawned on me that I could keep lying to myself, but where would it get me? After a while you have to wonder if so many people are telling you the same thing, is it possible that what they're saying might have some validity?"

Mr. Easton's insight, commitment, and, we might add, courage to accept responsibility for initiating changes in his lifestyle did not occur overnight, and the path toward change was not always smooth. However, even though painful and arduous at times, it was a necessary journey toward a more resilient, satisfying life.

Steps to Achieve Self-Control

Our interventions to help Mr. Easton become less impulsive and more reflective were guided by particular steps. As you read the following descriptions of these steps, consider the extent to which you lead a disciplined life characterized by thoughtfulness and self-control.

Step One: Accept Ownership for Your Behavior

This step was prominently featured in our earlier discussions about the necessity of assuming personal control and changing negative scripts if we are to nurture a resilient mindset and resilient behaviors. Mr. Easton would not have been able to improve his life had he continued to abdicate personal responsibility and blame others for his plight. The same obstacles faced by Mr. Easton were in evidence with many of the other people we have met in this book, including Mrs. Atkins, who feared her mother; Mr. Butler, who blamed his managers for his firm's difficulties; Ms. Nance, who was unhappy with her office environment but failed to take actions to improve it; or Mr. and Mrs. Savin, whose struggles with their son, Wade, to be more responsible initially focused on the changes he must make rather than on what they might do differently so that Wade would be more receptive to them.

Accepting ownership for our actions should not be confused either with blaming ourselves or justifying behaviors that are inappropriate. Acceptance implies that we assume responsibility for our actions. We don't resort to rationalizations such as "He made me get angry" or "She made me lose my temper" or "He was very persuasive, and that's why I did such a foolish thing." While it's true that others will do things that may make us angry, we must recognize that we have choices in terms of how we express anger or any feeling. We have control over whether we lead a disciplined, responsible life. If we do not accept ownership for our behavior, we will face serious roadblocks in becoming resilient.

"My Temper Seems So Out of Character" When we first met Mrs. Berkley, she had difficulty accepting responsibility for her behavior. She was prone to screaming at her two sons and to losing her temper on a regular basis. While she did not deny that she engaged in these behaviors, she pushed aside responsibility with the statement, "It's not really me." In many respects, she cast blame on some unknown entity that was apart from her.

Mr. Berkley challenged his wife's excuse. He told us, "It's difficult to have any kind of conversation with Arlene. Soon she's yelling and screaming. Almost anything can set her off, especially if she feels you don't agree with her or listen to her. I know that she keeps saying 'It's not really me,' but these aren't isolated incidents. They occur all the time, and I think they're getting worse. Arlene can be very kind and thoughtful, but these outbursts are really her. If they really weren't her, they wouldn't be happening so often."

On hearing these words, Mrs. Berkley said, "But I'm really not an angry person. I think I'm kind to others. Mason will tell you that I do volunteer work for the elderly in our town. When I lose my temper, it really isn't who I am as a person."

In listening to Mrs. Berkley's attempt to disown her behavior, one might wonder, "Why can't she just admit that she has a problem with her temper and get help controlling her actions? Her behavior is right out in the open. She's aware that she often loses her temper—why not accept it?"

These are important questions. Many individuals display the same kinds of coping strategies used by Mrs. Berkley. They know that what they are doing is wrong, but they conjure up reasons to justify or excuse their behavior. It represents a form of self-protection. For some, it is protection from the criticisms and possible negative consequences of others. For others, it is primarily protection from straying from one's inner set of values. If we see ourselves as kind and giving, it is painful to confront what we might consider our "dark side." While minimizing or dismissing our responsibility for certain behaviors may bring temporary relief, the distress and pain continue to fester, ready to burst forth at any moment.

We were reasonably certain that Mrs. Berkley's assertions that "it's not really me" and "it's out of character" served as a protective shield. We also knew that in order for her situation to improve, she would eventually have to lower her shield and confront her problems. However, we knew that we could not expect Mrs. Berkley to abandon a lifelong shield unless she felt safe.

Given these considerations, we said to her, "Sometimes people can be very kind and helpful, yet have trouble with their anger for different reasons."

While this observation may seem obvious, we thought it was important to state as an initial step in helping Mrs. Berkley to realize that we were not being judgmental or accusatory and that she could feel secure in our presence.

Mrs. Berkley nodded and we added, "What we find can be helpful is to understand why even kind people might lose their temper and, even more important, how they can find better ways to express their anger." This statement was intended to convey the notion that we all get angry at times, but what is important is the way we express this anger.

Mr. Berkley glanced at his wife. She didn't say anything. After a few more moments, we asked what they were thinking.

Mrs. Berkley answered, "I'm not sure. I know I'm not happy with myself when I yell. I know it hurts the kids. I tell them I'm sorry, but I realize that just saying you're sorry without changing what you're doing is not enough. Also, I sometimes blame them. I tell them that if they listened to me I wouldn't have to yell."

She looked at her husband and said, "I'm certain Mason is tired of my yelling."

"I am. It's very upsetting. I just don't know what to do. I love Arlene, but the tension in the household can be unbearable. When she yells I wish there was something I could say or do that would help, but I'm at a loss to know what it might be. Lately, I find the best thing to do is just walk away, but I know that's just a temporary solution."

We looked at Mrs. Berkley. "You said that you weren't happy with yourself when you yelled. You also mentioned that when that happens, it's not really you. Yet your husband feels it happens so often, that it is a part of you. What do you think?" We posed this question to facilitate our goal of helping Mrs. Berkley to accept ownership for the way in which she managed her anger.

"It's hard for me to say this. I want to see myself as a kind, understanding person. I try to act that way, but sometimes I can't seem to control myself. That's why I said that when I lose my temper it seems so out of character."

We wondered, "Out of character in terms of the way you would like to see yourself?"

"Maybe that's a better way of understanding things."

"What we're going to say may seem paradoxical. The more you can accept your temper as part of yourself and not as something out of character, the better chance you'll have of changing it."

"What do you mean?"

"When people behave in a way that seems to go against how they see themselves or their values and then say 'It's not me' or 'It's out of character,' they're basically excusing their behavior. When you excuse behavior, it can keep you from trying to change it. But when you don't excuse it, when you can say 'I behaved in a way I don't want to behave,' then you can focus on changing it."

"That makes sense. It seems like something any intelligent person would know. I wonder why I haven't thought about what you just said."

"Why do you think you haven't?"

"I'm not sure. Without thinking too deeply about it, I would say that when you act in a way that you don't feel is right or that might get you in trouble, it's easier to say it's not you. Then you don't have to feel as bad about having done it. However, as you pointed out, making excuses doesn't solve the problem."

"You've just done a good job of explaining why many people make excuses for their behavior. It's not easy to acknowledge that we've been doing things that go against our values. It actually takes a lot of courage, but it's a necessary step to change."

Mrs. Berkley looked at her husband. "OK, Mason, if I ever say 'It's really not me,' just remind me that it is me."

Mr. Berkley answered, "Oh, I will, but I'll always say it in a nice way."

Mrs. Berkley asked an important question: "But how can I stop losing my temper? What can I do not to yell?"

The answers to her question reside in Step Two.

Step Two: Think Before You Act—Become a Proactive Problem Solver

Most likely, we all have occasionally acted without thinking. At times it may be adaptive to do so, such as when we instinctively jump out of the way of an oncoming car. At other times no harm is done by an impulsive action. However, as we have witnessed with Mr. Easton and Mrs. Berkley, to act without thinking often results in negative consequences. A lack of self-control weakens a resilient lifestyle. Rather than being masters of our destiny, we fall prey to forces that work against personal control.

If we are to minimize being at the mercy of strong emotions and impulsive behavior, we must build into our everyday lives a problem-solving mentality, similar to what we outlined in Chapter 2 when we described strategies for overcoming negative scripts. The parallels between developing realistic self-control and changing negative scripts are to be expected, for they share many features in common. Negative scripts represent repeated actions that are counterproductive and sustained by a mindset in which there is limited reflection, thoughtfulness, or spontaneity. Problems with self-control are also rooted in a lack of reflection and spontaneity, whether taking the form of impulsivity or indecisiveness.

In Chapter 2 we described the following sequence for changing negative scripts once these scripts have been identified (identifying negative scripts is similar to the first step we defined in this chapter—accepting ownership for one's behavior). You might wish to review the problem-solving sequence we described in Chapter 2. The same sequence can be applied to becoming more reflective and less impulsive.

- Articulate your goals: what do you want to achieve?
- Consider a number of new scripts.
- Select the script with the greatest probability for success and define the criteria to assess its effectiveness.
- Consider possible obstacles to success.
- Perform the new script and judge its effectiveness.
- Modify or change the script if it proves unsuccessful.

Following this sequence will help to build or restore a more disciplined, resilient lifestyle. We will illustrate its use with Mrs. Berkley.

"How Can I Stop Losing My Temper?" Once Mrs. Berkley could accept rather than excuse her struggles with self-control, she placed herself in a position to consider what she might do to change her usual style of dealing with stress and anger. We not only described this problem-solving sequence to her, but we also asked her to think about several of the questions listed earlier in this chapter, especially the following two:

- In the past year or two, have there been any occasions when you feel you have acted without considering the consequences? If so, why do you think this occurred?
- Think about two situations you encountered that led you to have strong feelings: one in which you feel you expressed these feelings in an appropriate way, and one in which you did not. What was the difference between the two situations?

At our next session, Mrs. Berkley said that attempting to answer these questions was very revealing. "I immediately thought about two occasions when I got angry with my kids. Both involved their not listening to me when I asked them to clean up. Once was the time I mentioned to you when I actually threw one of their toys against the wall. The other time I was calmer and told them if they didn't put their toys away, they would not have them to play with the next day. They actually listened to me more when I didn't yell."

"Why do you think you had a different reaction on the two occasions?"

"The answer's really simple. The time I behaved more rationally, Mason's parents were over, and I didn't want to look like a raving fool in front of them."

"So you were able to keep from screaming and throwing things?"

"Yes."

"Which means that part of you stopped long enough to consider the possible consequences of screaming and shouting at your kids in front of your in-laws." We said this to emphasize that under certain conditions Mrs. Berkley showed greater control. We recognize that most people will refrain from saying certain things to their children or spouse when "outsiders" are present. Our intent in offering this observation to Mrs. Berkley was to reinforce her ability to display greater control.

"Yes."

"Is that usually the case?"

"What do you mean?"

"Do you usually show more control or handle your anger better when people who are not in your immediate family are present?"

"Yes, but don't most people do that?"

"Yes, but there are some who don't, so it's a good sign that you were able to control yourself in front of your in-laws."

"I'd like to be able to control myself even when my in-laws or others aren't around."

We wondered, "Can you think of a time you were able to control yourself without other people being around?" We were looking for possible "exceptions" to her usual behavior.

"I'm not sure."

Mr. Berkley said, "I remember a couple of months ago when our kids were acting up and it seemed like you were ready to scream. Instead you said that you needed a time-out and went to our bedroom. The kids were stunned and they actually stopped acting up."

Mrs. Berkley smiled. "I remember that. Actually, I had been listening to some talk show on TV and a psychologist was discussing discipline. He said that if you feel you're getting too angry, rather than take it out on your kids or your spouse or even someone at work, it might be best for you to take a time-out. So I did. I told my kids that I was really angry and ready to do something that I didn't really want to do, so instead I was giving myself a time-out to calm down."

"From what you said, it seemed to work."

"Yes."

"Have you done it again?"

"Not really."

"How come?"

"I don't know. When I was doing it, it seemed a little foolish. I felt like I was acting like a little kid. I mean, what kind of mother gives herself a time-out?"

"It sounds like a mother who's trying to show more restraint and have her kids listen to her. We all need to think about different options to handle situations. The more options we can choose from, the less likely we will act in an impulsive, out-of-control way."

The session was almost over. We said, "Before our next meeting it might be helpful to think about the sequence of steps we outlined for solving problems. Whether you realize it or not, you've already used parts of the sequence."

Mrs. Berkley seemed surprised. "I have?"

"Yes, by restraining yourself when your in-laws were visiting or by taking your own time-out."

"I hadn't really thought about that."

At our next meeting, Mr. and Mrs. Berkley reported that they had "spent hours" discussing the problem-solving sequence as well as the other questions we raised.

Mr. Berkley said, "We really did our homework."

We smiled, "What good students. What did you learn?"

Mrs. Berkley answered, "We talked a lot about our goals and what we wanted for our family. We looked at our relationships with the kids and our relationship with each other. We talked about some difficult things. As we did, we thought about the discussion we had in here about being empathic. It was helpful to keep in mind the other person's perspective, and I know that when I said something to Mason, I asked the question you suggested we always keep in front of our minds, *Would I want anyone to speak to me the way I am speaking with Mason?* Our discussion really helped."

"In what way?"

Mr. Berkley answered, "We talked about defining our goals, both short-term and long-term, and what we wanted in our relationship with each other and with the kids. I don't know whether we've ever had a conversation like that before. We know that there are going to be some difficult moments, but one of our goals was to be able to express what we want in a way that is not critical or judgmental or filled with such strong emotion that all you hear is the emotion and not the message. We felt if we could do that we would achieve the longer-term goal of having a calmer, less hectic, less angry home."

"Those are very important goals."

Mrs. Berkley said, "We think so."

"So, getting to the next part of the sequence, what would one possible new script look like?"

Mrs. Berkley answered, "At first, we were a little too vague or too one-sided in our discussion. What I mean is that we focused only on what not to do. We talked about not yelling at each other or not yelling at the kids.

Then we realized that other, more positive steps should be involved. We discussed expressing more appreciation to each other and to our kids when things went well. As you said in here once, 'Catch people doing something good.' We also talked about listening to each other and, if we disagree—and I know this is more my problem than Mason's—not to lose our temper."

Mrs. Berkley continued, "I've always had a problem with my temper, especially when I feel people aren't listening to me. I'm not sure where that comes from, but it's a part of me that I realize I have to change." This was a dramatic indication that Mrs. Berkley was assuming greater responsibility for her behavior rather than blaming others or excusing her actions.

"Did you discuss different options for dealing with frustrating situations?"

Mrs. Berkley answered, "Yes, but we also talked about why we get so angry in the first place. Actually, because Mason is much more even-tempered than I am, I think most of the discussion was about what got me so angry and why these things got me so angry."

Mr. Berkley said, "But I also had to look at things that got me angry. It was a joint project." The empathy and understanding conveyed in this brief statement were very apparent.

Mrs. Berkley said, "I appreciate your saying that, Mason. I've been doing a lot of thinking about my reactions to things. Rationally, I shouldn't get so angry with my kids if they don't immediately put away their toys or listen to what I have to say. But I just seem to lose it. I know that when they don't listen, I feel I'm losing control of the situation and I feel I have to gain control."

"What do you mean when you say you feel like you're losing control of the situation if your kids don't immediately listen to you?"

"This may sound silly, but I think that if they don't listen to me about putting their toys away, they won't listen to me about anything. Don't you think that kids should help out and put their toys away?"

"Our quick answer is that we feel kids should be responsible for cleaning up and putting things away that they've taken out. But the key question is how to encourage them to do so without yelling."

Mrs. Berkley offered a very perceptive observation that reflected several remarks we had made in earlier sessions: "I just realized something. I told you that I lose my temper because I don't want to lose control of my kids.

But by losing my temper I *am* losing control. That seems so obvious, but I never thought about it that way before."

"That's a very insightful remark. Now what we've got to figure out is what a new, more effective script would look like. You've already started to write it. You mentioned focusing on the positive and catching your kids when they do help out. You'll find that's one of the best ways to teach kids and help them develop self-control. However, even if you become more positive, there will be times when your kids still might not listen. Think about how you might react." We asked this to prepare the Berkleys for the obstacles that they would face in the process of changing their scripts.

Mrs. Berkley answered, "I was thinking about how I don't yell when Mason's parents are visiting. Maybe I should make-believe that Mason's parents or other people are there."

Mr. Berkley smiled and said, "That's an interesting technique. I know that something that has helped me is the time-honored strategy of counting to five or ten before saying anything so that I have a little time to think about what I'm going to say or do."

Mrs. Berkley said, "I've tried that, but found that although it may work the first time, if the kids still don't listen I lose it. I know I start to feel that the only way they'll listen is if I yell."

"If you count to ten and the kids don't listen the first time you ask, you might think of what else you can do. Earlier you mentioned another strategy you used that worked, but you didn't continue using—taking a time-out. The more strategies you have available, the more likely it is that you will remain in control."

"If I could just remember to use them."

"In our experience, the more you use these kinds of strategies the easier it becomes to remember to use them. This doesn't mean that you won't lose your temper again, but it should occur less and less."

In the months ahead, Mrs. Berkley rewrote her script. She began to use the strategies we discussed in our meetings. Mr. Berkley was very supportive of his wife's efforts. With each success, Mrs. Berkley attempted new strategies. For example, she found that giving her kids a choice of cleaning up by themselves or having her help them was very effective. "They often chose to have me help them clean up, but I didn't mind, especially because they also cleaned up."

With each new strategy, Mrs. Berkley's stance as a proactive problem solver solidified. It is a sign of self-control when one becomes proactive rather than reactive. It is also a sign of a resilient approach to life.

Step Three: Be Consistent, Not Rigid

Self-discipline or self-control that is associated with a resilient lifestyle is characterized by consistency over time and in different situations. When we first met Mrs. Berkley, she demonstrated self-control with her children in the presence of her in-laws but not in their absence. Consistency was lacking.

One source of inconsistency is arbitrariness. We often witness this in people whose mood on a particular day determines their behavior and their level of self-control. Their response to similar situations varies based on how they are feeling at the moment rather than on the reality of the situation.

This scenario was evident with Russ Needham, a thirty-five-year-old manager of an auto parts store. He came to see us after a couple of incidents, one in which he had berated one of his employees in front of other employees for a seemingly minor error, and another in which he had slapped his eight-year-old son for not coming down immediately to dinner when he was called.

Mr. Needham said, "I think I'm losing it. One day I'm fine, and the next I lose my temper."

We asked Mr. Needham to elaborate on his statement.

"Take my slapping my son. He's the kind of kid who gets really involved with different activities. It's hard for him to break away from something, whether he's playing a video game or drawing a picture or building something with Legos. I know that. When I'm feeling in a good mood and he doesn't come down for dinner, I will go up and calmly remind him that he can return to what he's doing after dinner. When I'm not feeling stressed, I even remember to tell him about ten minutes in advance that he will have to come down for dinner, which also helps.

"The same is true at work. When I yelled at my employee, there was no reason for me to handle it that way. I should have spoken to him calmly and by himself. I embarrassed him, but I embarrassed myself even more."

As we worked with Mr. Needham, it became increasingly evident that he was vulnerable to both depression and anxiety. Not surprisingly, on those days in which his mood was more upbeat, he demonstrated compassion and self-control. However, when feeling anxious or sad, he could respond angrily and impulsively to the same situation in which he had acted calmly the previous day. To the people in his life, his behavior was arbitrary and puzzling. They didn't know which Mr. Needham would show up.

Given the intensity of these shifts in mood, we recommended a medication consultation, which resulted in his being treated with an antidepressant. In addition to the medication, Mr. Needham continued in psychotherapy with us. We used the problem-solving sequence listed in Step Two to reinforce a more structured, consistent approach to leading a self-disciplined life. The combination of medication and psychotherapy served to help Mr. Needham remain more even-tempered and to become more consistent and less arbitrary in his response to a wide range of situations.

Consistency should not be mistaken for being rigid or refraining from spontaneity. As we noted earlier in this chapter, resiliency involves a balanced life. Self-control involves flexibility, not impulsivity or rigidity. To quote psychiatrist Joseph Strayhorn again, "Obviously not every decision to delay or forgo gratification is a good one. Miserliness, puritanical sexual joylessness, workaholism, overexercise, and anorexia nervosa may be conditions representing overavoidance of certain types of pleasure."[5]

People who are burdened by the need to control, who fear spontaneity or change, can engage in the same steps to modify their behavior that we have outlined for those who are impulsive. They must first assume ownership for their behavior and not blame others. Once this step is accomplished they can follow the sequence we described in Step Two that will assist them to become proactive problem solvers. We must remember that changing longstanding patterns of behavior is not easy. It takes time. We must be prepared for setbacks. But the rewards of persevering and reaching a more balanced life are worth the struggles involved in attaining these goals.

Concluding Thoughts: Self-Discipline, Self-Control, and Being True to Our Values

Each feature of a resilient mindset is interwoven with all of the other features. Self-discipline and self-control are tied intimately to leading a balanced life and behaving in ways that are in concert with our goals and values.

When self-control is lacking, we are vulnerable to neglecting our values and priorities, to succumbing to dishonesty, to compromising fulfilling relationships with others, and to displaying behaviors that are not in accord with a resilient mindset. When realistic, flexible self-control is present it is rooted in self-acceptance and represented by behaviors that nurture our life and the lives of those with whom we interact. We might do well to remember the following thoughts of Alfred, Lord Tennyson: "Self-reverence, self-knowledge, self-control. These three alone lead life to sovereign power."

11

The Lessons of Resilience

Maintaining a Resilient Lifestyle

In March 1513, Ponce de Leon set sail from Puerto Rico with three ships in search of the fountain of youth. A Spanish explorer and soldier, he was the first European to set foot in Florida. His search for the legendary spring that gave people eternal life and health led him to a spot along the east coast of Florida. He named the land *Pascua de Florida*, meaning "feast of flowers," because the land was first spotted on Palm Sunday, April 2, 1513. Ponce de Leon did not find the fabled fountain of youth. He returned to Florida in 1521 but was wounded by Native American warriors. He died of his wounds in July of that year in San Juan, Puerto Rico.

Ponce de Leon sought a quality of life that is, as far as we are aware, unattainable. In contrast, the quality of life we describe and advocate in this book—the resilient lifestyle—is attainable, but it cannot be discovered in an eternal spring or obtained through a simple act. As we have emphasized, the process of developing and maintaining the components of a resilient mindset can be fraught with obstacles requiring ongoing commitment and hard work. It is our hope that you have come to realize that, unlike the elusive fountain of youth, these components are tangible and attainable. They can be described, observed, and successfully developed. The more you are aware of the features that nurture resilience as well as the roadblocks to achieving a more satisfying, fulfilling life, the better prepared you will be to promote resilience and stress hardiness within yourself.

In the preceding chapters we described these building blocks of resilience, including communicating effectively, managing stress, developing empathy, accepting oneself and others, dealing effectively with mistakes, and developing self-discipline, self-control, compassion, and islands of competence.

We also posed questions for you to consider as you assess the extent to which you practice a resilient lifestyle.

While we believe the ideas we have conveyed in our book have the intuitive feel of being common sense, an important quality, they are also supported by scientific research. Because this book was not intended as a textbook, we chose to limit the amount of research we reported, confining ourselves to citing a few studies relevant to the content housed in each chapter. However, the work of many other clinicians and researchers served as sources of information for our book.

For example, there are a handful of longitudinal studies that have followed individuals exposed to a variety of childhood risks into their adult lives, identifying the qualities that promote resilience. Many of the longitudinal studies of resilience have involved samples of youth who, as Dr. Emmy Werner has pointed out, have "pulled themselves up by their bootstraps" without the benefit of prescribed intervention.

These studies have included children raised in families with parents who have mental illnesses or substance abuse problems. The research evidence suggests, as we have elaborated in this book, that a common core of individual attributes, socialization, and family and community support acts to help individuals overcome adversity. These factors buffer responses to both constitutional risks in parents, such as alcoholism or mental illness, as well as stressful life events, such as economic hardship.

In their most recent book, *Journeys from Childhood to Midlife: Risk, Resilience, and Recovery*, Emmy Werner and Ruth Smith report the results of forty years of study of a population of children born in Hawaii. They describe five major factors that appear to define good adult outcome:

1. Being employed or enrolled in school and satisfied with work and scholastic achievement
2. Strong relationships with spouses or significant others (this included a long-term, committed marital relationship and satisfaction in parental roles)
3. Positive relationships with parents and siblings extending into adulthood
4. Several close friends who can provide emotional support and affiliation
5. Accurate self-assessment that involved individuals being happy and mostly satisfied with the present state of their lives

Werner and Smith report that when asked about their strengths, resilient men and women focused on similar assets, including compassion and caring, the ability to get along with others, a sense of optimism, a sense of humor, the capacity to plan and solve problems, creativity, and hard work. Many of these individuals came to view the adversities in their lives as important learning experiences that served as challenges to overcome rather than as great tragedies or mistakes from which to suffer. The assets detailed by Werner and Smith parallel our description of resilient mindsets and resilient lifestyles.[1]

In his 1993 book *American Lives: Looking Back at the Children of the Great Depression*, John A. Clausen wrote about the concept of *planful competence*. This concept consisted of self-confidence, intellectual investment, and dependability as the organizing principles in the life course of resilient individuals. Clausen emphasizes that although some qualities, such as level of intelligence, physical attractiveness, or temperament, may represent the luck of the genetic draw, many other protective buffers, such as being raised by caring and supportive adults, learning to manage stress, finding a comfortable niche in life, and learning to communicate effectively, are qualities that can be taught and mastered throughout life. These protective factors contribute to the nurturance of a resilient mindset that flourishes throughout one's life.

One other interesting finding from resilience research is an appreciation for the complexity in predicting outcome. Future research may help us to gain a better understanding of how one protective factor might compensate for the absence of another or, for that matter, balance the scales for exposure to a risk factor. We hope that in reading our descriptions of the lives of many individuals in this book, you have gained a better understanding and appreciation of factors that direct one toward a resilient life.

To mention just a few of these people, reflect on the lives of psychiatrist Viktor Frankl, who found purpose in his existence even while confined in a concentration camp; Stacy Lamsted, the foster mother who learned of the impact that one evening spent in her house had on a teenaged foster child; Melissa Atkins and George Larsen, both of whom displayed the courage to confront abusive parents; Lou Bauer, who brought purpose and passion back to his life as he reminded himself of why he became a teacher; Mark Holland, who escaped a lifestyle in which he felt out of control and that distanced him from his family; Meg, the woman we were fortunate to meet at one of our workshops, who found comfort in her friendships after the death of her son and husband, but gave to her friends as much as she received from them; Jeremy Butler, who assumed increasing responsibility for the events that occurred in his business and personal life rather than blaming others; Peter Hopkins, a man with severe learning disabilities who, with the support of his wife, found avenues for success; and Arlene Berkley, who confronted her anger rather than making excuses for it.

Although these individuals were different in many ways and faced different kinds of challenges, they shared one very important attribute: a willingness to assume personal control of their lives and to change their negative scripts in order to lead a more balanced, satisfying, resilient existence.

Maintaining a Resilient Lifestyle

Throughout this book we have emphasized that developing a resilient mindset and leading a resilient lifestyle take time and energy. It is a lifelong process. We will not wake up one morning and declare, "We have now reached the pinnacle of resilience." Even as we become more skilled in embracing and applying the characteristics of resilience outlined in this book, we must practice these skills on a regular basis lest we fall back to old, self-defeating patterns of thinking and behaving.

We believe that there are questions we can ask ourselves and exercises we can do on a daily basis, as well as guideposts we can reflect on from time to time, to help us maintain a resilient lifestyle. This short-term and long-term self-examination will keep the concept of resilience at center stage, in order that we have a clearer image of our goals and values and the manner in which we pursue our lives.

Exercising Resilience on a Daily Basis

Set aside a few minutes each day for a resilience exercise. It might be the same time each day, but need not be. Whatever works out best in your schedule is what is most likely to succeed. To facilitate this task, we offer the following questions for you to consider. Feel free to create additional ones. These responses need not be written down. As you think about your answers, reflect on what you have read in this book and the questions that appear in Appendix A.

- Have I truly listened during the past day and attempted to understand the viewpoints of others?
- How have I related to others? Have I practiced empathy and respect?
- How have I responded to stress, mistakes, and setbacks? If I am not happy with my response, what will I do differently next time?
- In what areas did I do well? How do I maintain or reproduce these positive behaviors tomorrow?

We believe that spending even a few minutes on a daily basis thinking about these or similar questions will help to fortify and maintain a resilient mindset.

Guiding Principles for the Long Term

It is never too late to develop a resilient mindset and to apply skills necessary for resilience. Just as we have listed questions you can ask yourself on a daily basis, we recommend guidelines that you can consider weekly or monthly as you take a long-term view of your life. These guidelines are related to our daily questions but assume a broader perspective. They represent the features of a resilient mindset that we have articulated in previous chapters.

Revisit the principles of a resilient mindset. Remember, nurturing resilience is a lifelong, open-ended process, one that constantly changes in a dynamic way.

Periodically assess your progress in terms of leading a resilient life. You can facilitate this by engaging in resilience exercises on a daily basis and periodically considering the questions in Appendix A.

Do not wait for other people to change first for you to achieve your goals and happiness. Remember, you hold the key to your changes. You are master of your destiny and must assume personal control for your life. You are the main force responsible for changing any negative scripts that you might possess.

Articulate and evaluate short- and long-term goals that are realistic, achievable, and in concert with your values. Be optimistic, but don't forget that change takes time and cannot be realized overnight.

Anticipate mistakes and setbacks. Be prepared with a backup plan. Remember that mistakes serve as the basis for learning.

Relish your accomplishments. We are not talking about being immodest or bragging, but simply taking credit for your achievements and successes. You deserve to pat yourself on the back for a job well done. Experience the joy of success.

Develop and maintain connections with people, ideals, causes, and faith. In nurturing connections, participate in activities that benefit the lives of others. Be a vital, contributing member of society.

Engaging in daily resilience exercises and reflecting throughout one's lifetime on the assumptions and characteristics that are the underpinnings of a resilient mindset will reinforce an attitude of perseverance, caring, and hope. Such an attitude is essential for your emotional and physical health.

It's Never Too Late: The View from a Northern Exposure

It is never too late to seek and achieve our dreams and change our lives. We have emphasized that doing so requires diligence, time, perseverance, and effort, all of which are rooted in a sense of hope and living a life in concert with one's values. In ending this book, we would like to share with you the life of one woman who captures many of the admirable qualities we have described. Although we did not know her personally, we feel comfortable in assuming that she regularly considered the questions we have posed related to developing and maintaining a resilient mindset. Most likely, if she had read this book, she would have offered us many other questions and insights.

Margaret "Peg" Phillips died in 2002 at the age of eighty-four. Although many people might not know her name, if they saw her photo they would instantly recognize her as one of the stars of the popular TV series "Northern Exposure." Her obituary in the *Boston Globe* illustrated the power of mindsets to determine our behavior.

In an interview she noted, "I never wanted to do anything but act. I wanted to go to the University of Washington drama school, but when I got out of high school, there was no money; it was 1935." Given the reality of the Depression, she moved to California, worked as a bookkeeper and accountant, married and divorced twice, and raised four children mostly as a single mother. For almost fifty years she spent whatever spare moments life afforded her acting in community theater. She retired in the early 1980s, but if she were asked the question, "Is it ever too late?" she would probably laugh and offer a resounding "No."

After her so-called retirement, she returned to the Seattle area and enrolled at the age of sixty-seven at the University of Washington, almost fifty years later than intended. The *Boston Globe* obituary reported, "She acquired an agent in her freshman year. She soon had so much work—radio and television commercials and bit parts in eight movies—that she never had time to finish her degree. She found her signature role in 1990 when she was cast as the gruff but kindly Ruth-Anne in 'Northern Exposure.' Envisioned as a minor recurring role, Ruth-Anne proved to be so popular that after sixteen episodes she became a regular."[2]

In 1993, at the age of seventy-five, she was nominated for an Emmy Award. Her attire at the awards ceremony included blue jeans, a red-and-white checked blouse, suspenders, and sandals. When asked who designed the outfit, she replied, "Me."

Imagine if Peg Phillips could have counseled Ponce de Leon. She would have informed him that the fountain of youth does not reside in an illusory spring of water but rather in the reality of minds filled with dreams and hope, challenges and achievements, and a mindset of attitudes, behaviors, and beliefs that can best be attained through the power of resilience.

It is our wish that this book will help you to harness the power of resilience and develop a mindset that encourages you to plan and dream, to bring joy to others, to laugh, and to appreciate that we are truly the authors of our lives.

Appendix A

Worksheets for Resilient Living

Chapter 2 Changing the Words of Life: Rewriting Your Negative Scripts

List three things in your life that you would like to change. _____

_____

_____

_____

List steps you have taken in the past to make these changes. _____

_____

_____

_____

What did you do if you were unsuccessful initially? _____

_____

_____

_____

Why do you think you were unsuccessful? _____

_____

_____

_____

List three times you have made successful modifications to a script. _____

_____

_____

_____

Explain why you think these modifications were effective. _____

_____

_____

_____

What is a negative script in your life? _____

_____

_____

_____

What are your goals in this situation? _____

_____

_____

_____

What could define a new script? _____

_____

_____

_____

What steps will be required to put the new script into place? _____

_____

_____

_____

What obstacles might interfere with the new script being effective? _____

_____

_____

_____

What is your backup plan? _____

_____

_____

_____

Chapter 3 Choosing the Path to Become Stress Hardy Rather than Stressed Out

Commitment

What are two or three things that give meaning and purpose to your life?

_____

_____

_____

What energizes you? _____

_____

_____

_____

Do the main activities you engage in give meaning to your life? _____

_____

_____

_____

Do you derive satisfaction from each of these activities? _____

_____

_____

_____

Why did you go into your profession? _____

_____

_____

_____

Why did you become a parent? _____

_____

_____

_____

Why did you get married? _____

_____

_____

_____

What satisfactions do each of these activities or roles provide you? _____

_____

_____

_____

What frustrations have been associated with these activities or roles? _____

_____

_____

_____

How do you cope with the frustrations? _____

_____

_____

_____

Challenge

When difficult situations arise, do you become more stressed or do you see
the challenges you can meet? _____

_____

_____

_____

How do you generally cope with difficult situations? _____

_____

_____

_____

Personal Control

List three things in your life that you would like to change. _____

_____

_____

_____

Does someone else have to change before you can make these changes?

_____

_____

_____

Do you have control over the things you would like to change in your life?

_____

_____

_____

Chapter 4 Viewing Life Through the Eyes of Others

How do I hope other people would describe me? _____

_____

_____

_____

How do I interact with these people so that it is likely that they would describe me in this way? _____

_____

_____

_____

How would these other people actually describe me? _____

_____

_____

_____

How do I interact with these people to cause them to describe me in the ways that they do? _____

_____

_____

_____

Is there a significant discrepancy between how I hope people would
describe me and how they actually would describe me? _____

_____

_____

_____

If there is a discrepancy, how can I change my attitudes and behaviors so
that others will begin to describe me in the way I would like to be
described? _____

_____

_____

_____

_____

In anything I say or do, what do I hope to accomplish? _____

_____

_____

_____

Am I saying or doing things in a way that others will be most willing to
listen and respond to me? _____

_____

_____

_____

Am I behaving toward others in the same way that I would like to be
treated? _____

_____

_____

_____

What are two positive interactions you have had with others? _____

_____

_____

_____

What are two negative interactions you have had with others? _____

_____

_____

_____

How did you feel and react in each case? _____

_____

_____

_____

_____

Do you use these interactions and experiences to guide your current behavior? _____

_____

_____

_____

Chapter 5 Communicating Effectively

What are two important situations in which I had to communicate with others? _____

_____

_____

_____

What goal was I attempting to achieve in each of the two situations?

_____

_____

_____

In general, do I say or do things in a manner in which others will be most responsive to what I have to say? _____

_____

_____

_____

Would I want anyone to speak to me the way I speak to others? _____

_____

_____

_____

How would others describe me as I communicate with them? _____

_____

_____

_____

What makes it easiest for me to listen to what others have to say? _____

_____

_____

_____

What do others say or do that turns me off and keeps me from listening to their message? _____

_____

_____

_____

Even if I disagree with someone, do I at least validate his or her point of view? _____

_____

_____

_____

These are goals I would like to accomplish that involve changes I would like to see occur in my life. _____

_____

_____

_____

Have my past communications moved me toward reaching these goals?

_____

_____

_____

Will my planned communications move me toward reaching these goals?

_____

_____

_____

Chapter 6 Accepting Oneself and Others

What words would you use to describe the person you would like to be, or your ideal self? _____

_____

_____

_____

What words would you actually use to describe yourself? _____

_____

_____

_____

How far apart are the words you would use to describe your ideal self and the words you would use to describe your actual self? _____

_____

_____

_____

Describe a time in your life when you believe you came closest to your ideal self. What occurred in this situation that made you feel this way?

_____

_____

_____

Describe a time in your life when you felt far removed from your ideal self. What occurred in this situation that made you feel this way? What, if anything, did you do to change the situation? _____

_____

_____

_____

List two or three goals or expectations that are a priority. For each goal or expectation, list one or two activities in which you engage to achieve that goal. Are there expectations you have for yourself that may be unrealistic?

_____

_____

_____

List three values or priorities in your life that are of greatest importance to you. _____

_____

_____

_____

Is the way in which you conduct your life in accord with these values and priorities? _____

_____

_____

_____

Are there certain feelings you experience more often than others? _____

_____

_____

_____

_____

In what situations do these feelings typically occur? _____

_____

_____

_____

_____

Make a list of different feelings you experience, such as happiness, sadness, anger, or anxiety. _____

_____

_____

_____

Next to each feeling, describe one or two specific situations that prompted you to feel that way. _____

_____

_____

_____

When you experienced the feeling in question, how did you show or deal with it? _____

_____

_____

_____

Describe a couple of times when you felt you did not handle your feelings very effectively. What happened? Why do you think it happened? Did it lead to changes in how you handled these feelings the next time they occurred? _____

_____

_____

_____

Describe a couple of times when you felt you handled your feelings effectively, especially feelings such as anger and frustration. What helped you to handle these feelings effectively? _____

_____

_____

_____

List two or three activities that you enjoy doing. _____

_____

_____

_____

How frequently do you engage in these activities? _____

_____

_____

_____

List several areas that you believe represent your strengths. _____

_____

_____

_____

How important are these strengths in terms of your daily routine? _____

_____

_____

_____

List several areas that you believe represent your vulnerabilities or areas of weakness. _____

_____

_____

_____

How important are these vulnerabilities in terms of your daily routine?

_____

_____

_____

What steps have you taken to strengthen those vulnerabilities that affect your daily living? _____

_____

_____

_____

List three or four short-term or long-term expectations or goals you have for yourself. _____

_____

_____

_____

_____

How do these goals relate to what you perceive to be your strengths and weaknesses? _____

_____

_____

_____

_____

Next to each goal, list what steps you have taken to achieve that goal.

_____

_____

_____

_____

What expectations about yourself or others have you modified in the past year? _____

_____

_____

_____

What led you to modify these expectations? _____

_____

_____

_____

When you do not achieve a goal, what do you usually do? Think of a specific example. _____

_____

_____

_____

_____

Make a list of four or five roles or activities that you believe are most important to you. _____

_____

_____

_____

_____

Next, evaluate whether your behavior is in concert with your priorities.

_____

_____

_____

Chapter 7 Making Connections and Displaying Compassion

Who were the charismatic adults in your life when you were a child or adolescent? _____

_____

_____

_____

What are two or three examples of what these charismatic adults said or did that caused you to consider them to be charismatic adults? ._____

_____

_____

_____

When you were a child or adolescent, were there people who interacted with you in ways that were contrary to the qualities of charismatic adults?

_____

_____

_____

What did these people say or do that disqualified them from being considered charismatic adults? _____

_____

_____

_____

Who are the charismatic adults in your life today? _____

_____

_____

_____

What are the things they say or do that make them charismatic adults?

_____

_____

_____

_____

_____

What people would list you as a charismatic adult in their lives? _____

_____

_____

_____

What do you say or do that would prompt them to call you a charismatic adult? _____

_____

_____

_____

Are there any people who would say that your behavior toward them is contrary to your being a charismatic adult? If so, what would lead them to believe this? _____

_____

_____

_____

If you were encountering some personal difficulties, who are the two or three people you would turn to for help, and why would you feel comfortable turning to them? _____

_____

_____

_____

Who are the people you would not turn to, and why wouldn't you turn to them? _____

_____

_____

_____

_____

Who would turn to you for help and support? Why would they do so?

_____

_____

_____

Who would not turn to you for help and support? Why wouldn't they?

_____

_____

_____

As you think about the quality of your relationships, what are one or two things you might change to feel more connected to others? _____

_____

_____

_____

How would you like friends, relatives, and colleagues to describe you?

_____

_____

_____

Are you interacting with them in ways that would lead them to describe you this way? _____

_____

_____

_____

If not, what must you change? _____

_____

_____

_____

Where are your current connections located? How well balanced are they?

_____

_____

_____

Who are five people in your life with whom you feel most connected? In
what ways do you feel connected to each? _____

_____

_____

_____

_____

What do you do to express this feeling of connectedness and keep it alive?

_____

_____

_____

In addition to your relationship with people, what are three other things in
your life with which you feel connected—that is, areas of your life that are
important to you and provide you with a sense of connectedness and
belonging? _____

_____

_____

_____

In what ways are you involved with these areas? _____

_____

_____

_____

Chapter 8 Dealing Effectively with Mistakes

List three situations in the past year or two in which you made a mistake or
failed at a task. _____

_____

_____

_____

Before you attempted each of the tasks, how confident were you of
succeeding? Did your confidence level differ from one task to the next?

_____

_____

_____

When you experienced a failure, can you recall how you explained this
situation to yourself? _____

_____

_____

_____

As you examine the three situations, did you have the same explanations for
why you failed in each? _____

_____

_____

_____

How did you react to each situation? _____

_____

_____

_____

With hindsight, would you respond differently to any of the situations now? If so, how would you respond differently? _____

_____

_____

_____

Of the three situations in which you made a mistake or failed, in which situation did you react in a way that pleased you most? Why did it please you? _____

_____

_____

_____

What is the worst thing that has happened to you when you made a mistake or failed in a situation? _____

_____

_____

_____

What memories do you have about how your parents or other important adults in your life handled mistakes? _____

_____

_____

_____

If you make a mistake or fail in the future, what do you want to tell yourself? Is this different from what you told yourself in the past? _____

_____

_____

_____

If it is different, how do you think it will affect your behavior? _____

_____

_____

_____

What difficulties do you anticipate encountering as you use new words and actions to deal with mistakes? _____

_____

_____

_____

How will you manage these difficulties so that you can move forward?

_____

_____

_____

Chapter 9 Dealing Well with Success in Building Islands of Competence

List three islands of competence that you possess. _____

_____

_____

_____

How important are these islands to you in terms of your everyday life?

_____

_____

_____

Think of three significant people in your life. What would each say about
the importance of the islands of competence you have listed? _____

_____

_____

_____

List three situations in the past year or two in which you were successful at
a task. _____

_____

_____

_____

Before you attempted each of the tasks, how confident were you of
succeeding? Did your confidence level differ from one task to the next?

_____

_____

_____

_____

When you experienced success, can you recall how you explained the
situation to yourself? _____

_____

_____

_____

As you reflect on these three situations, did you entertain the same reasons
why you succeeded at each? _____

_____

_____

_____

How did you react to each situation? _____

_____

_____

_____

_____

What memories do you have about how your parents or other important
adults in your life handled success? _____

_____

_____

_____

_____

Chapter 10 Developing Self-Discipline and Self-Control

List a couple of important decisions you have made in the past year. _____

_____

_____

_____

_____

When you made these decisions, did you define both short-term and long-
term goals? _____

_____

_____

_____

If these decisions involved interactions with other people, did you consider how they would respond to your words and actions? Did the way you communicated and acted increase the likelihood of these other people understanding and responding constructively to your point of view? _____

_____

_____

_____

_____

_____

Did you think about several possible alternatives when making these decisions? _____

_____

_____

_____

Looking back at the decisions you made, would you change them in any way? _____

_____

_____

_____

In the past year or two, have there been any occasions when you feel you have acted without considering the consequences? If so, why do you think this occurred? _____

_____

_____

_____

_____

Think about two situations you encountered that elicited strong emotions in you: one in which you believe you expressed these emotions in an appropriate and effective way, and one in which you did not. What was the difference between the two situations? _____

_____

_____

_____

Do you feel that you have difficulty making decisions? Are you hesitant to make decisions or take certain action? If so, why might you be hesitant?

_____

_____

_____

Appendix B

A Guide to Resilient Living

Chapter 1 Resilient Mindsets, Negative Scripts, and Personal Control

Ten Keys for Resilient Living

1. Rewrite your negative scripts.
2. Choose the path to become stress hardy rather than stressed out.
3. Develop the ability to view life through the eyes of others.
4. Learn to communicate effectively: listen, learn, and influence.
5. Accept yourself and others.
6. Make connections and display compassion.
7. Learn to deal effectively with mistakes.
8. Learn to deal well with success in building islands of competence.
9. Develop self-discipline and self-control.
10. Learn the lessons of resilience: maintain a resilient lifestyle.

Chapter 2 Changing the Words of Life: Rewriting Your Negative Scripts

Obstacles That Prevent Progress

1. A lack of awareness of the role negative scripts play in your life
2. Insisting that others must change first
3. Being overwhelmed by the stress of everyday life
4. Giving up

Become the Author of Your Life

1. Identify negative scripts in your life and assume responsibility to change them.
2. Define short- and long-term goals related to the particular issue at hand.
3. Consider new scripts or plans of action that accord with your goals.
4. Select from these new scripts the one that you believe has the greatest probability for success. This step also requires considering criteria for assessing the success of the new script.
5. Anticipate the possible obstacles that might interfere with reaching your goal and consider how these obstacles might be handled.
6. Put the new script into action and assess its effectiveness.
7. Change your goals, scripts, or approach if they prove unsuccessful.

Chapter 3 Choosing the Path to Become Stress Hardy Rather than Stressed Out

1. Are you committed to the important things in your life?
2. Do you view difficult situations, mistakes, and problems as challenges to learn from?
3. Do you practice personal control?

Chapter 4 Viewing Life Through the Eyes of Others

Obstacles to Becoming an Empathic Person

1. Practicing what you have lived
2. Harboring disappointment or anger
3. Making assumptions about the motives of others
4. Fearing that if you're too empathic people will take advantage of you

Steps to Becoming an Empathic Person

1. Exercise empathy. Consider how you would like other people to describe you versus how they might actually describe you. Act on the discrepancy.
2. Use your experience as a guide.
3. Put empathy into practice every day.

Chapter 5 Communicating Effectively

Obstacles to Successful Communication

1. Being trapped by models from the past
2. Harboring disappointment, anger, or frustration
3. Losing sight of how best to achieve your goals

Steps to Improve Communication

1. Practice, and then practice some more.
2. Become an active listener.
3. Validate; let others know they have been heard.
4. Live by the Golden Rule.
5. Avoid all-or-none statements.
6. Serve as a model of honesty, integrity, and dignity.
7. Make humor an essential part of your communication.

Chapter 6 Accepting Oneself and Others

Paths to Self-Acceptance

1. Recognize your feelings, thoughts, and coping style.
2. Define realistic expectations and goals for yourself and others.
3. Live in concert with your values.

Chapter 7 Making Connections and Displaying Compassion

Guidelines for Nurturing Connectedness

1. Make connectedness a top priority in your life.
2. Remember that connections come in many forms.
3. Be proactive in developing connections and learn to take risks.
4. Be compassionate and assume the role of a charismatic adult.
5. Remember that connections are constantly changing.

Chapter 8 Dealing Effectively with Mistakes

Steps to Manage Mistakes and Setbacks

1. Examine your assumptions about mistakes.
2. Challenge self-defeating attributions.
3. Learn something positive from every situation.
4. Decide on a plan of action to attempt new scripts based on new attributions.

Chapter 9 Dealing Well with Success in Building Islands of Competence

Steps to Develop a Resilient Outlook About Success and to Nurture Islands of Competence

1. Examine your assumptions about success.
2. Challenge self-defeating attributions.
3. List your interests and islands of competence and pursue them.

Chapter 10 Developing Self-Discipline and Self-Control

Steps to Achieve Self-Control

1. Accept ownership for your behavior.
2. Think before you act—become a proactive problem solver.
3. Be consistent, not rigid.

Problem-Solving Sequence

1. Articulate your goals: what do you want to achieve?
2. Consider a number of new scripts.
3. Select the script with the greatest probability for success and define the criteria to assess its effectiveness.
4. Consider possible obstacles to success.
5. Perform the new script and judge its effectiveness.
6. Modify or change the script if it proves unsuccessful.

Chapter 11 The Lessons of Resilience: Maintaining a Resilient Lifestyle

Exercising Resilience on a Daily Basis

1. Have I truly listened during the past day and attempted to understand the viewpoints of others?
2. How have I related to others? Have I practiced empathy and respect?
3. How have I responded to stress, mistakes, and setbacks? If I am not happy with my response, what will I do differently next time?
4. In what areas did I do well? How do I maintain or reproduce these positive behaviors tomorrow?

Guiding Principles for the Long Term

1. Revisit the principles of a resilient mindset.
2. Periodically assess your progress in terms of leading a resilient life.
3. Do not wait for other people to change first for you to achieve your goals and happiness.
4. Articulate and evaluate short- and long-term goals that are realistic, achievable, and in concert with your values.
5. Anticipate mistakes and setbacks. Be prepared with a backup plan.
6. Relish your accomplishments.
7. Develop and maintain connections with people, ideals, causes, and faith.

Endnotes

Preface

1. Willie Stargell, "Yes, I Am Ready," *Parade*, April 3, 1983.

Chapter 1

1. "One More Reason to Be Your Own Boss," as cited in the *Boston Globe*, July 25, 1997.
2. Ibid.
3. Patricia Wen, "Doctors Seek Insight into Our Outlook," as cited in the *Boston Globe*, November 27, 2001.
4. Edward M. Hallowell, *Connect: 12 Vital Ties That Open Your Heart, Lengthen Your Life, and Deepen Your Soul* (New York: Pantheon, 1999).

Chapter 3

1. "Stress," www.well-connected.com/report.cgi/fr000031.html (Atlanta: A.D.A.M., Inc., 2002).
2. Ibid.
3. "One Minute Retreat," www.healthatoz.com/healthatoz/Atoz/dc/cen/ment/alert07132000.html (Cranbury, NJ: Medical Network, Inc., 2000).
4. Suzanne C. Kobasa, "The Hardy Personality: Toward a Social Psychology of Stress and Health," in *Social Psychology of Health and Illness*, eds. G. S. Sanders and J. Suls (Hillsdale, NJ: Erlbaum, 1982), 3–28.
5. Julius Segal, "Life Crisis! The Five Techniques You Need to Survive," *Parents*, July 1986.
6. Roger von Oech, *A Whack on the Side of the Head: How You Can Be More Creative* (New York: Warner, 1998), 163.

Chapter 4

1. Daniel Goleman, Richard Boyatzis, and Annie McKee, *Primal Leadership: Realizing the Power of Emotional Intelligence* (Boston: Harvard Business School Press, 2002), 50.
2. Ibid, 23.
3. Ibid, 50.

Chapter 5

1. Steve Sainsbury, "Stress in the Workplace: Five Great Ways to De-Stress," *Outposts* March/April (1997): 10–11.

Chapter 6

1. Goleman, Boyatzis, and McKee, 40.
2. Ibid, 40.

Chapter 7

1. K. Dwyer, D. Osher, and C. Warger, *Early Warning, Timely Response: A Guide to Safe Schools* (Washington, DC: U.S. Department of Education, 1998), 3–4.
2. Hallowell, xvi.
3. Ibid, 5–6.
4. James M. Kouzes and Barry Z. Posner, *Encouraging the Heart: A Leader's Guide to Rewarding and Recognizing Others* (San Francisco: Jossey-Bass, 1999), 9–10.
5. Ibid, 11.
6. Ibid, 11.
7. His Holiness the Dalai Lama, *The Art of Living: A Guide to Contentment, Joy and Fulfillment* (London: Thorsons, 2001), 119.
8. George E. Vaillant, *Aging Well: Surprising Guideposts to a Happier Life from the Landmark Harvard Study of Adult Development* (New York: Little, Brown, 2002).
9. As cited in Conari Press, eds., *Random Acts of Kindness* (Berkeley, CA: Conari Press, 1993), 76.

Chapter 8

1. Willie Stargell, "Yes, I Am Ready," *Parade*, April 3, 1983, 11.
2. California Department of Education, *Toward a State of Esteem: The Final Report of the Task Force to Promote Self-Esteem and Personal and Social Responsibility* (Sacramento, CA: The California Self-Esteem Report, 1990), 1.

Chapter 9

1. Jim Collins, *Good to Great: Why Some Companies Make the Leap . . . and Others Don't* (New York: HarperBusiness, 2001).
2. Kouzes and Posner, 13.

Chapter 10

1. Joseph M. Strayhorn, "Self-Control: Theory and Research," *Journal of the American Academy of Child and Adolescent Psychiatry* 41 (2002): 7–16.
2. Goleman, Boyatzis, and McKee.
3. Strayhorn, 8.
4. Strayhorn, 8–9.
5. Strayhorn, 8–9.

Chapter 11

1. Emmy E. Werner and Ruth S. Smith, *Journeys from Childhood to Midlife: Risk, Resilience, and Recovery* (Ithaca, NY: Cornell University Press, 1992).
2. Obituary, *Boston Globe*, November 13, 2002.

Recommended Reading

Brooks, Robert, and Sam Goldstein. *Raising Resilient Children: Fostering Strength, Hope, and Optimism in Your Child.* Chicago: Contemporary Books, 2001.

Brooks, Robert, and Sam Goldstein. *Nurturing Resilience in Our Children: Answers to the Most Important Parenting Questions.* Chicago: Contemporary Books, 2003.

Clausen, John A. *American Lives: Looking Back at the Children of the Great Depression.* New York: Free Press, 1993.

Covey, Stephen R. *The Seven Habits of Highly Effective People.* New York: Simon & Schuster, 1989.

Frankl, Viktor E. *Man's Search for Meaning.* Boston: Beacon Press, 1998.

Goleman, Daniel. *Emotional Intelligence.* New York: Bantam, 1995.

Goleman, Daniel, Richard Boyatzis, and Annie McKee. *Primal Leadership: Realizing the Power of Emotional Intelligence.* Boston: Harvard Business School Press, 2002.

Hallowell, Edward M. *Connect: 12 Vital Ties That Open Your Heart, Lengthen Your Life, and Deepen Your Soul.* New York: Pantheon, 1999.

———. *Human Moments: How to Find Meaning and Love in Your Everyday Life.* Deerfield Beach, FL: Health Communications, 2001.

———. *The Childhood Roots of Adult Happiness.* New York: Ballantine Books, 2002.

Higgins, Gina O'Connell. *Resilient Adults: Overcoming a Cruel Past.* San Francisco: Jossey-Bass, 1994.

His Holiness the Dalai Lama. *The Art of Living: A Guide to Contentment, Joy and Fulfillment.* London: Thorsons, 2001.

Katz, Mark. *On Playing a Poor Hand Well.* New York: Norton, 1997.

Kouzes, James M., and Barry Z. Posner. *Encouraging the Heart: A Leader's Guide to Rewarding and Recognizing Others.* San Francisco: Jossey-Bass, 1999.

Levine, Saul, and Heather Wood Ion. *Against Terrible Odds.* Palo Alto, CA: Bull Publishing Company, 2001.

McGraw, Phillip C. *Self Matters: Creating Your Life from the Inside Out.* New York: Simon & Schuster, 2001.

Oech, Roger von. *A Whack on the Side of the Head: How You Can Be More Creative.* New York: Warner, 1998.

O'Hanlon, Bill. *Do One Thing Different.* New York: William Morrow, 1999.

Reivich, Karen, and Andrew Shatté. *The Resilience Factor: 7 Essential Skills for Overcoming Life's Inevitable Obstacles.* New York: Broadway Books, 2002.

Seligman, Martin E. P. *Learned Optimism: How to Change Your Mind and Your Life.* New York: Pocket Books, 1990.

———. *Authentic Happiness.* New York: Free Press, 2002.

Vaillant, George E. *Aging Well: Surprising Guideposts to a Happier Life from the Landmark Harvard Study of Adult Development.* New York: Little, Brown, 2002.

Werner, Emmy E., and Ruth S. Smith. *Journeys from Childhood to Midlife.* Ithaca, NY: Cornell University Press, 2002.

———. *Vulnerable but Invincible: A Longitudinal Study of Resilient Children and Youth.* New York: Cornell University Press, 1992.

Index

Acceptance, 14–16, 123–50, 299
    and dealing with success,
        212–13
    defining realistic
        expectations as step
        in, 143–48
    recognizing your feelings,
        thoughts, and
        coping style as step
        to, 136–43
    and resilience, 124–36
    and values alignment,
        148–50
    worksheet for, 278–84
Achievements, 219
Acting, counterproductive
        patterns of, 186
Action plans, 203–7
Active listening, 13, 116–17
Adaptability, 240
Adversity, preparation for, x
Affection, 156–57
Alcoholics Anonymous, 7
Alexander, Jill, 18
Allen, Woody, 125
All-or-none statements, 120–21,
        196
Altruism, 57
American flags, 167
American Lives (John A.
        Clausen), 263

Andover, Millie and Dave,
        138–42
Anger, 85–86, 108–11
Anticipation (of obstacles), 40,
        203–4
Anxiety, 49, 50, 59
Anxiety disorders, xi
Arsdale, Drew, 209–10, 219–25
The Art of Living (Dalai Lama),
        175–76
Assessment, 40, 41
Assumptions
    about mistakes, 191–95
    about motivations of
        others, 86–90
    about success, 224–27
Atkins, Melissa, 37–39, 44–46,
        65, 247, 263
Attribution theory
    and mistakes, 184–92, 206
    and self-control, 245
    and success, 210–13, 221,
        222
Attributions
    challenging self-defeating,
        195–200, 228–32
    for mistakes, 187
    of success, 219
Awareness
    of negative scripts, 28–30
    social, 74

Baker, Marian, 19, 226–27
Balance
    and connections, 166–70
    overcontrol vs., 240–41
Balfour, Jennifer, 9
Baseball, 185
Bauer, Lou, 53–56, 69–71,
    166–67, 170, 263
Behavior
    accepting ownership for
        your, 247–50
    learned, 82–85
Behavior rehearsals, 206
Benard, Bonnie, xiii
Bereavement, 57
Berkley, Arlene, 264
Berkley, Arlene and Mason,
    238–40, 248–50, 252–57
Berkman, Lisa, 155
Boston Globe, 266, 267
Boyatzis, Richard, 74, 77, 91,
    137, 138
Brainstorming, 39–40
Braude, Jacob, 183, 207
Breast cancer, 151–52, 155
Buffering process, x
Burnout, 55
Butler, Jeremy, 5–6, 29–30,
    41–44, 78–79, 137, 247,
    264

Caldwell, Jessica, 103–6, 113
California Task Force to
    Promote Self-Esteem
    and Personal and Social
    Responsibility, 201
Carter, Len, 196–203
Castor, Paul, 26–28

Celester, Frank, 58–60
Center for Creative Leadership
    (CCL), 156
Challenges, 58–64
Change
    burnout and drastic, 33–34
    potential for, x
    in relationships, 178–81
    responsibility for, 30–32
Charismatic adult(s), ix
    assuming role of, 173–78
    and connections, 16–17
    and making connections,
        152–54, 157–58, 162
    and mistakes, 206
Charles, Ray, ix
Childhood, factors contributing
    to stress and
    vulnerability in, x
Child(ren)
    and charismatic adults, ix,
        152–53, 174
    feelings of, 91
    and honesty, 122
    loss of a, 57
    resilience factors in,
        262–63
CHUCK. *See* Committee to
    Halt Useless College
    Killings
Clark, Mary, 60–62, 167
Clausen, John A., 263, 307
Clowning, 24–25
Collins, Jim, 212–13
Commitment, 52–58, 162–63
Committee to Halt Useless
    College Killings
    (CHUCK), 57, 167

Communication, 43,
99–124
active listening skill in,
116–17
all-or-none statement
avoidance in,
120–21
anger and disappointment
as obstacles to,
108–11
effective, 13–14
experience as obstacle to,
103–8
Golden Rule in, 119–20
honesty, 121–24
humor in, 123–24
improving skills of, 112–24,
299
losing sight of goals as
obstacle to,
111–12
obstacles to successful,
103–12, 299
practicing to improve,
112–16
and resilient mindset,
99–103
validation skill in,
117–19
worksheet for, 276–78
Community, 167
Compassion, 16–17
and connections, 173–78
Charles Dickens on, 181
and stress hardiness, 57
Walt Whitman on, 181
worksheet for, 284–88
Compassionate Friends, 57

Competence
islands of. *See* Islands of
competence
planful, 263
Compliments, 106, 134
Concentration camps, 57–58,
177, 263
Confidence levels, 186–87,
219
Connect (Ned Hallowell), 154
Connectedness
guidelines for nurturing,
163–81, 300
qualities of, 154–56
as top priority, 164–65
Connections, making, 16–17,
151–81
and adults, 153–54
and balance, 166–70
and being compassionate,
173–78
and change, 178–81
and children, 152–53
proactiveness and
risk-taking in,
170–73
and values, 168–70
in the workplace, 156–57
worksheet for, 284–88
Consistency, rigidity vs.,
257–58
Contributions of others, 213
Control, personal. *See* Personal
control
Controlling behavior, 27–28,
138–42
Coping styles, recognizing,
136–43, 187

Couples
  and changing nature of
    relationships,
    178–80
  and communication, 13–14,
    109–11
  and connectedness, 164–65
  expectations of, 8
  and ghosts of the past,
    66–69
  and resilient mindset, 8
  and self-acceptance, 138–42
Courage, 41–48
Covey, Stephen, 7, 116, 307

Dalai Lama, 175–76, 307
Dangerfield, Rodney, 123
Decision making, 241–42
Dembar, Lisa and Alex, 109–11,
    113
Depression, 14, 50
Depressive disorders, xi
Devotion (to a higher cause),
    57
Dickens, Charles, 181
Dignity, 121–24
Disappointment, 86, 109
Disney, Walt, 201
Disneyland, 201
Dissonance, 77–78
Do One Thing Differently (Bill
    O'Hanlon), 105, 229

Early Warning, 153
Easton, Tyler, 237–40,
    242–47

Edison, Thomas, 201
Einstein, Albert, xiii, 201
Eitinger, Leo, 57
Elderly, 176–77
Emerson, Ralph Waldo, 176,
    235
"Emotional cripples," 132–33
Emotional self-control, 240
Emotions, expression of, 242,
    252
Empathy, 12–13, 73–87
  anger and disappointment
    as obstacles to,
    85–86
  assumptions about motives
    as obstacle to,
    86–90
  and communication,
    99–100
  definition and role of,
    74–75
  exercising, 92–95
  experience as guide to,
    95–96
  failures in, 76–82
  fear of weakness as obstacle
    to, 90–92
  and feedback, 121–22
  guidelines for gaining,
    92–97, 299
  learned behavior as obstacle
    to, 82–85
  obstacles to, 82–92, 298
  practicing, 96–97, 113–14
  and self-control, 242
  worksheet for, 274–76

Empowerment, 64–66
"Exception rule," 133
Expectations
    and attributions of failure,
        187
    and attributions of success,
        219
    realistic, 143–48
    unrealistic, 33–34
Experience
    as communication obstacle,
        103–8
    as guide to empathy,
        95–96
    learning from, 242

Failure, fear of, 18
Faith, 152
Family support, 152
Fear
    of commitment, 162–63
    of failure, 18
    of making mistakes,
        187–91
    of success, 213–18
    of weakness, 90–92
Federman, Irwin, 157
Feedback
    and empathy, 121–22
    offering, 89
    positive, 66, 134
    soliciting, 76–77
    from supervisors, 198–200,
        231
Feelings, recognizing, 136–43
Flexibility, 19–20

"Fostering Family Closeness
    and Respect"
    workshop, 11
Frankl, Viktor, 57–58, 177, 263,
    307
Friends, support from, 152
Friendships
    changing nature of,
        179–80
    with younger people,
        176–77
Frustration, 109, 110

Gallup poll, x–xi
Gateman, Lenore, 131–37, 150
"Gathering strength," ix, 152
Germany, 165
Ghosts of the past, 67–69,
    130
"Giving purpose to your pain,"
    56–57
Giving up, 34–35
Goals
    and assessment of success,
        40
    defining, 11
    and islands of competence,
        233
    losing sight of, 111–12
    realistic, 143–48
    and rewriting your negative
        scripts, 39
    and self-control, 241
    short-term, 33
    unrealistic, 33–34, 145
Golden Rule, 119–20, 156

Goleman, Daniel, 12, 19, 74, 77, 91, 137, 138, 240, 307
Great Depression, 263
Greatness, defining, 212–13
Greeting card industry, 164–65
Growth, continued personal, x
"Guidelines" for better communication, 111

Hallowell, Edward (Ned), 16, 154–56, 307
Hamlet (William Shakespeare), 148
Harris, Max and June, 93–95
"Helper's high," 16, 175
Helplessness, learned, 35, 186
Higgins, Gina O'Connell, 307
Holland, Mark, 128–31, 145–48, 171, 263
Honesty, 121–24
Hopkins, Peter, 205–7, 264
"Human moments," 16
Humility, 212
Humor, 123–24

Integrity, 121–24
Interests, pursuing your, 232–34
Ion, Heather Wood, 308
Islands of competence, 18, 219
    identifying, 218
    and mistakes, 192
    pursuing your, 232–34
    steps for nurturing, 300
    and success, 221–22, 224, 230
    worksheet for, 291–93
Isolation, 155, 171

Katz, Mark, 307
Kindness, 152
Kobasa, Suzanne, 52, 64
Kouzes, James, 156–57, 213, 308
Kubzansky, Laura, 9

Lamsted, Stacy, 107–8, 263
Lancet, 9
Lapora, Miss, 54–55, 69–71, 167
Larimer, Luke, 125–26
Larsen, George, 66–69, 263
Larsen, Melinda, 66–69
Leaders, Level 5, 212–13
Learned behavior, 82–85
Learned helplessness, 35, 186
Learning disabilities, 1–2, 205
Learning from mistakes, 200–204
Level 5 leaders, 212–13
Levine, Saul, 308
Lewis, Richard, 125
Lifestyle, 20
Listening, active, 13, 116–17
Logotherapy, 57
Lowell, Gerald, 183–84
Luck, 210

Managers
    affection expressed by, 156–57
    feedback from, 198–200, 231
Man's Search for Meaning (Viktor Frankl), 57
Manter, Alan and Barbara, 8
Marmot, Michael, 9
Married couples. *See* Couples

Marty, 176–77
"Martyr act," 141
McGraw, Phillip C., 308
McKee, Annie, 74, 77, 91, 137, 138
Meaning therapy, 57
Meaning (to our lives), 52–53, 56–57
Meg, 151, 263–64
Memories, 187, 219
Mental disorders, xi
Millis, Sam, 49–50, 71–72, 193–94
Mindset, resilient. *See* Resilient mindset
Mistakes, dealing with, 17–18, 183–207
    action plan as step in, 203–7
    and attribution theory, 184–91
    challenging self-defeating attributions as step in, 195–200
    examining your assumptions as step in, 191–95
    learning from the situation as step in, 200–203
    and rewriting negative scripts, 35
    steps for, 300
    worksheet for, 289–91
Models
    parents as, 219
    positive, 106–8
Motivation, 86–90

Nance, Marjorie, 66, 247
Narcissism, 212–13
National Institute for Occupational Safety and Health, 51
National Institute of Mental Health, xi
Needham, Russ, 257–58
Negative scripts, 4–7, 105
    awareness of, 28–30, 29–30
    courage to change, 41–44
    identification of, 37–39
    rewriting your. *See* Rewriting your negative scripts
Newman, Gene, 49, 72, 193–95
"Northern Exposure" (television show), 266, 267
Norwood, Michelle, 183, 187–91
Nurturing Resilience in Our Children (Robert Brooks and Sam Goldstein), ix

Obstacles, anticipating, 11, 40, 203–4
Oech, Roger von, 65–66, 308
O'Hanlon, Bill, 105, 229, 308
Opportunities
    learning, 58–60
    missed, 158–63
Optimism, 9
Ownership (for your behavior), 247–50

Pace, Carl and Andrea, 13–14, 118

Palmer, Carla, 213–18, 225, 228–33
Parents
    acceptance from, 131–36
    bereavement of, 57
    and honesty, 122
    impact of baby on relationship of, 178–80
    as models, 103–6
    relationships with, 38–39, 44–46, 65
Parsons, Warren, 96–97, 119
Past
    as communication factor, 103–8
    and self-acceptance, 130, 146, 147
    as stress hardiness factor, 67–69
Penn, Dr., 198–203
Personal control
    and empathy, 75
    and mistakes, 203
    and self-acceptance, 212
    and self-discipline, 246
    significance of, 7–10
    and stress hardiness, 64–71
Personal humility, 212
Perspective, 32
Pessimism, 17
Petrie, Ruth, 86–90
Pets, 167–68
Phillips, Margaret "Peg," 266–67
Planful competence, 263

Polonius (fictional character), 148
Ponce de Leon, 261
Positive feedback, 66, 134
Positive models, 106–8
Positive scripts, 4
Posner, Barry, 156–57, 207, 308
Primal Leadership (Daniel Goleman, Richard Boyatzis, and Annie McKee), 74
Priority(-ies)
    and connectedness, 168–70
    connectedness as top, 164–65
    and stress hardiness, 56, 58
    and values, 128
Problem-solving sequence, 251–57, 301
Proctor, Alex, 1–2
Purpose to life, 57–58

Raising Resilient Children (Robert Brooks and Sam Goldstein), ix, 67, 91, 143, 152, 229
Randolph, Lorraine, 171–73, 184
Realistic expectations, 143–48
Rehearsals, behavior, 206
Reivich, Karen, 308
Relationships, satisfying, 12
"Reserve capacity," x
Resilience, 10–21
    accepting oneself and others for, 14–16
    and communication, 13–14

definitions of, x, 3
and displaying compassion,
16–17
empathy for, 12–13
keys for, 10–20, 297
lifestyle for, 20
and making connections,
16–17
and mistake handling,
17–18
rewriting negative scripts
for, 10–12
self-discipline development
for, 19–20
stress hardy path choices
for, 12
and success handling,
18–19
Resilient lifestyle, maintaining
a, 264–67, 301–2
Resilient mindset, 2–7
and attribution theory,
184–91
and communication,
99–103
and dealing with success,
210–18
features of, 3
negative scripts as obstacles
to, 4–7
and personal control,
7–10
and self-discipline and self-
control, 240–47
and stress hardiness, 51–72
Resonance, 77

Responsibility
accepting realistic, 212
for change, 9, 11, 30–32
taking, 65–66
Rewriting your negative scripts,
10–12, 23–48
anticipation of obstacles as
step in, 40
and assessment of new
script, 41
and awareness of negative
scripts, 28–30
brainstorming step in,
39–40
courage for, 41–48
and giving up, 34–35
goal definition step in, 39
identification step in, 37–39
for mistake handling, 204
modification step of, 41
obstacles to, 28–35, 297
and putting new script into
action, 41
responsibility for change in,
30–32
selection step in, 40
steps in, 36–41, 298
and stress, 32–34
worksheet for, 269–71
Rigidity, consistency vs., 257–58
Risk taking, 170–73, 187–91
Roper Starch Worldwide
Study, 51

Sainsbury, Steve, 123
Sarcasm, 123

Sargent, Ross, 15, 53, 149, 168–71, 180
Satisfaction, lack of, 211–12
Satisfying relationships, 12
Savin, Mr. and Mrs., 31–32, 46–48, 247
Schools, 153
Scripts. *See* Negative scripts; Rewriting your negative scripts
Security, 7
Segal, Julius, ix, 56–57, 152
Self-acceptance. *See* Acceptance
Self-assurance, 210
Self-awareness, 137–43
Self-blame, 9
Self-defeating attributions, 195–200, 212, 228–32
Self-destructive habits, 51
Self-discipline (self-control), 19–20, 237–59
  Robert Burns on, 237
  and consistency vs. rigidity, 257–58
  ownership of behavior as step in achieving, 247–50
  and resilient mindset, 240–47
  steps to achieving, 247–58, 301
  thinking before acting as step in achieving, 251–57
  and values, 258–59
  worksheet for, 293–95

Self-discovery, 37
Self-doubt, 196–97, 202–3, 220, 224
Self-esteem, 185, 210, 220
Self-management, 240
Self-reflection, 138
Seligman, Martin, 35, 308
Semper, Joshua, 100–103, 113–16
September 11, 2001, terrorist attacks, x, 150, 167
Serenity Prayer (Alcoholics Anonymous), 7
The Seven Habits of Highly Effective People (Stephen Covey), 7
Shakespeare, William, 148
Shatté, Andrew, 308
Short-term goals, 33
Shyness, 131–36
Significant others, 219
Smith, Roslyn, 2
Smith, Ruth, 262–63, 308
Social awareness, 74
"Social skills investigators," 116
"Special times," 48, 180
Spiegel, David, 155
Spontaneity, 6, 19
Stargell, Willie, 185, 186
Sterling, Rachel, 118
Stevens, Eileen, 56–57, 167
Stevens, Marcia, 24–26, 79–80
Strayhorn, Joseph, 240, 241, 258
Strengths, 14, 144, 218, 219, 232–33
Stress, x–xi, 32–34, 49–51

Stress hardiness, 12, 51–72, 298
    challenge feature of, 58–64
    commitment feature of,
        52–58
    components of, 52
    personal control feature of,
        64–71
    and resilient mindset, 51–72
    worksheet for, 271–74
Stress hardy personality, 52
"Stress in the Workplace" (Steve
    Sainsbury), 123
Success, 3
    attributions of, 219
    criteria for assessment of, 11
    Ralph Waldo Emerson on,
        235
    fear of, 213–18
Success, dealing with, 18–19,
        209–35, 300
    and acceptance, 212–13
    and attribution theory,
        210–18
    challenging self-defeating
        attributions as step
        in, 228–32
    examining your
        assumptions as step
        in, 224–27
    pursuing your interests and
        islands of
        competence as step
        in, 232–34
    and satisfaction, 211–12
    worksheet for, 291–93
Syme, Leonard, 9

Taylor, Jeremy, 83–85
Temperament, 12, 51–52
Tennyson, Alfred, Lord, 259
Teresa, Mother, 151
Thinking
    before acting, 251–57
    counterproductive patterns
        of, 186
Thoughts, recognizing, 136–43
Tradition, 7
Transparency, 240

Unrealistic expectations, 33–34
U.S. Bureau of Labor
    Statistics, 51

Vaillant, George, 176, 308
Validation, 13, 14, 117–19, 243
Values
    and connections, 168–70
    and self-acceptance, 148–50
    and self-control, 258–59
Vaughn, Alisa, 81–82, 112
Videka-Sherman, Lynn, 57
Vintor, Duane, 80–82

Walton, Bea, 158–63, 170
Weakness, fear of, 90–92
Well-being, 9
Werner, Emmy, x, xiii, 262–63,
    308
*A Whack on the Side of the
    Head* (Roger von
    Oech), 65
Whitaker, Larry, 33–35, 145
Whitman, Walt, 181

Workplace
  connections in the, 156–57
  control in the, 9
  humor, 123–24
  negative environment
      in, 66
  stress in the, 51
Worksheet(s), 269–95
  for acceptance, 278–84
  for communication,
      276–78
  for compassion, 284–88
  for dealing with mistakes,
      289–91

  for dealing with success,
      291–93
  for empathy, 274–76
  for islands of competence,
      291–93
  for making connections,
      284–88
  for rewriting your negative
      scripts, 269–71
  for self-discipline and self-
      control, 293–95
  for stress hardiness, 271–74

Yalom, Irvin, 57